BRITISH-AMERICAN RELATIONS
1917-1918

Supplementary volume to *The Papers of Woodrow Wilson*

BRITISH-AMERICAN RELATIONS,

1917-1918,

The Role of Sir William Wiseman

BY W. B. FOWLER

PRINCETON UNIVERSITY PRESS

PRINCETON, NEW JERSEY 1969

327.42073
F789b

153581

ACKNOWLEDGMENTS

I thank the following:

Yale University, for financial assistance;

Lady Wiseman, Miss Sheila Wiseman, Mrs. Winifred Mood, Sir Arthur Willert, Mr. Arthur Walworth, Mr. Robert Bunselmeyer, Dr. F. Brittain, Mr. and Mrs. W. F. Lyons, and Cdr. and Mrs. A. Cameron, for information and special courtesies;

Mr. Julian Amery, for permission to quote from the Diary of L. S. Amery; Mr. George Lodge, for permission to quote from the Henry Cabot Lodge Papers; and the Trustees of the Beaverbrook Foundations, for access to the Lloyd George Papers;

the staffs of Yale University Library (especially Miss Judith A. Schiff), Harvard University Library, Massachusetts Historical Society, Library of Congress, National Archives (Washington), Public Record Office (London), British Museum, Foreign Office Library, Plunkett Foundation (London), New College (Oxford) Library, University of Birmingham Library, Scottish Record Office, and National Library of Scotland, for making available records in their care;

Mrs. Anne J. Granger and Roy A. Grisham, Jr., for help in preparing the book for publication;

Lewis L. Gould, Robert H. Johnston, William S. McFeely, and D. A. Smith, for suggestions as to style;

and, especially, Professors Gaddis Smith and Arthur S. Link, for their expert and sympathetic criticisms.

I alone bear the responsibility for the contents of this book.   W.B.F.

CONTENTS

NOTE ON FOOTNOTE CITATIONS

THE TWO most heavily used sources, the Sir William Wiseman Papers and the Edward M. House Papers (both in Yale University Library), are abbreviated as WWP and HP respectively. The number following each WWP identifies the folder; the number following each HP identifies the drawer and folder. Wiseman cable numbers (e.g. CXP 25) are given only when necessary to distinguish between cables of the same date. A recent addition to Yale's collection of Wiseman Papers is cited as New WWP. The few items still in the possession of Sir William's widow are identified as London WWP.

Identifying file numbers for records of the State Department and the Foreign Office are preceded by the abbreviations SD and FO.

The location of other manuscript collections is indicated only in the initial citation, unless, as in the case of Cecil and Balfour papers, clarity requires the location as well as the name of the collection.

Unless otherwise indicated, a cable message is cited by the names of the actual sender and receiver, rather than by the names of ambassadors and other agents who merely relayed the cable.

The State Department serial publication *Papers Relating to the Foreign Relations of the United States* is abbreviated as *Foreign Relations*.

BRITISH-AMERICAN RELATIONS
1917-1918

CHAPTER ONE

INTRODUCTION

IN THE waning days of the Paris Peace Conference, Arthur J. Balfour, British Foreign Secretary, acknowledged the resignation of Lord Reading from the post of ambassador to the United States in these words:

> The heavy responsibilities and the unceasing anxieties which weigh upon the Diplomatic representatives of belligerents and neutrals when half the world is fighting are known to all observers. Very different, but not less formidable, were the problems which faced the Associated Governments after America entered the War; and which had to be solved if the co-operation of the two countries was to bear its full fruits. . . .
>
> The difficulties were great, they were without exact precedent, they were quite outside ordinary Diplomatic routine. They involved most complicated questions of finance, shipping, food supply, troop transportation and armaments. Though they profoundly affected the fortune of all the Allies, they had to be dealt with in the main between Britain and America. . . .[1]

Balfour's words remain remarkably apt for the historian concerned with Anglo-American diplomacy during the First World War years. No one as experienced as he was in international affairs could doubt that the drama of the Paris Peace Conference and the range of decisions it made would ensure it a prominent place in the history books. Nor, he seemed to anticipate, were the problems in Anglo-American relations during America's neutrality any less likely to engage the attention of future observers. Not so the diplomatic difficulties of co-belligerency. These rarely captured the headlines during 1917-18, and it is perhaps

[1] Balfour to Reading, May 24, 1919, Balfour Papers 49741, British Museum.

not too much to infer that Balfour expected them to be overshadowed by the questions of neutrality and the peace settlement in historical accounts.

In any case, the diplomacy of co-belligerency has been overshadowed in such accounts. There are only a handful of specialized studies of American wartime diplomacy.[2] By contrast, a list of studies on the neutrality and Peace Conference periods would require several pages.[3] Why this relative neglect? Several reasons can be suggested. First, as Balfour implied, the diplomatic questions during neutrality and the peace talks were more exciting. During the months of American belligerency there were no summit meetings of the Casablanca or Yalta sort to lure attention away from military developments. Second, regarding the Peace Conference, governmental and private records have been, until recently, more generally available to scholars than have been the records of the war period, which could be withheld from historians on the basis of military security. Third, since historical precedents are frequently invoked for guidance in current situations, both the neutrality and Peace Conference periods were searched for les-

[2] In the bibliography, see the titles by Bailey, Gelfand, Gerson, Kennan, Mamatey, Martin, Mayer, Trask, and Unterberger. General coverage is provided in the books by Dos Passos, Daniel M. Smith, and Walworth. The only book specifically concerned with Anglo-American relations is Sir Arthur Willert's memoir, *The Road to Safety*, London, 1952.

[3] See the bibliographies in Ernest R. May, *The World War and American Isolation, 1914-1917*, Cambridge, Mass., 1959; Seth P. Tillman, *Anglo-American Relations at the Paris Peace Conference of 1919*, Princeton, 1961; and Arno J. Mayer, *Politics and Diplomacy of Peacemaking; Containment and Counterrevolution at Versailles, 1918-1919*, New York, 1967. Also see the survey articles, Richard W. Leopold, "The Problem of American Intervention, 1917: An Historical Retrospect," *World Politics*, II (1950), 405-25; Ernest R. May, "Emergence to World Power," in John Higham, ed., *The Reconstruction of American History*, New York, 1962; Daniel M. Smith, "National Interest and American Intervention, 1917: An Historical Appraisal," *The Journal of American History*, LII (1965), 5-24; Robert C. Binkley, "Ten Years of Peace Conference History," *Journal of Modern History*, I (1929), 607-29; and Paul Birdsall, "Second Decade of Peace Conference History," *Journal of Modern History*, XI (1939), 362-78.

sons during the 1930's and 1940's. The lesson, if any, taken from American wartime diplomacy was that there had not been enough of it—that Wilson had mistakenly overlooked the opportunity to come to agreement on political matters with his co-belligerents *during* the war. Which leads to a fourth answer to the question: by and large, the telling of American negotiations with the Allies in such matters as finance, munitions, food, manpower, and shipping —the means by which American power was exerted— has been left to technical or official histories.[4]

There is some justification for the diplomatic or political historians' neglect of the technical side of American-Allied negotiations. They could take their cue from President Wilson, who himself took careful pains to separate the mechanical means of war-making from the political ends of the war. Indeed, the salient feature of American diplomacy from April 1917 to October 1918 was Wilson's attempt to impose a moratorium on political consultation with the Allies. It was as if he had announced to the Allies, as he did to domestic politicians, that politics was adjourned. There would be no alliance, and there would be no negotiations over objectives. Wilson's distinctive approach to relations with fellow members of the anti-German coalition imposed on that coalition a particularly tenuous quality, sometimes overlooked. Without a commitment from America to fight on until the coalition unanimously agreed to end the war, the Allies could never be sure that the United States might not negotiate a separate peace. Formally, and to an extent actually, this approach made the association between America and the Allies an "open-ended" one, in which the Allies constantly had to be on guard against so offending Wilson in matters such as war aims that he might desert them. And as the American contribution to the war effort increased, the Allies became proportionately more dependent on Wilson. Practically, however, the le-

[4] A notable exception is David F. Trask, *The United States in the Supreme War Council; American War Aims and Inter-Allied Strategy, 1917-1918,* Middletown, Conn., 1961.

verage over and independence from the Allies which Wilson expected to enjoy lost force under the exigencies of war-making. To cite one example described in this study: American troops, once in Europe, became something of an American hostage to an Allied victory, and the transportation of them and their supplies provided the British with a bargaining point with the United States. Similarly, Wilson came to appreciate, if he did not before, that strategic considerations, nominally military, were unfortunately fraught with political implications. The diplomatic moratorium he wished to maintain was in fact, as we shall see, several times roused—by the Supreme War Council, by his Secretary of the Treasury, even by his confidant, Colonel Edward M. House.

Indirectly, Wilson's insistence on diplomatic independence for the United States illuminates the well-worn question of whether his neutrality beforehand was genuine. Indeed, students of the neutrality problem who conclude their investigation at April 6, 1917, may fall into the logical fallacy of assuming, if only unconsciously, that since the American government declared war on Germany it was and had been pro-British. Similarly, students who conclude that the Treaty of Versailles was essentially an Anglo-American document might infer that Anglo-American harmony prevailed during 1917-18. Close inspection of the period does not bear out such an inference. There is little evidence to indicate that Wilson veered from his December 1916 opinion that Britain's ambitions were as objectionable as Germany's. After he became a belligerent he several times expressed distrust of the motives of the British government and looked sceptically on attempts to unite the policies of the two nations, feeling that such attempts could produce only an artificial entente. For its part, the British government chafed under Wilson's stubbornness and idealism, particularly concerning intervention in Russia, and despised his aloofness from the Allies.

Credit for keeping the animosities that developed between the American and British governments in check, or anesthetized, must go to several men. Among them, Sir William Wiseman occupies a front rank. In a time when unorthodox procedures became orthodox, when the State Department and the Foreign Office found themselves sharing traditional responsibilities—and power—with other government departments and with emergency boards, few things were more unusual than this young man's sudden rise to great diplomatic importance.

COALITION diplomacy, novel to and grudgingly practiced by the United States in 1917-18, within 25 years became an identifying and permanent characteristic of American foreign policy. To a remarkable extent, the difficulties of co-belligerency in the First World War and the methods by which they were met reappeared in the Second World War. Even during the interwar years, and certainly in the years following the Second World War, the United States found itself obliged to work jointly with other nations on economic, military, and political problems similar to those first encountered by the Wilson Administration. In part this new obligation resulted from America's relative gain in power and wealth over the war-exhausted great powers of Europe. In addition, rapid communications, economic interdependence, and similarity of political attitudes forced the United States into an unaccustomed but inescapable filiation with other nations. General intercourse with these nations came to resemble the relations with the co-belligerents of 1917-18 and required the same speedy, direct, yet comprehensive access of virtually all the departments of the American government to dependent or cooperating governments.

Sir William Wiseman and the others who built the Anglo-American war partnership thus were pioneers in twentieth-century diplomacy. Their unfamiliar tasks became the routine ones of their successors. Their improvisations reformed the method and widened the scope of diplomacy and made it fit for modern usage.

7

CHAPTER TWO

WISEMAN AND THE BEGINNING
OF THE WAR PARTNERSHIP

> I had a conference with Sir William Wiseman yesterday. He is the most sensible Englishman that has been connected with the Embassy here since the war began. He has intelligence enough to go with friends of the Administration rather than with its enemies.
>
> Colonel S. M. House
> to President Woodrow Wilson,
> January 16, 1917

FUNDAMENTALLY, Anglo-American cooperation in the First World War was an embrace of necessity. There was no formal alliance. Each country, however, for reasons of expediency, became the other's chief partner. In 1917 the United States was Germany's sole enemy with fresh reserves of men, money, and materials. Britain, having underwritten her Allies for three years, was on the brink of financial exhaustion and was beginning to run short of manpower. Still, Britain was in much better shape morally and materially than her Allies. All were dependent on the British Treasury. The French army was suffering from widespread desertion, as was, at a more alarming rate, the Russian army. And the Italians were incurring casualties at the rate of two for every one of Austria's. Only Britain appeared, however deceptively, unweakened.[1] So it was natural for the United States to look to the strongest member of the Entente for support and guidance.

From the American standpoint, Britain's most necessary strength lay in her maritime tonnage. Despite great effort and even greater publicity the American "bridge of ships" to Europe never materialized. Consequently the

---

[1] Cyril Falls, *The Great War*, New York, 1959, pp. 232, 261-62, 279-80; Viscount Grey of Fallodon, *Twenty-five Years, 1892-1916*, 2 vols. London, 1925, Vol. 2, p. 131.

majority of American troops and supplies went to Europe in British vessels.[2] Without British ships America's overwhelming might would never have been transmitted to Europe. Without American soldiers and supplies—and the credits to pay for the latter—Britain would never have won a military triumph. The capacities of the two nations were nicely complementary, their partnership imperative.

But imperative circumstances, like natural affinities, did not make cooperation a sure thing. Men, more than the requirements of the situation, made the partnership work. Yet before the men who perfected the partnership assumed their stations, other men, notably the two ambassadors involved, unintentionally hindered the integration of the two countries' war efforts. Because of their training and experience the American and British ambassadors logically should have reached a zenith of usefulness in wartime. Ironically, their experience made them ineligible to function as the intermediaries between the governments. Each exhausted himself trying to maintain Anglo-American cordiality during the period of American neutrality. In the process, each lost his sense of perspective and the confidence of his government.

Sir Cecil Spring Rice, the British ambassador at Washington, brought wide learning and considerable literary talent to his embassy. A career diplomat, he had served as secretary at the Washington embassy during the Harrison and second Cleveland administrations. In 1886 he acted as best man in Theodore Roosevelt's wedding, and from that year forward he enjoyed close friendships with numerous prominent Republicans, particularly Roosevelt, John Hay, and Henry Cabot Lodge. His appointment as ambassador to Wilson's Democratic administration was therefore of questionable wisdom. For a time, Spring Rice seemed acceptable to Wilson, but as the war progressed his zealous defense of British interests against American neutrality,

[2] American ships carried 46 percent of the American troops, British ships 51 percent. John J. Pershing, *My Experiences in the World War*, 2 vols. New York, 1931, Vol. 2, p. 84.

his ranting about German spies, his consorting with Republicans, and his indiscreet wit (which victimized even Wilson) became more and more irksome. By late 1915 Spring Rice was to Wilson a "highly excitable invalid" whom he rarely received. The Foreign Office, less dissatisfied than Washington with Spring Rice, nevertheless found his reports "bewildering" and saw little value in asking him questions.[3]

The American ambassador at London, Walter Hines Page, like most American envoys at the time, was not a career man. He was a North Carolinian, educated (like Wilson) at the Johns Hopkins University, and had been the editor of the *Atlantic Monthly*, the founding editor of *World's Work*, and one of the earliest supporters of Wilson for the presidency. Despite what seemed to be a genuine affection between the two men they became estranged over Wilson's neutrality policies. As early as October 1914 Wilson detected too much Anglophilia in Page. By January 1917 Wilson was seldom reading Page's dispatches and was preparing to dismiss him. For the next several weeks the ambassador's future seemed uncertain, causing his son to ask the State Department for clarification. At last Wilson, in what he labeled a misguided moment, decided to continue Page in his post, complaining that he could find no suitable replacement and would have to endure being represented by a "British-American." The British, though pleased by Page's sympathetic attitude, knew that his opinions were not consonant with Wilson's.[4]

[3] Details of Spring Rice's life may be found in Stephen Gwynn, ed., *The Letters and Friendships of Sir Cecil Spring Rice*, 2 vols. London, 1929. E. M. House, Diary, Nov. 28, 1915, HP. Hereafter cited as House Diary; Lord Robert Cecil to Lord Milner, Dec. 25, 1916, Lord Robert Cecil's Private Papers, FO 800/190, Public Record Office. According to American Ambassador Page, the British government was thinking of dismissing Spring Rice in February 1917. Page to Wilson, Feb. 3, 1917, Page Papers, folder 1482, Harvard University Library.

[4] Details of Page's life are in Burton J. Hendrick, *The Life and Letters of Walter Hines Page*, 3 vols. New York, 1925-26. Wilson to House, Oct. 23, 1914, Wilson Papers, Series 6, Box 258, folder 1303,

It is astonishing that collaborating governments in time of war should retain ambassadors whom they knew to be unsatisfactory. Yet Spring Rice remained at Washington until January 1918 and Page at London until September 1918. How were the governments able to effect the frequent and candid consultation required of co-belligerents? As so often in problems of foreign affairs during the Wilson administration, Colonel Edward M. House provided the answer. The anomalous situation was in fact condoned, even encouraged, by House, for it dovetailed with his desire to keep the direction of foreign policy in his own hands.

House, who fancied himself a Democratic party king-maker, was an honorary Texas colonel who seemed the very antithesis of the image evoked by his title. Rather, he was a discreet and cosmopolitan progressive. He may have owed his cosmopolitanism to formal schooling in England, Virginia, and the northeast, but his appreciation of political realities grew out of extracurricular though ardent firsthand observations—begun at an early age—in Washington, New York, and Austin. Financial security allowed him leisure for speculation on noble if not always practical schemes of domestic and international reform. Not surprisingly, he developed a yearning for political power, the attainment of which, however, seemed doomed by his physical frailty. He was, he said, "like a disembodied spirit seeking a corporeal form. I found my opportunity in Woodrow Wilson." A close friendship ripened between the two almost immediately after their meeting during Wilson's first presidential campaign. House became Wilson's adviser, confidant, intimate friend—his alter ego. In

---

Library of Congress; William Phillips to House, Feb. 3, 1917, HP 15:51; House Diary, Jan. 12, 1917; Spring Rice to Balfour, Sept. 20, 1917, Sir C. A. Spring Rice's Private Papers, Vol. 2, 1916-18, Foreign Office Library. Spring Rice said: "I venture *again* to warn you against accepting Mr. Page's opinion as proof that the President and United States Government approve of any arrangement proposed to him unless and until he is expressly authorised to express it." (Emphasis added.)

foreign affairs, or at least in those relating to the war, House became the second most powerful man in the land.[5]

Before and during the war House's Manhattan apartment had the aspect of a super foreign office. Unencumbered by any official position, he received ambassadors and unobtrusively gave guidance to the State Department, kept in touch with Republican leaders, and gave the "right steer" to newsmen. Pilgrimages to his home became *de rigueur* for visiting dignitaries. Before the United States entered the war he twice visited European capitals as the President's personal envoy.

The British were fully aware of House's power in the formulation of foreign policy. They, like Secretary of State Robert Lansing, found means of accommodating to the peculiar circumstance. Lansing established a liaison with House through State Department Counselor Frank Polk, who eventually perfected the arrangement by taking House's son-in-law, Gordon Auchincloss, into his office as assistant counselor. Couriers plied between Washington and New York to keep the Colonel abreast of developments at the State Department and to collect his recommendations. Later a private telephone line, financed by Auchincloss's law partner, David Hunter Miller, put House in instant touch with the State Department.[6]

The British liaison with House came about through less calculation, at least on the part of the British government. It began quite accidentally when Spring Rice entrusted to a British intelligence officer the delivery of an inquiry to House. Previously Spring Rice assigned errands of this type to his naval attaché, Commander (later Admiral) Guy

[5] House's early life and meeting with Wilson are described in Charles Seymour, ed., *The Intimate Papers of Colonel House*, 4 vols., New York, 1926-28, Vol. 1, chaps. 2, 3. Also see Arthur S. Link, *The New Freedom*, Princeton, 1956, pp. 93-96. For House's speculations on reform see his anonymously published novel, *Philip Dru: Administrator*, New York, 1912. House, whose middle name was Mandell, named a hotel in his novel the "Mandell House."

[6] Auchincloss began work as Polk's assistant on May 25, 1917. Auchincloss to House, May 26, 1917, HP 2:4; House Diary, March 29, 1917.

Gaunt. In December 1916, however, Gaunt, a talkative bon vivant, was on leave, and (Army) Captain Sir William Wiseman, on duty in New York, substituted for him. Wiseman's interview required only a few minutes, but House invited him to stay for a conversation. Wiseman made an excellent first impression. House described him as "the most important caller I have had for sometime." Within a month, during which the two men had three more conversations, House decided that Britain would be "far better" represented by Wiseman than by "the older and experienced diplomat, Sir Cecil Spring-Rice." A friendship, which caught fire as rapidly as had House's and Wilson's, and of vital importance to Anglo-American regulations, had begun.[7]

Several factors accounted for the almost instantaneous confidence between House and Wiseman. Most important, House was looking for a liaison with the new British government. The coalition government headed by David Lloyd George replaced the Asquith ministry on December 7, 1916. House was on close terms with the old government, often communicating directly with his friend Foreign Secretary Sir Edward (later Viscount) Grey. Grey did not join the Lloyd George cabinet, which House feared would be reactionary and dictatorial. The change in government occurred just as Wilson was planning a dramatic offer of mediation to the belligerents. House, by his own account, was therefore busy trying to create "a proper background" in England for the reception of the American proposal. But with Grey's departure his best entree into the British government vanished. House still had friends in the British liberal press, and he was rather well acquainted with the new foreign secretary, Arthur J. Balfour, and Balfour's private secretary, Sir Eric Drummond. Nonetheless, House no longer had his previous direct channel to the top echelon of the British government.[8] And

[7] House Diary, Dec. 17, 1916; Jan. 15, 1917; Willert, *Road to Safety*, p. 61; Sir Guy Gaunt, *The Yield of the Years*, London, 1940, p. 172 and *passim*.

[8] Seymour, *Intimate Papers*, Vol. 2, 397-99; House to Wilson, Dec. 1, 4, 10, 1916, HP 49:7.

after the break in German-American relations (February 3) he searched for a means of establishing himself as the direct contact between Wilson and the British government. One of House's ideas for placing himself in the center of events, if war came, was reported to London by Commander Gaunt: "House considers it important that some American of Cabinet rank should be sent to England as a resident special mission so as to be medium of direct quick communication with the President *eliminating despatch through Embassies*. He thinks a similar mission should be sent here."[9]

For the time being, however, Wiseman presented an acceptable alternative. As head of the British intelligence operations in the United States he could relay House's views to his superiors in London. Because of his position he could be presumed (and later proved) to be discreet. Though young and unknown, he might as a Unionist and with House's backing be expected to get a hearing from that greatest of Unionists, Balfour. Despite his Unionist affiliation he seemed sufficiently liberal to House, and he affirmed his sympathy to the Administration by deploring Spring Rice's and Gaunt's association with Wilson's enemies.[10] Wiseman's conversation revealed him as a knowledgeable and capable man, and on January 26 he completely won House over by confessing (as House wrote): "in the gravest confidence a thing which I had already suspected and that is that he is in direct communication with the Foreign Office and that the Ambassador and other members of the Embassy are not aware of it. I am happy beyond measure over this last conference with him, for I judge he reflects the views of his government."[11]

Reflect as he might the views of his government, Wiseman exercised commendable prudence in making his revelation in gravest confidence. He was not, at the mo-

[9] Gaunt to Director of [Naval] Intelligence Division (Adm. Reginald Hall), Feb. 14, 1917, FO 371/3112. (Emphasis added.)
[10] House Diary, Jan. 15, 1917.
[11] House to Wilson, Jan. 26, 1917, HP 49:8.

ment, in direct touch with the Foreign Office proper. Rather, he was an agent for the Secret Service (M.I. 6), the espionage organization which, though financed by the Foreign Office, operated with nearly complete autonomy. His reports, like other intelligence reports, doubtless circulated anonymously in the Foreign Office, and his reports on conversations with House must have attracted special attention. But not until April did Wiseman become primarily an agent of the Foreign Office instead of a Secret Service officer who happened to send in useful political information. One of his January reports to the Secret Service gave a more accurate glimpse of his status than did his confession to House. In it he said that he was taking "a more active interest in politics than he would ordinarily have considered his duty because the Ambassador and his staff have practically all their friends among the leaders of the Republican Party. . . . This has produced an unfortunate situation in that the Administration has come to regard the British officials as Republican partisans."[12]

The prevarication, or half-truth, to House can be excused. It was merely a means by which Wiseman propelled himself into a position to do good, in his own eyes, for Anglo-American relations. Wiseman recognized that House liked him and saw in their developing friendship the potential for drawing Britain and America closer. To heighten his importance in House's eyes he intimated that he was a

[12] Willert, *Road to Safety*, p. 52. In a memorandum of November 16, 1925, and printed in Seymour, *Intimate Papers*, Vol. 2, p. 400, Wiseman says of this period that he "communicated to the Foreign Office, through my Chief in London, certain information and suggestions which Colonel House thought they ought to have." "Chief" here meant Wiseman's superior in the Secret Service.

Information about the Secret Service is understandably scarce. David Wise and Thomas B. Ross, *The Espionage Establishment*, New York, 1967, pp. 97-98, present a credible account, based on unidentified sources. They name Sir Mansfield Cumming as "C," or the chief of the Secret Service, during World War I. See also Sir Samuel Hoare, *The Fourth Seal*, London, 1930, pp. 26-28 for a discussion of "C" as well as of the Director of Military Intelligence, Sir George Macdonogh, and the Director of Naval Intelligence, Adm. Reginald Hall.

special emissary for the Foreign Office. Impressed, House confided in him more and more and never seemed to feel duped, even when it appeared that Balfour knew nothing of Wiseman's work. Instead House caused the State Department to inform Balfour of Wiseman's cooperation with the Department. If Balfour understood what the State Department's message really meant, he knew that the Foreign Office without any initiative on its part now had a representative at the court of Colonel House. The only thing to do was to make of Wiseman the special emissary he had pretended to be.[13]

What kind of man was Wiseman the interloper diplomat? In the early 1930's when theories abounded that slick Old World diplomacy, together with Wall Street conniving, had tricked the United States into the First World War, Wiseman's name was one of those mentioned in the alleged conspiracy. At that time, circumstantial evidence seemed to give credence to the suspicions about Wiseman. He was a prosperous partner in Kuhn, Loeb and Company —an international banker—and his involvement in First World War diplomacy was widely if not precisely known. But in April 1917 Wiseman carried negligible weight in the circles that formulated British policy, even less in financial circles. His prominence in both came later. Initially his chief assets were his own drive and finesse and House's patronage.[14]

In 1917 Wiseman was a quiet man of 32, rather plump, of average height and round features. Despite a mustache he looked "the merest boy." He chose friends with care and ceaselessly cultivated them (as well as useful men not necessarily friends) with small attentions. To House he paid

[13] House to Polk, Mar. 11, 1917, Polk Papers, 77:124, Yale University Library; Polk to Page, Mar. 12, 1917, *ibid.*, 73:100.

[14] See *New York Times*, Oct. 2, 1919 and Jan. 12, 1930, for allegations (false) made about Wiseman to the Senate Naval Affairs Committee. As a Kuhn, Loeb partner, Wiseman was also a director of Paramount Publix, which he helped reorganize as Paramount Pictures in 1935. *Ibid.*, June 19, 21, and Oct. 12, 1935.

flattery, devotion, and a protégé's admiration. Himself fatherless at age eight, he came to think of his relation to House as that of a son. His well-bred manners and sense of propriety recommended him to House and Wilson, both rather punctilious men. In many ways Wiseman was a young House with an Oxbridge accent.

His title was no drawback. House throughout his life enjoyed associating with great, famous, or titled people and no doubt liked having a "sir" in his entourage. Status-conscious Englishmen could reflect that Wiseman was the tenth holder of a baronetage dating from 1628 and that he could trace his lineage even farther back to Sir John Wiseman, a knight by leave of Henry VIII. In the nineteenth century Wiseman's family, not a wealthy one, based its moderate distinction on service in the Royal Navy. His father, Captain Sir William Wiseman, annexed the Pacific island of Tongareva in 1888. Twenty years earlier, his grandfather, Rear Admiral Sir William Wiseman, commanded naval units in the same area. His great-grandfather, too, had been a naval captain.[15]

Wiseman did not continue the family tradition of naval service. After attending Winchester College he spent the year 1904-1905 in residence at Jesus College, Cambridge. There he enrolled in the miscellaneous course but did not stay long enough to earn the "pass degree" toward which the course led. In athletics, however, the 20-year-old Wiseman qualified as a "boxing Blue" and successfully represented Cambridge in a bantam-weight contest against Oxford in 1905. For the next two years or more he worked as a reporter on the London *Daily Express*. During those days he wrote a satirical play titled "The Way to Tim-

---

[15] Willert, *Road to Safety*, pp. 62, 64. L. S. Amery, Diary, Nov. 29, 1917, L. S. Amery Papers, in the possession of Mr. Julian Amery, London. Hereafter cited as Amery Diary.

My conversations with Mrs. Winifred Mood, Wiseman's sister, on Aug. 8-9, 1964, and with Joan, Lady Wiseman, Wiseman's widow, on July 1, 1964.

Burke's Peerage, London, 1963, pp. 2,607-2,608; W. P. Morrell, *Britain in the Pacific Islands*, Oxford, 1960, pp. 99, 286.

buktu," but it, like two plays he wrote in later life, was never commercially staged. By late 1908 he had concluded that there was no money in journalism and that banking was his field. In 1909 he came to North America and made modest returns from ventures in Canadian real estate and Mexican meat-packing. While in Mexico he met the dictator Porfirio Díaz and developed an interest in the country which he retained for life.[16]

Married and the father of two children by the outbreak of the war, he left family and business to become an artillery lieutenant in the British army. Later he was promoted to captain in the 6th Battalion, Duke of Cornwall's Light Infantry. While serving with this unit he was gassed in Flanders in 1915. Back home in England to recuperate, he was chosen, because of his familiarity with America and on the recommendation of an old shipmate of his father, to work for M.I.6 in the United States. About the beginning of 1916 Wiseman took charge of the American operation, which was camouflaged as part of the American and Transport Department of the Ministry of Munitions. The cover was appropriate, for his duty consisted mainly in stymying the efforts of Austrian, German, Irish, and Hindu groups in the United States who sought to sabotage the flow of munitions to the Allies or plotted sedition in the British Empire. With one or two exceptions, British espionage (or counterespionage) in America was, contrary to versions remembered later, probably no more exciting than a contemporary description of it by the British consul general in New York: "watching suspicious ships, shipments and persons; and . . . obtaining information asked for by the Foreign Office and . . . Embassy." Still, Wiseman's work introduced him to similarly commissioned Poles, Czechs, and Slovaks;

[16] Dr. F. Brittain (Keeper of the Records, Jesus College) to the author, Oct. 2, 1967. Interviews with Wiseman in the *Mexico City Herald*, Dec. 20, 1945 and the [Kingston, Jamaica] *Daily Gleaner*, Jan. 28, 1955; Wiseman to Lord Elibank, May 17, 1956; all in New WWP. My conversations with Mrs. Mood and Lady Wiseman, as cited in the preceding footnote.

as will be seen, these acquaintances in the spy network later proved useful in his political work.[17]

WISEMAN's first visit to House on December 17 was an attempt to learn unofficially the terms underlying Germany's offer of a peace conference five days earlier. House did not know, but promised to try to find out if the British government would delay its answer to Germany for a few days. London refused to delay, so nothing came of this first House-Wiseman scheme.[18] As an attempted behind-the-scenes maneuver, however, it typified the modus operandi Wiseman and House would follow in the next three years. Foremost in the minds of each was the desire to put British and American diplomacy in tandem—in December 1916 to end the war, later to win it.

President Wilson, afraid that the Allies would categorically reject the German peace overture and thereby rule out all chance for a negotiated peace, rushed out his own plea for peace on December 18. He did so contrary to House's advice, and as House foresaw neither Germany nor the Allies accepted Wilson's proffered good offices. On the contrary, the British were incensed and hurt by Wilson's remark that the objects of the belligerents on both sides seemed virtually the same. House passed on to the President Wiseman's reaction: "No matter who brought on the war or what the governments knew the cause to be for which they were fighting, the people, he said, of every belligerent nation had worked themselves up to an exalted enthusiasm of patriotic fervor and they resent any

[17] *Burke's Peerage*, pp. 2,607-2,608; Willert, *Road to Safety*, pp. 18-31; Edmund Phipps (Ministry of Munitions) to Foreign Office, June 25, 1917, FO 371/3119; Clive Bayley (Consul General, New York) to Spring Rice, Jan. 18 and Mar. 7, 1916, FO 115/2139. Attached Embassy statements show that about $2,000 per month was being spent in New York for Secret Service work. Such scattered evidence as remains in the Wiseman Papers concerning Secret Service activity relates to the guarding of munitions and to reports and rumors about persons suspected of being pro-German.

[18] Seymour, *Intimate Papers*, Vol. 2, pp. 400-403.

19

suggestion that they have selfish motives and are not fighting solely for a principle."[19]

Wiseman expressed similar disappointment at Wilson's next essay on peace, his "peace without victory" address of January 22, 1917, to the Senate. In that speech Wilson outlined a concert of nations for the enforcement of arbitration, invoking the principles later to be enunciated in the Covenant of the League of Nations. Wiseman, whose report on Allied reception of the speech Wilson asked to see, related the Allies' deep resentment at the speech. The Allies felt, he reported, that they were at present doing exactly what Wilson suggested for the future—punishing an aggressor which had refused arbitration. Personally Wiseman thought that Wilson, by pressing the Allies too hard for peace, might harm the cause of democracy.

> He asserts [House wrote Wilson] that every belligerent Government is now in the hands of the reactionaries and must necessarily be in their hands when the war ends. He believes if we are not careful we will find that these forces in the belligerent Governments will all come together when peace is made, and it is not at all unlikely that their concentrated hate for democracy will be centred upon this country.
>
> Peace, he says, must come first, and then a plan to enforce arbitration afterwards. He thinks it is possible that after peace is signed, and before the arbitration agreement is made, the reactionary forces might refuse to go into any league for future peace and make some pretext to turn upon us in order to save autocracy.[20]

These views, coming from the man House had already described to Wilson as a friend of the Administration and "the most sensible Englishman that has been connected with the Embassy here since the war began,"[21] could

[19] *Ibid.*, pp. 403-409; House to Wilson, Dec. 20, 1916, HP 49:7.
[20] Seymour, *Intimate Papers*, Vol. 2, pp. 414-21; Wilson to House, Jan. 24, 1917, HP 49:18; House to Wilson, Jan. 25, 1917, HP 49:8.
[21] House to Wilson, Jan. 16, 1917, HP 49:8.

hardly have improved Wilson's opinion of the belligerents. They meant there was no immediate hope for
peace. They confirmed Wilson's suspicion that Allied as
well as Central governments were reactionary. They gave
a cogent reason for Wilson's later (and much criticized)
insistence on incorporating the Covenant of the League of
Nations in the peace treaty.

No doubt fearing that Wilson might be angry at Wiseman as well as at Wiseman's views, House acted quickly to
put Wiseman in the President's good graces. To the latter
he wrote; "I do not want you to think that anything that
Wiseman said . . . reflected his own views. He had been
saturated with the unfriendly attitude of Spring-Rice and,
for the moment, it warped his vision. Wiseman seems to be
a sincere liberal and a devoted adherent to the principles
of democracy. He is working intelligently in the direction we desire. For instance, he is cabling to his government the favorable editorials like those in the World and
is trying to give them a different viewpoint from that which
they must necessarily get from Spring-Rice."[22]

Temporarily warped vision or not, Wiseman soon had no
further cause to criticize Wilson's attempt at peacemaking. Germany blasted those attempts by resuming un-
restricted submarine warfare. On January 31 Wiseman informed House that during the night before there was
furious activity in the German and Austrian consulates,
probably in preparation for a new departure in policy for
the Central Powers. The same day the German ambassador, Count von Bernstorff, handed the American government a note announcing the resumption of unrestrained
submarine warfare on February 1. On February 3 the
United States severed diplomatic relations with Germany.
The way was clear for Wiseman and House to begin their
program of Anglo-American cooperation.[23]

Or almost clear. Guy Gaunt returned from leave on Jan-

[22] House to Wilson, Jan. 27, 1917, HP 49:8.
[23] House Diary, Jan. 31, 1917; Seymour, *Intimate Papers*, Vol. 2,
pp. 431-42.

uary 30 to discover that Wiseman was in the process of supplanting him as the British contact with House. Gaunt soon sought to discredit Wiseman by telling House that London (no official was named) was complaining of Wiseman's activities. Wiseman countered by saying that Gaunt communicated only with the naval intelligence office, whereas Wiseman, so he led House to believe, communicated directly with the Foreign Office. House had earlier concluded that it was more profitable to work through Wiseman, but he left the resolution of the scrap to the contenders. Wiseman won. Apparently he did so by explaining to Spring Rice his close relations with House and receiving the ambassador's approval of his political work. In return, Spring Rice instructed Wiseman to let him know "at once any *political* information which you may receive or give in order that I may check it against other information."[24]

In early March Wiseman had some political information to report. It was a memorandum on American attitudes toward Britain and the war for the information of the Imperial War Conference, due to convene in London in late March. Wiseman persuaded House in late February that such a message should be sent. House talked the matter over with the President during the weekend of the latter's second inauguration. Wiseman and House then drafted a statement which Wiseman gave Spring Rice to forward to London. Although House authorized Wiseman to say that the President had read the statement and thought it just, Wiseman cautioned Spring Rice that it was not a state document.[25]

[24] House Diary, Jan. 19, 30, Feb. 9, 23, 1917; Spring Rice to Wiseman, Feb. 12, 1917, WWP 121. (Italics in the original.)

[25] House Diary, Feb. 23, Mar. 7, 1917; Wiseman to Spring Rice, Mar. 6, 1917, WWP 121. Copies of the memorandum are in WWP 4 and HP 48:292. The latter copy bears this notation: "This is the form Sir Wm Wiseman and I agreed upon to be sent to the meeting of the chiefs of the British Empire now in conference in London. I told him that the President had read it and thought it a just statement. E.M.H. March 8/17." House's diary does not indicate when Wilson read the

22

The memorandum warned that although broader-minded Americans supported the Allies as defenders of democracy, the mass of the people possessed little pro-Ally and less pro-British sentiment. Britain was the least popular of the Allies because of her war measures—the blockade, blacklists, and censorship. There was animosity toward and misunderstanding of British policy in Ireland. Nor, the memorandum continued, did Americans understand the connection between Russia's domestic struggle and the war against reactionary Germany. Unless care were taken, German intrigue might create bad feeling between Britain and the United States in unsettled Mexico. Having indicated points where British and American policies might come into conflict, the memorandum condemned Englishmen and Anglophilic Americans antipathetic to the Administration: "Some of our most fervent partisans in this country have done our cause much harm. Unintentionally, no doubt, they have drawn the whole question of the neutrality of the United States into domestic politics, which has been very much to the detriment of a proper understanding between the two Governments." In summary, the memorandum said, "the people of the United States wish to be entirely neutral as far as the European war is concerned. The Administration, however, have always understood the cause of the war and have been entirely sympathetic to the Allies. The people are beginning to realise that it may not be possible for them to remain at peace with Germany. There is a feeling among the Americans that if they tolerate too much they will lose their prestige and authority as a world power. If the United States goes to war with Germany—which she probably will—it will be to uphold American rights and assert her dignity as a nation."

The memorandum went to Spring Rice for dispatch on March 6 or 7. He forwarded it despite its implicit criti-

---

draft memorandum. Received by the Foreign Office on March 9, the memorandum was circulated to the King and the Cabinet as "the views of President Wilson and the majority of the people of the U.S.A." Balfour Papers, 49740, British Museum.

23

cism of himself. The British government now had one more indication that the United States was on the verge of declaring war. Already the Zimmermann telegram and the sinking of the *Laconia* had intensified German-American animosities. As important, the memorandum warned that United States belligerency would not mean any great sympathy toward Britain nor automatic acceptance of Britain's war aims, and that there would be obstacles—Ireland, Russia, and Mexico—to full Anglo-American cooperation. Much of this Spring Rice had previously reported,[26] but never with the authority of this memorandum.

For the remaining three weeks preceding American belligerency, Wiseman busied himself with conferences with House and in plans to mesh British and American intelligence operations. In February he had revealed his Secret Service identity to Frank Polk, Counsellor of the State Department. He now passed on to Polk such information as possible German submarine positions and the procedures used to protect British supplies and shipping.[27] On a pettier level, he investigated the background of Indian nationalist poet Sir Rabindranath Tagore, who wished to dedicate a book to President Wilson. Wiseman advised against the dedication, on the grounds that Tagore was mixed up with "Indian plotters," and the poet's tender of respect was rebuffed.[28]

A few days prior to Wilson's war address, House briefed Wiseman on what the President would say, with the intent

[26] Spring Rice to Balfour, Feb. 23 and Mar. 1, 1917, printed in Gwynn, *Spring Rice*, Vol. 2, pp. 381-85.

[27] House Diary, Mar. 8, 23, 24, 1917; Frank Polk Confidential Diary, Polk Papers, Feb. 16, 1917 (hereafter cited as Polk Confidential Diary). House to Polk, Mar. 11, 1917, Polk Papers, 77:124. The Secret Service was anxious that Wiseman, in cooperating with the State Department, not be "brought into the open." Balfour to Spring Rice, Mar. 15, 1917, FO 371/3112. See also [Secret Service] to Wiseman, Mar. 13, 1917, WWP 4.

[28] House to Wilson, Apr. 6, 1917, HP 49:9. None of the four books by Tagore published in the United States in 1917 bore a dedication to Wilson.

that the British arrange a favorable reception by the press. Wiseman thus knew in advance more about Wilson's war message than Cabinet members, for Wilson gave none of them the details of what he would say. Wiseman returned the compliment by asserting that Shakespeare himself could not have improved on Wilson's prose.[29]

WITH THE United States at last in the war, the British lost no time in appealing for American aid. To outline the Allies' needs, and to welcome the United States into the war, the War Cabinet decided to dispatch a high-powered mission headed by Balfour to Washington. The decision, relayed to the United States government on April 6, was made without first determining directly whether the President would welcome such a mission. Lloyd George did secure Page's approval and may have assumed that Page spoke for the President. Page did not. Wilson, who seemed reluctant to make war despite his demand for it, foresaw "manifest dangers" from the Balfour mission. He feared that the public would interpret the mission "as an attempt to in some degree take charge of us as an assistant to Great Britain, particularly if the Secretary of State for Foreign Affairs heads the commission." House worried that Wilson might give offense by delaying to respond to the War Cabinet's overture. In a prod to the President, House stated that Wiseman had learned that the War Cabinet unanimously desired Balfour to come to Washington. Wiseman, according to House, thought that to discourage the Balfour visit would have a bad effect throughout the British Empire. The President agreed that under the circumstances he must receive the mission. He therefore suggested to Lansing the possibility of cloaking the political aspect of the mission by describing it as a delegation of experts come to share their experience in war administration with the Council of National Defense. Lansing replied

[29] House Diary, Mar. 29, Apr. 2, 1917; House to Wilson, Apr. 4, 1917, HP 49:9.

that such a guise would offend the British, for Balfour wished to discuss the "whole international situation."[30]

This first exchange between Washington and London as co-belligerents revealed a pattern that was to distinguish Anglo-American relations in the succeeding months. First, there was the tendency of the British to spring a plan on Wilson without first preparing the way for it. There was Wilson's reluctance to adopt any course which might make him appear to be following the British lead. He was determined to steer a separate diplomatic course for the United States. Finally, there was the intervention of House and Wiseman to prevent the development of friction between the two governments.

This first exchange also pointed up the difference in outlook of Washington and London. The United States, sensing no immediate military peril, began the war with a slate virtually clean of war plans. Wilson's war message committed the country to cooperation with and material aid to the Allies. He also promised to strengthen the navy and army, but that did not necessarily mean that the Administration envisaged a large American army in France. Counsel among Wilson's advisers was divided. Secretary of the Treasury William G. McAdoo, Wilson's son-in-law, doubted that the United States could furnish soldiers for the front and declared that the chief means of aiding the Allies would be through extending them financial loans. House, too, questioned the wisdom of trying to form a large army. Despite Secretary of War Newton D. Baker's wish to send an army to Europe immediately, through most of April the Administration conceived of America's role in the war chiefly as that of a warehouse for the Allies. And whatever form American participation took, there seemed plenty of time to proceed deliberately.[31]

[30] House Diary, Apr. 6, 1917; Page to Secretary of State, Apr. 6, 1917, *Foreign Relations, 1917*, Sup. 2, Vol. 1, p. 11; David Lloyd George, *War Memoirs*, 6 vols., London, 1933-36, Vol. II, p. 1,677; Lansing to Wilson, Apr. 6, 1917, SD 763.72/3669-1/2; Wilson to House, Apr. 6 and 9, 1917, HP 49:18; House to Wilson, Apr. 8, 1917, HP 49:8.

[31] Wilson's war message is printed in Ray Stannard Baker and

The government in London took a less placid view of American participation in the war. True, Lord Milner, a leading member of the War Cabinet, wondered if America should not concentrate on building an air force instead of an army, and, true, Lloyd George had doubts that an American army could reach Europe in time to be effective. But all agreed that immediate American action of some sort was imperative. Germany's submarine offensive was taking a terrible toll of British shipping. Balfour thought the most pressing need of the moment was American ships to replace British losses. American cargoes, especially steel and food, were also desperately needed, as were credits to pay for the cargoes. The British also hoped, though perhaps without expectation, that American troops would be able to take over a quiet sector of the Western front in August or September. The task of Balfour's mission was to impress the urgency of these needs on the Administration.[32]

Despite Wilson's forebodings, Balfour's party, consisting largely of technical experts, enjoyed a cordial reception from the American public and press. After a stopover in New York for a briefing by Colonel House (arranged by Wiseman), Balfour arrived in Washington on Sunday, April 22. He was met by streets full of Washingtonians waving miniature Union Jacks. Installed in the mansion of Breckinridge Long, an Assistant Secretary of State, the one-time Prime Minister embarked on a month-long routine of

---

William E. Dodd, eds., *The Public Papers of Woodrow Wilson*, 6 vols., New York, 1925-27, Vol. 5, pp. 6-16.

Robert Lansing, "Memorandum of the Cabinet Meeting 2:30–5 P.M. Tuesday, March 20, 1917," Lansing Private Diaries, Box 1, Vol. 2, Lansing Papers, Library of Congress; House to Wilson, Mar. 19, 1917, in Seymour, *Intimate Papers*, Vol. 3, pp. 6-7.

According to Arthur Willert (who was in Washington at the time), "the overriding idea, before the Allied Missions arrived, was for an all-out naval war, for generous financial and material aid to the Allies, and only for limited land-warfare." Willert, *Road to Safety*, p. 78. See also Trask, *United States in the Supreme War Council*, p. 9.

[32] Milner, "Memorandum to War Cabinet on War Policy," June 7, 1917, Milner Papers, Vol. 8, New College, Oxford; Pershing, *My Experiences*, Vol. 1, pp. 15-17; Lloyd George, *War Memoirs*, Vol. 3, pp. 1,678-80.

ceremony and conference. He laid a wreath on Washington's tomb, visited Richmond and Chicago, patiently withstood threats and rude letters from Irish extremists, paid his respects to Theodore Roosevelt, and addressed prominent New Yorkers gathered together by former Ambassador to Britain Joseph Choate (who, possibly overexcited by the manifestation of Anglophilia, died immediately afterward). Balfour's subordinates put themselves at the disposal of American officials for the explanation of British policies and experiences in the war. One of them, General Tom Bridges, dispelled, as did a similar French mission, the notion that large numbers of American soldiers might not be needed in France. He asked that 500,000 men be amalgamated into the British army. But in this as in other questions, arrangements for cooperation were left tentative and vague.[33]

Balfour himself opted for tacit rather than written understandings. In his first interview at the White House, he heard Wilson rule out the possibility of a treaty of alliance or any arrangement which committed America to fight until Allied claims were satisfied. Wilson wanted a free hand in diplomacy, free to make a separate peace if necessary. Balfour the diplomatist appreciated Wilson's position and, in repeating it to London, remarked, "Were I in his place I should have decided as he has done." But Balfour wanted Wilson to understand Britain's position also, so he explained his country's contractual obligations to the other Allies and gave the President copies of the secret Allied treaties. Balfour's candor and his philosophical manner won the admiration of Wilson, who indicated his respect for the visitor by appearing in the gallery of the House of Representatives during Balfour's May 5th address to Mem-

[33] The papers relating to Balfour's visit (including letters from Irish partisans) are filed in a portfolio entitled Lord Balfour's Mission to the United States, America 1917, in the Foreign Office Library (hereafter cited as Balfour's Mission). Charles Hanson Towne, ed., *The Balfour Visit*, New York, 1917. Sir Tom Bridges describes the visit in *Alarms & Excursions*, New York, 1938, pp. 169-90. Trask, *United States in the Supreme War Council*, p. 10.

bers of Congress. Arthur Willert, the Washington correspondent for the London *Times*, was able to cable his editor in mid-May that "Balfour has been in broad sense conspicuously successful though his subordinates [are] handicapped in concrete work."[34]

Meanwhile London was growing anxious for proof of American participation in the war. The cordiality of Balfour's reception could not obscure the failure of his mission to achieve immediate tangible results. A Foreign Office cable told Balfour that the War Cabinet "do not think American people are taking war quite seriously enough and are beginning to doubt whether their assistance (except in the matter of finance) is going to be as valuable as they had hoped." The War Cabinet particularly wanted more American destroyers to fight submarines in European waters and American steel for ship-building. When Lloyd George instructed Balfour to urge the Administration's intervention to divert steel from private uses to the construction of ships, Balfour replied in a vein which characterized his attitude on how to influence the American government. Any prodding from the British which might look like an attempt to manage the Americans would be harmful, he said. It was "absolutely necessary to rely entirely on U.S. Government" to mobilize American resources. Balfour demonstrated this attitude by conceding to the American Shipping Board the right to requisition British ships under construction in United States yards.[35]

[34] Balfour to Lloyd George, Apr. 26, 1917, FO 371/3119; Wilson to Balfour, May 19, 1917, FO 200/208. This is Wilson's acknowledgment, in his own hand, of receipt of the treaties. Willert to Lord Northcliffe, May 18, 1917, quoted in Reginald Pound and Geoffrey Harmsworth, *Northcliffe*, New York, 1960, p. 528.

Lord Eustace Percy, the blockade specialist in Balfour's party, wrote Drummond on May 14 urging that Balfour "put something on paper" before he left Washington. Percy feared the Americans would wreck British procurement organization in the United States, for example, the purchasing arrangement with J. P. Morgan and Company, without providing adequate substitutes. Percy to Drummond, May 14, 1917, Balfour's Mission. For Balfour's discussion with House and Wilson, see Seymour, *Intimate Papers*, Vol. 3, pp. 29-63.

[35] Lord Robert Cecil to Balfour, Apr. 25, 1917; Lloyd George to

Balfour's posture of deference was appropriate for the occasion, if for no other reason than that Britain was the suppliant, with almost no means of pressuring the United States. He realized that any attempt directly to steer the American government would be futile. For the American government, he reported home, was "the President, and nobody but the President," and the only way to move him was by persuasion. Persuasion would require close and constant communication with the President. Britain did not have that through her ambassador, for, as House told Balfour, Spring Rice no longer had access to the President. House also told Balfour how to get the requisite communication: keep Spring Rice on as ambassador but route really important messages through Wiseman to House, who would then take them up with Wilson. Balfour agreed and delegated his private secretary, Sir Eric Drummond, to work out the details for a direct cable link between the Foreign Office and Wiseman. Wiseman's importance was thus recognized and his status upgraded.[36] In House's words, "The coming of Balfour and Drummond has given Sir William a tremendous 'Boost.' They found out how much I think of him and how much I trust both his integrity and ability, and they reciprocated by following my lead. I am looking forward to Wiseman's future career in English politics. I should like to see him go far."[37]

Balfour, May 1, 1917; Balfour to Lloyd George, May 4, 1917, Balfour's Mission. Balfour to William Denman, May 4, 1917, HP 2:22.

[36] Balfour to Cecil May 27, 1917, Balfour's Mission; House Diary, Apr. 22, 26, 1917. Concerning the direct line of communication, Wiseman wrote about 1926: ". . . Colonel House arranged, with the President's approval, that Balfour should cable in a special British Government code direct to me in New York, and that I should make it my chief duty to attend to these cables and bring them immediately to Colonel House, who could telephone them over a private wire to the State Department or to President Wilson. In this way Balfour, speaking for the British Government, could get an answer from President Wilson, if necessary, within a few hours. This would have been utterly impossible had the communications gone through ordinary diplomatic channels." Seymour, *Intimate Papers*, Vol. 3, p. 65.

[37] House Diary, May 23, 1917.

Balfour, however, was not so sure that a makeshift arrangement could substitute for a properly constituted embassy. Wiseman, after all, was an unknown quantity, young and inexperienced. Balfour probably had not met him previously. Spring Rice obviously could not function as ambassador, but neither was it clear that Wiseman, under some cover, could. Balfour therefore urged the War Cabinet to send over Lord Grey, his predecessor as foreign secretary, to replace Spring Rice for the duration of the war. Grey, known to be highly acceptable to Wilson and House, was a happy choice. But the War Cabinet, some of whose members considered Grey to be "too pacifist," failed to persuade him to take the post. In the opinion of Lord Robert Cecil, Balfour's deputy in the Foreign Office, the War Cabinet did not seriously try. Instead they quickly accepted Grey's objections and moved on to consider appointing Austen Chamberlain, favored for the job by the King. Balfour approved the suggestion of Chamberlain but, informed by Cecil of the War Cabinet's perfunctory offer to Grey, requested that no decision be taken until he returned to London.[38]

Four days later Cecil cabled that the War Cabinet proposed to send Lord Northcliffe, the proprietor of the London *Times* and a string of other newspapers, to Washington as their special representative. Contrary to Lloyd George's memory later, Balfour and his assistants reacted strongly and negatively to this proposal. Drummond cabled home his belief that the appointment of Northcliffe would be "quite disastrous." Cecil deeply regretted the decision, thinking that to send out a "business hustler" instead of Grey was "a very dangerous experiment." Balfour, on the eve of his departure from North America, agreed with the War Cabinet that British procurement missions in the United States needed coordination and that there were grave defects in America's mobilization for war. He doubted, however, whether Northcliffe, a "vigorous hustler

[38] Balfour to Cecil, May 5, 19, and 22, 1917, Cecil to Balfour, May 17 and 21, 1917, in Balfour's Mission.

and loud voiced propagandist," would provide the remedies. At any rate, Balfour advised, the British government should solicit, through Colonel House, the President's opinion of a Northcliffe mission.[39]

Lloyd George did not query the President, nor was he deterred by Balfour's objections. He did secure an endorsement of Northcliffe from Page and again possibly mistook Page's opinion for the President's. In fact, Wilson emphatically deplored the choice of Northcliffe. So did Wiseman and Spring Rice, both of whom interpreted the hurry with which Northcliffe was nominated as a maneuver on the part of Lloyd George to avoid the opposition Balfour could rally if he were in London. The Prime Minister may have thought Northcliffe the best available man to look after the war missions. Possibly he also saw the chance, by taking Northcliffe into the government, to silence the potentially hostile Northcliffe newspapers, which had been instrumental in bringing about the fall of Asquith. Whatever the motive, flamboyant Northcliffe sailed into New York on June 11. House lamented to Wilson that Balfour had been unable to head off the press lord.[40]

In a sense, Lord Northcliffe was, as he thought and as

[39] Cecil to Balfour, May 26, 1917, *ibid.*; Lloyd George, *War Memoirs*, Vol. 3, p. 1,689. See also Lord Beaverbrook, *Man and Power, 1917-1918*, New York, 1956, pp. 67-72. Drummond to Sir Maurice Hankey, May 27, 1917, Balfour's Mission; Cecil to Hankey, May 17, 1917, Lord Robert Cecil's Private Papers, FO 800/188, Public Record Office, Balfour to Cecil, May 27, 1917, Balfour's Mission. Balfour in a "strictly personal" cable to Cecil said he wished to continue Spring Rice in the Washington embassy unless Grey could come over. "To send Northcliffe might in my opinion have an unfortunate effect on the present and future relations of the two countries and I earnestly trust that no such decision will be taken until I have had opportunity of explaining situation here, which perhaps Cabinet hardly appreciate." Balfour to Cecil, May 19, 1917, *ibid.* Balfour did not like Northcliffe personally. See Beaverbrook, *Men and Power*, p. 148.

[40] Lloyd George, *War Memoirs*, Vol. 3, p. 1,689; Pound and Harmsworth, *Northcliffe*, p. 530; House Diary, June 1, 1917; House to Wilson, June 7, 1917, HP 49:8. In the preceding February House told Wilson that, according to Wiseman, Northcliffe wanted Spring Rice removed. House to Wilson, Feb. 11, 1917, HP 49:8.

the press announced, Balfour's successor. He did not, however, have any diplomatic responsibilities. Officially the British government announced that he was in America to combine and coordinate the activities of the various governmental missions. Styled the Chairman of the British War Mission, he was to oversee the recruiting of British citizens and the manufacture, purchase, and transport over land and sea of all supplies. If diplomatic support were necessary he was to apply to the embassy.[41]

The scope of the instructions and the reputation of the envoy nevertheless caused Spring Rice to fear that his own authority would be usurped. Apparently that is why he sent no one to the dock to meet Northcliffe. The latter was enraged by the snub and was not consoled by Spring Rice's explanation that the arrival was supposed to be secret. (The excuse suffered from the fact that members of the New York press met Northcliffe at the ship.) There followed an acrimonious confrontation, during which Spring Rice accused Northcliffe of being a personal enemy. Actually, both men quickly gave way to their country's best interest and at least superficially resolved personal animosities. Spring Rice said, "We have got to work together, whatever we may feel about each other."[42]

Wiseman and Arthur Willert soothed the hurt pride of Northcliffe, who for his part set up office in New York to keep clear of the ambassador. Wiseman was able to retain Spring Rice's confidence and gain Northcliffe's. To the latter he gave his private secretary and use of cable facilities. Two weeks after Northcliffe's arrival, House, Wiseman, and Spring Rice, assembled at House's Magnolia,

[41] Pound and Harmsworth, *Northcliffe*, pp. 530-31; War Cabinet to Balfour, May 31, 1917, HP 20:45. Northcliffe's mission was explained to the House of Commons by Bonar Law, the government's parliamentary leader. *Parliamentary Debates, House of Commons*, 5th series, Vol. 94 (June 5-22, 1917), p. 607. Lloyd George, *War Memoirs*, Vol. 3, p. 1,690.

[42] Pound and Harmsworth, *Northcliffe*, p. 541. Accounts of the Northcliffe–Spring Rice confrontation are also given in Lloyd George, *War Memoirs*, Vol. 3, pp. 1,693-96, and Willert, *Road to Safety*, pp. 95-104.

Massachusetts home, agreed to make the best of an unhappy situation by helping Northcliffe in his mission as much as possible. Wiseman became a sort of chaperon to Northcliffe. For instance, after an interview with the President on June 30, Northcliffe handed Wiseman a report on the interview to be cabled to Lloyd George. Wiseman first let House read the report, than cabled it. "Northcliffe does not realize," House recorded, "how he is being moved on the chessboard, and how carefully he is being watched to keep him from making mistakes." Wiseman, in extending cable facilities, seemed as concerned to keep affairs under his own surveillance as in meeting Northcliffe's convenience.[43]

Once in harness, the "dictator of Fleet Street" worked hard on supply problems and kept clear of Spring Rice's premises. One of his first dispatches to Lloyd George revealed that there were in America six different British purchasing agencies, some of which competed with one another. Together they spent some two million pounds (approximately $9,500,000) per day. Later reports showed his major concerns to be procuring petroleum for the navy, ferreting out tonnage to carry supplies, and transferring general purchasing responsibility from J. P. Morgan and Company, the British buyer since 1915, to his own office. In all his work he found Wiseman to be "one of our most valuable people here. . . . He is young, alert, and knows these people well."[44]

As June drew to a close America's participation in the war was still largely indirect. Six destroyers were operating in European waters and Gen. John J. Pershing was in France setting up facilities to receive the American Expeditionary Force.[45] The main theater of activity, however, was in Washington, where representatives of virtually all

[43] *Ibid.*, p. 102; House Diary, June 23, 30, 1917.

[44] Pound and Harmsworth, *Northcliffe,* p. 545. Copies of the numerous cables sent by Northcliffe in his work are in WWP 91 and 92.

[45] Hendrick, *Page,* Vol. 2, p. 276. Pershing arrived in Britain on June 10, in France on June 13. Pershing, *My Experiences,* Vol. 1, pp. 44, 57.

the Allies were clamoring for loans and goods. No way had yet been found to meet the Allies' needs orderly and in accordance with some sound system of priority. Within the British ranks uncertainty and resentment added to the disorder. American officials somewhat bewilderedly conducted business with both the embassy and War Mission staffs. The latter seemed no surer of their specific responsibilities than did their hosts. The division of British authority between "two political nonentities, . . . one [Spring Rice] prematurely aged and one [Northcliffe] a boy who had never grown up,"[46] could not last. The first crisis in Anglo-American relations, arising partly out of the ramshackle scheme of representation, proved the scheme unworkable. Well before the crisis came Wiseman determined to go to London to explain the American situation and his place in it to the Prime Minister. He had decided that the best way to overcome the Spring Rice–Northcliffe tangle was to bring over a prominent statesman to replace both men and consolidate their work under one head. He would find that the crisis in relations paved the way for the reception of his ideas.

[46] Lord Eustace Percy, *Some Memories*, London, 1958, p. 55.

CHAPTER THREE

DOLLARS IN DIPLOMACY

> . . . holding the command of the purse [Secretary of the Treasury McAdoo] is entitled to a controlling voice in war expenditure and indeed in the conduct of the war. . . . The State Department naturally falls into abeyance and the Treasury becomes supreme.
>
> Sir Cecil Spring Rice to Foreign Office, July 20, 1917

THE BRITISH government interpreted the American entry into the war as putting an end to British financial worries. The War Cabinet, when complaining to the Balfour mission concerning American dilatoriness, took cheer only from the promise of American financial aid. Hours before the War Cabinet cabled Balfour, Congress passed the first Liberty Loan act, authorizing the Secretary of the Treasury to loan up to three billion dollars to the Allies. A few days later McAdoo handed over $200 million to the British. The American vaults were swinging open just at the point when Britain's purse was about to collapse. When the vaults abruptly closed at the end of June, panic broke out among the British and Wiseman was given his first chance to shape Anglo-American relations.[1]

Chancellor of the Exchequer Bonar Law promptly thanked McAdoo for the first loan, and with good cause.

[1] Cecil to Balfour, Apr. 25, 1917, Balfour's Mission. A description and copy of the first Liberty Loan act of April 24 are contained in the *Annual Report of the Secretary of the Treasury 1917*, Washington, D.C., 1918, pp. 5, 83. William G. McAdoo, *Crowded Years*, Boston, 1931, p. 394. Authorizations for loans to Britain are located in Record Group 39, Bureau of Accounts, Treasury Department, Country File, Box 117, GB 132.1, National Archives (hereafter cited as Country File).

For accounts of government finance during the war see Alexander D. Noyes, *The War Period of American Finance, 1908-1925*, New York, 1926; Randolph E. Paul, *Taxation in the United States*, Boston, 1954, pp. 110-18; and Sidney Ratner, *American Taxation*, New York, 1942, pp. 364-96.

Because of the one-sided trade with the United States since 1914, Britain was suffering an ever worsening shortage of dollar credits. In 1915 a special financial mission had come to New York and secured a £50,000,000 (approximately $240,000,000) loan from private bankers. A few months earlier J. P. Morgan and Company signed a contract with the British government to coordinate purchases and maintain the pound sterling's exchange standing in the United States. To pay for purchases and to peg the pound at a constant value required the shipment from Britain of vast quantities of gold and the mortgaging of virtually all British-owned securities in the United States. British expenses mounted so in the fall of 1916 that additional loans amounting to $550 million had to be raised in New York. By early 1917 Britain urgently needed yet more credits. As she waited to see whether the United States would enter the war, she covered her deficits in the U.S. by a fluctuating overdraft (or demand loan) from Morgan's.[2] On April 3 Law happily told the Imperial War Cabinet that President Wilson's war message, promising financial aid, gave hope that Britain would not have to go off the gold standard. At that moment Britain was making purchases in the United States at the rate of $75,000,000 per week and possessed remaining resources convertible into dollars of only $219 million. On the eve of Wilson's war message Law was toy-

---

[2] Law to Balfour, May 3, 1917, and Balfour to Lansing, May 5, 1917, both in Balfour's Mission. The [2nd] Marquess of Reading, *Rufus Isaacs First Marquess of Reading*, 2 vols., London, 1939-45, Vol. 2, pp. 22-50, 54-56, describes the negotiations for private loans. See also Link, *Wilson*, Vol. 3, pp. 627-28.

U.S. Congress, 74th Cong., 2nd Sess., Senate, *Munitions Industry*, 7 vols., Washington, D.C., 1936, Vol. 6, p. 121. This is the report of Senator Gerald Nye's special committee investigating the munitions industry. Chapter 7 of Volume 6 deals with Anglo-American finances on the eve of American entry into the war and concludes (p. 158) that because Britain expected the United States to declare war she purposely overextended her credit in the United States in the belief that the United States government would pay it off. Confirmation of this conclusion would depend on full access to the records of the Morgan firm and the British Treasury. See also Arthur S. Link, *Wilson*, 7 vols. to date, Princeton, 1947-65, Vol. 4, p. 148, and Vol. 5, pp. 178-84.

ing with the idea of converting Canadian Pacific Railroad stocks (worth about £40,000,000) into dollar securities, so that they could be negotiated on the New York market. Now that the United States was offering loans, such a step would not be necessary.[3]

Despite American willingness to loan and British eagerness to borrow, negotiations over money produced the first crisis in the Anglo-American war partnership. The crisis centered on the question of whether the United States Treasury was liable for Britain's overdraft at Morgan's. The Treasury said no, Britain yes. Domestic American political considerations, personal vanity, and incoherent diplomatic organization were the circumstances which allowed dispute over this question to reach crisis proportions. By explaining the first, appeasing the second, and untangling the third, Wiseman helped engineer a solution to the crisis.

The already described confusion of British diplomatic organization in Washington had something of a counterpart in the American government. No longer was the State Department solely responsible for international negotiation. The Liberty Loan act of April 24 invested full power for the allocation of loans to the Allies in the President and the Secretary of the Treasury. As a consequence, McAdoo demanded and the President agreed that Allied representatives deal directly with his department and not indirectly through the State Department.[4] McAdoo, perhaps the most capable administrator in Wilson's cabinet, was determined to disburse the loans in the most economic and efficient way possible. Appalled that the financial needs of both the United States and the Allies were much greater than he anticipated, he devoted his long working days principally to finding revenue to meet the needs. In May and June he toured the country to promote the Liberty Loan bond

[3] "Mr. Bonar Law's Statement on Finance . . . 3rd April, 1917," Chamberlain Papers, AC 20, University of Birmingham.

[4] Spring Rice to Balfour, July 13, 1917, in Gwynn, *Spring Rice*, Vol. 2, p. 402.

sale, leaving his newly appointed assistant secretary, Oscar T. Crosby, to handle the loans to the Allies. Crosby qualified for his post by graduation from West Point, fluency in French, experience as a civil engineer, and a 20-year friendship with McAdoo. Full of ideas on the control of war and international organization, he had vainly sought an appointment in the State Department. Now with the Treasury Department assuming international responsibilities Crosby needed to look no further for outlets for his diplomatic propensities. It was his decision which set off the financial crisis.[5]

The other circumstances of the crisis had to do with McAdoo's personality and ambition. From the beginning McAdoo's handling of war finance indicated a more than casual regard for domestic politics. As an aspirant to his father-in-law's job he based his program of tax increases on the income tax, highly favored among Democrats, especially those in the South. His life insurance policies for soldiers, costly to the government, proved to be popular with the servicemen and their dependents. War bonds were sold, upon McAdoo's insistence, in small denominations to the public in order to personalize common citizens' interest in the war and to diminish the traffic in bonds by the bankers. Indeed, the Treasury Secretary took every precaution against giving or appearing to give opportunities for profiteering to Wall Street. And the greatest name in Wall Street was J. P. Morgan and Company, anathema to Democrats and agents for the British government. As Wiseman was quick to note, British claims on the Treasury suffered a major liability by their connection with Morgan's.

[5] McAdoo, *Crowded Years*, p. 402; Arthur Walworth, *Woodrow Wilson*, 2 vols., New York, 1958, Vol. 2, pp. 114-15. William Phillips to House, Jan. 8, 1917, HP 15:51, encloses a letter from McAdoo recommending Crosby for a diplomatic appointment. See Crosby to McAdoo, Feb. 24, 1917; R. C. Leffingwell to Crosby, Aug. 22, 1917; Crosby to McAdoo, Mar. 8, 1918; and Crosby to House, June 10, 1918, all in Crosby Papers, Box 5, Library of Congress, for Crosby's interest in the control of war and international organization.

McAdoo, Wiseman found, believed the British relied too heavily on the advice of Morgan's.[6]

Beside a suspicion of the correctness of the Morgan-British connection, McAdoo exhibited a personal vanity at least commensurate with his importance and ambition. There was no disputing his heightened importance once war was declared, for all the American government departments as well as the Allies had to come to him for their funds. As financial arbiter he stood a good chance of influencing the course of the war and, incidentally, gaining public applause. He therefore demanded acknowledgment of his importance, for example by reminding the President that in Europe all the finance ministers took part in the highest counsels of war strategy. This sense of importance made McAdoo reluctant to deal with the subaltern, Sir Hardman Lever, sent over by the British Treasury to negotiate loans. In addition, McAdoo disliked Lever personally. With Northcliffe, McAdoo was willing to deal as an equal, but the fact that Northcliffe lacked technical financial knowledge and shared financial responsibilities with Lever, Spring Rice, and Sir Richard Crawford (commercial attaché to the embassy) prevented his establishing straightforward and confident relations with the United States Treasury. Balfour, who presumably qualified as McAdoo's peer, during his visit explained the state of British finances to McAdoo but, as in other matters, failed to secure any written agreements.[7]

When Balfour left Washington he took with him the impression that McAdoo had agreed to pay off the overdraft at Morgan's. He did not realize his mistake until the clos-

[6] McAdoo's ambition for the presidency was well known. See Walworth, *Woodrow Wilson*, Vol. 2, pp. 66, 92, 176; McAdoo, *Crowded Years*, pp. 378-80, 408, 428-35; Wiseman to Drummond, July 3, 1917, WWP 42.

[7] McAdoo to Wilson, May 12, 1917, McAdoo Papers, Box 522, Library of Congress; Spring Rice to Balfour, July 13, 1917, in Gwynn, *Spring Rice*, Vol. 2, pp. 402-403; Polk Diary, July 9, 1917, Polk Papers, Yale University Library; McAdoo, *Crowded Years*, pp. 400-401, 371, 397; McAdoo to Lansing for the British Government, July 11, 1917, Country File, Box 116, GB 132.4.

ing days of June.[8] Then the mistake was revealed by the U.S. Treasury's announcement that it was suspending all loans to Britain. Crosby, acting in McAdoo's absence, dropped this bombshell and did so because Morgan's attempted to collect the amount of the overdraft—$400,000,000—from him. Henry P. Davison, a Morgan partner, visited Crosby on June 28 to ask for payment of the overdraft. Davison related that his firm understood from Lever that McAdoo had promised Balfour to advance the $400 million on July 1. Both Crosby and Sir Richard Crawford, who happened to be in Crosby's office when Davison called, denied knowledge of any such agreement. Crosby remembered that although McAdoo had consented to consider Balfour's request to cover the overdraft, he had distinctly declined to make a firm commitment. Crawford's failure to remember such a commitment seriously weakened the British and Morgan position. Crosby immediately informed Lansing (and presumably McAdoo) of the misunderstanding. He then telephoned Spring Rice, on vacation at Woods Hole, Massachusetts, that not only would an advance for the overdraft not be forthcoming but in addition loans of every sort would be stopped "until we could be assured that the funds usually available during each month would be used for meeting their commercial commitments."[9]

Crosby's insistence that loans be spent on current commercial commitments in the United States indicated his grave doubts (1) that the Treasury possessed enough money to meet all the Allies' demands, and (2) that Congress had intended that American loans be used to support exchange, pay off old debts, or pay for the Allied purchases

[8] Colville Barclay to Lansing, July 1, 1917, Country File, Box 119, GB 132.17-3.

[9] Crosby to Lansing, June 28, 1917, Lansing Papers, Library of Congress, Vol. 28; Crosby, "Report on Treasury Loans to Allies Prepared for Ambassador [to Germany, Alanson B.] Houghton," no date [ca. 1922], Crosby Papers, Box 6. Crawford's contemporary account of the meeting in Crosby's office bears out Crosby's memory. Spring Rice to Balfour, July 4, 1917, FO 371/3115.

outside the United States. He subsequently secured from the Attorney General the opinion that the loans could not be applied to debts contracted before the United States entered the war, that is, debts like the Morgan overdraft. Although others in the Treasury Department disagreed and eventually prevailed, Crosby in June was unwilling to go out on a legal limb. In addition, he yearned to influence the political outcome of the war. Prior to American belligerency Crosby had prepared a pamphlet on a league to enforce peace, and he accepted appointment in the Treasury Department with the understanding that his major interest in life was the question of an international tribunal.[10] Now that he was in charge of making loans to the Allies, Crosby advocated a political role for the Treasury Department. He urged the following considerations on McAdoo:

> The magnitude of our loans to foreign governments is such as to justify on the part of the United States Government a more searching inquiry than it has yet made into the general conduct of the European War . . . our own military preparations and operations would be the more wisely conducted if we had carefully weighed the financial, political, and military conditions of those with whom we are associated in a war which will be exhaustive to our own country if expenditures are continued at the present rate.
>
> [There is an] uneasiness on the part of the small nations in Europe as to the results to be gained from the war, even on the supposition of a marked success for the arms of the Allies, unless the power of the United States should be felt in the political field as well as on the field of battle.[11]

[10] U.S. Senate, *Munitions Industry*, Vol. 6, pp. 164-65, 176; Crosby to McAdoo, Mar. 8, 1918; Crosby to House, June 10, 1918; Crosby Papers, Box 5.

[11] Crosby to McAdoo, July 21, 1917, in U.S. Senate, *Munitions Industry*, Vol. 6, pp. 175-76.

Crosby was suggesting that the Treasury Department concern itself with both strategy and war aims, and his suspension of loans to Britain (causing panic in Whitehall) vividly illustrated the power the United States government could wield in such matters. Crosby in addressing his ideas to McAdoo was preaching to the already converted, for McAdoo fully realized the power he possessed and scarcely veiled his desire to use it to influence the policy of the Allies. McAdoo informed the President that he drafted one section of the Liberty Loan legislation "for the specific purpose of enabling this government to impose such terms and conditions upon the borrowing powers as would give us potential voice in the use of such credits." McAdoo gave a sample of the kind of voice he would have the United States speak in a message to Bonar Law. In so many words he told Law that the British naval construction program was designed as much for postwar supremacy as for present needs and should be reduced. He went on to demand whether Britain in her capacity as lender to the other Allies had received any preferential trade agreements or territorial concessions.[12]

Here was the potential for iron-fisted diplomacy. McAdoo followed up with a proposal to force Allied adherence to American war aims. He asked the State Department to announce that ". . . the President desires that I should be guided by the principle that sums lent should be used, as far as possible, to the defeat of the German arms and to the accomplishment of such aims as this Government may have announced or may later announce in regard to its participation in the war against Germany." Secretary of State Lansing vetoed this move and upon McAdoo's further insistence on sending the circular replied that he was "not at all afraid that any of the powers will attempt to construe our silence into acquiescence in the

[12] McAdoo to Wilson, Apr. 30, 1917, McAdoo Papers, Box 522; McAdoo to Bonar Law, June 30, 1917, Country File, Box 117, GB 132.17-3.

national objectives of the various countries." The President sustained Lansing's position. McAdoo had to content himself with demanding that copies of all communications exchanged with the Allied governments be routed to him as well as to the State Department. He insisted that without full information he could not be in the best position to judge when the power of the purse could be exerted to the best advantage.[13]

Fortunately for their equanimity, British officials in London did not know all that was in the minds of McAdoo and Crosby. They were shocked by the suspension and could not, so Wiseman learned, understand what had gone wrong. Lloyd George forgot that Northcliffe had no diplomatic standing and ordered him to find a way to turn the loans back on. Similar instructions went out to Spring Rice, Lever, and Crawford. Balfour cabled House via Wiseman, saying, "You know I am not an alarmist, but this is really serious. I hope you will do what you can in proper quarters to avert calamity."[14] And indeed the British were on the

[13] McAdoo to Lansing, July 17, 1917, Lansing Papers, Vol. 29; Polk to McAdoo, Aug. 11, 1917, Polk Papers, 89:86; McAdoo to Wilson, July 17, 1917, ibid.; McAdoo to Lansing, Aug. 14, 1917, Lansing Papers, Vol. 30. In this letter McAdoo warned that if the United States failed to reach an understanding on war aims with the Allies, "we may be confronted at the peace conference, if we have to raise an objection to the demands of some of the Allied Powers, with the claim that as we furnished money for the purpose of enabling the Powers to prosecute the war to a successful conclusion, we tacitly consented to or acquiesced in the national objectives they had in view." Lansing to McAdoo, Aug. 20, 1917, ibid.; McAdoo to Wilson, July 18, 1917, McAdoo Papers, Box 253.

[14] Balfour to House, June 30, 1917, WWP 42; Northcliffe to Balfour, June 29, 1917 (cable no. 43725 via J. P. Morgan and Company cable facility), Private Secretary's Archives, A. J. Balfour 1917-24, FO 800/200. Northcliffe refers to instructions sent him and from their subsequent actions it may be assumed that Spring Rice, Lever, and Crawford received similar instructions. Northcliffe warned Balfour that for him to negotiate with the United States government would bring him into conflict with Spring Rice. Balfour to Spring Rice, June 30, 1917, Balfour Papers, 49740, British Museum, explained that Northcliffe was entering the diplomatic field only "because of great urgency of situation." Balfour to House, June 29, 1917, in Seymour, Intimate Papers, Vol. 3, p. 101.

verge of calamity. Despite the American loans they had been obliged in June to ship $150 million in gold and to sell $10 million in American securities. As an additional strain on British reserves, American banks withdrew over $100 million from their sterling balances in London, apparently to buy Liberty Loan bonds. Total British gold reserves in July stood at £140,000,000 ($665,000,000). Bonar Law argued that to ship enough gold or sell enough securities to cover the Morgan overdraft would destroy the economic basis of the European Alliance.[15]

On July 1 the British chargé in Washington, Colville Barclay, described the perilous state of his government's finances to the State Department. He pointed out that the $150 million loaned in June covered only half of British requirements in the United States for that month. He requested (1) that proposed loans for Belgium and Russia be diverted to Britain, who was still financing these weak Allies in Europe, (2) that $100,000,000 be credited to the British account by July 4, and (3) that the United States government assume responsibility for the Morgan overdraft. Lansing responded sympathetically and arranged for Spring Rice to present the British case to the President. The latter heard Spring Rice out but referred him to McAdoo for a final decision.[16] McAdoo was still fuming over Lever's pledge to Morgan's. He declared that he would not "allow New York bankers and their Allies to use the British Government as a club to beat the United States Treasury with." Northcliffe, also engaged in the flurry of negotiations at the Treasury Department, assured Crosby that the overdraft was a purely British affair and would not "come up to you." Apparently this assurance, which turned out to be completely invalid, along with demonstrations of Britain's near bankruptcy in America, caused the Treasury to relent.

[15] The figures are taken from a statement by Law transmitted in Page to Lansing, July 30, 1917, *Foreign Relations 1917*, Sup. 2, Vol. 1, pp. 549-54.
[16] Lansing to Wilson, July 2, 1917, enclosing Barclay to Lansing, July 1, 1917, Country File, Box 119, GB 132.17-3, Spring Rice to Balfour, July 5, 1917, Gwynn, *Spring Rice*, Vol. 2, pp. 405-406.

On July 5 McAdoo extended a credit of $100 million care-
fully marked "as an independent and detached transaction
having no relation whatever" to Colville Barclay's three-
part request.[17]

The July 5 loan was, as McAdoo stated, an isolated ex-
pedient. Several weeks of entreaty and persuasion, the bulk
of which was not recorded, were required before loan
operations were put on a regular basis. For the British the
first order of business, as Wiseman realized, was to win the
confidence of McAdoo. This was no small undertaking.
McAdoo's reaction to the British contention that he had
promised to make good the overdraft was a flat denial of
any promises. In a long and barely polite cable to Law he
expressed regret "that general expressions of good will and
a general discussion of the needs of foreign Government,
and of the possibility of the United States Government's
meeting these needs, should have been construed as posi-
tive undertakings on the part of the United States to meet
requirements which had not then been stated in definite
terms." He demanded "far more complete and detailed information" so that he could assess the ability of Britain to
make payments in America. Noting the $100,000,000 ad-
vance for July, he indicated that he was giving consideration to a further request for $85,000,000. But before he
would make any additional commitment he wanted "an understanding . . . about a purchasing commission to be set
up in Washington through which all purchases for the
Allied powers in the United States should be made, and in
connection therewith an agreement should be arrived at for
the establishment of an Inter-Allied Council to sit in London or Paris to determine the relative needs and priorities
of the different powers in the markets of the United Satates."
Finally, McAdoo complained, as he was to do again,

[17] Northcliffe to Law, July 5, 1917, WWP 91; "Memorandum of a
Conference held in the Office of Assistant Secretary of the Treasury
Crosby on July 4, 1917," Country File, Box 116, GB 132.4; McAdoo
to Spring Rice, July 5, 1917, McAdoo Papers, Box 495, letterbook 50.

of the confusing number of British financial agents in Washington.[18]

Since an inter-allied council did not immediately materialize, and in view of McAdoo's threatening tone, it was a bit surprising that in the first half of August the Treasury lent Britain $235 million. Two developments accounted for McAdoo's leniency. The British Treasury began sending him details on the British financial situation.[19] More important, the efforts of Wiseman and House were beginning to bear fruit. Wiseman was involved in the crisis from the start. As soon as Northcliffe received the distress signal from London he telephoned for Wiseman's advice. The latter, afraid that Northcliffe might do something foolish, got busy on a behind-the-scenes settlement. First he warned London that British financial agents did not enjoy good relations with McAdoo's department. Then he explained the crisis to House, who in turn got in touch with McAdoo and the President. House cabled Balfour that the crisis would receive his undivided attention and that it had arisen because of "the lack of some directing mind here that would have inspired general confidence." Wiseman, House went on, was "in sympathetic touch with everyone, and while possessing both the ability and tact necessary to keep a difficult situation composed, he lack[s] the authority."[20]

[18] McAdoo to Lansing for British Ambassador, July 9, 1917, *Foreign Relations 1917*, Sup. 2, Vol. 1, pp. 539-40; McAdoo to Lansing for British Government, July 11, 1917, *ibid.*, pp. 543-54. In a memo to Crosby on July 22, McAdoo said he really did not know with whom he was supposed to deal on behalf of the British government. McAdoo to Crosby, July 22, 1917, Country File, Box 117, GB 132.1. On August 21 Crosby still did not know whether Spring Rice or Northcliffe's office was in charge of financial negotiations. Crosby to Spring Rice, Aug. 21, 1917, *ibid.* A British government warrant dated Sept. 3, 1917, authorized Spring Rice, Lever, Crawford, Barclay, Northcliffe, and Lord Reading to sign for loans; *ibid.*

[19] Lansing to Page for Bonar Law, Aug. 14, 1917, *Foreign Relations 1917*, Sup. 2, Vol. 1, pp. 561-64. "Memorandum for Mr. Crosby from Mr. [W.P.G.] Harding Re Collateral for British overdraft of $400,000,-000," c. July 25, 1917, Country File, Box 116, GB 132.4; Page to Lansing for McAdoo, July 20, 1917, *ibid.*

[20] Wiseman to Drummond, June 29, 1917, WWP 42; House to

Wiseman substituted audacity and an appreciation of the American financial hierarchy for his lack of authority. He called in an influential Anglophile, Benjamin Strong, whom he could not have known well, to lay the British case before House and McAdoo. Strong's position as governor of the New York Federal Reserve Bank made him about as powerful an advocate as Britain could have desired. He answered Wiseman's plea to talk to House and then, with House's blessing, set off to see McAdoo.[21] How Strong would offer advice in a matter that was formally none of his business was explained by Wiseman to Northcliffe.

> When Strong receives your request for advice he will immediately go to McAdoo, tell him that you have sought his advice, and ask McAdoo whether he thinks it advisable that he should try to help you. Strong would rather put it that he would be willing to give you his advice if by doing so he could render any service to McAdoo. McAdoo is fairly certain to ask him to assist in the matter. If it works out in this way, you will have a really able financial man who knows the local situation and the political difficulties at Washington, and is gen-

Balfour, June 29, 1917, HP 2:22; Wiseman to Drummond, July 3, 1917, WWP 42; House to Wilson, June 29, 1917, HP 49:8:

Things began to break yesterday afternoon in British headquarters. Spring Rice is at Woods Hole and McAdoo at Buena Vista and the machinery became clogged. As usual Sir William took hold and is trying today to see what can be done.

Northcliffe received a message from Lloyd George to come here and advise with me before moving further. . . . I received, through Sir William, the June 28 cable from Balfour which I sent you by Lansing. I therefore advised Northcliffe to go to Washington immediately rather than come here which he has done.

By putting together what I gather from Washington and Sir William, the trouble that has come about concerning finances is largely a matter of misunderstanding with some fault on both sides. . . .

[21] Wiseman to Drummond, July 3, 1917, WWP 42; House Diary, June 30, and July 2, 1917. Lester V. Chandler, *Benjamin Strong, Central Banker*, Washington, D.C., 1958, makes no mention of the episode described here.

uinely friendly to you and your Cause. . . . At the same time he would be in this way almost a nominee of McAdoo's.[22]

Both McAdoo and Northcliffe welcomed Strong's assistance. Strong upon investigation found that McAdoo's "trouble is that he does not understand the matter himself and is not willing to delegate authority to others."[23] What exactly Strong recommended is not clear, but there is reason to think that he outlined the plans for the inter-Allied priority board that McAdoo was soon demanding.[24] Probably Strong also recommended the other step which McAdoo soon took—direct discussion with the Morgan firm.

After the overture by Strong, House and Wiseman decided it was time for Wiseman personally to encounter McAdoo. House wrote McAdoo a letter introducing Wiseman as "the ablest of the British officials over here" and as one who sympathetically appreciated the Treasury's difficulties. Then House arranged for Gordon Auchincloss to bring Wiseman and McAdoo together, noting in his diary that Auchincloss was to tell McAdoo the meeting was of the greatest importance.[25] The two met for lunch, and afterward Wiseman reported that the financial crisis was easing and that McAdoo seemed genuinely concerned to solve the overdraft problem. But he considered McAdoo condescending toward the Allies and reluctant "for party

[22] Wiseman to Northcliffe, July 3, 1917, WWP 22.

[23] House Diary, July 4, 7, 1917.

[24] An undated memorandum outlining an inter-Allied finance and supply council and a joint Allied-American purchasing board is in the House Papers, 34:41. The author of the memorandum obviously was well acquainted with Federal Reserve procedures, and his proposal is almost identical to the one put forward by McAdoo. It is also significant that on July 7 the State Department received from the British Embassy a council scheme dated July 2, by which time Strong was advising the British. See British Embassy to State Department, July 2, 1917, *Foreign Relations 1917*, Sup. 2, Vol. 1, pp. 537-39.

But McAdoo was already thinking of ways to coordinate Allied purchasing before Strong intervened. See McAdoo to Wilson, Apr. 30 and May 16, 1917, both in McAdoo Papers, Box 522.

[25] House to McAdoo, July 1, 1917, HP 13:5; House Diary, June 29 and July 10, 11, 1917.

and personal political reasons to ask Congress for more money and the country for anything but the minimum war expenditure." McAdoo in turn gained a good opinion of Wiseman but remained disgruntled by the disorderly nature of Britain's dealing with the Treasury. "The truth is," he wrote House, "they need a big man over here to deal with these financial and war problems."[26]

The Wiseman-Strong-House intervention achieved several things. First, it established personal contact with McAdoo, which was especially important considering McAdoo's refusal during the crisis to see Lever,[27] the most technically competent British representative. Strong was able to explain the technical points to McAdoo and did so from the American standpoint. House, whose patronage was important to an aspiring Democratic politician, communicated his personal interest in a solution to the crisis by sending Wiseman to see McAdoo. Wiseman, after taking his measure of McAdoo, was able to coach Northcliffe on how best to approach McAdoo. The strongest argument to advance, he wrote Northcliffe, would be the urgent necessity for America to pour money and materials into the present military campaign, in which her army was not yet able to participate. To impress that necessity, as well as the vastness of British expenditures in Europe, would, in Wiseman's opinion, accomplish more than threatening McAdoo with House's displeasure. Wiseman was confident of House's support, but he preferred to bring McAdoo around on the merits of the case.[28] This strategy combined with McAdoo's fondness for Northcliffe to effect a temporary solution. Loans for current needs were resumed and the overdraft was shelved for the moment.

A lasting arrangement would have to await an overhauling of the Anglo-American method of doing business. Wise-

[26] House Diary, July 12, 13, 1917; [Wiseman], memorandum, July 14, 1917, HP 34:38. This memo is unsigned but internal evidence identifies it as written by Wiseman for Northcliffe. McAdoo to House, July 14, 1917, HP 13:5.
[27] Polk Diary, July 9, 1917.
[28] [Wiseman], memorandum, July 14, 1917, HP 34:38.

man considered it more important than ever that he go to London to explain matters.[29] He had the full backing of House, who agreed that British representation in the United States had become unmanageably snarled. House had already decided that Wiseman's credentials in London would be stronger if he could say that he knew the President. Consequently he arranged for Wiseman to attend a diplomatic reception where he could be introduced to Wilson. Since House had spoken so highly of Wiseman, it was not surprising that Wilson greeted him with more than a routine handshake.[30] Auchincloss witnessed the meeting and recorded this description of it:

> The night of Sec'y Lansing's reception [June 26] to the Russian Ambassador and the Commission Sir W. went with us so as to meet the President—I had previously asked Miss [Helen Woodrow] Bones [Wilson's first cousin] to ask the President to speak to him. The President went around the room in about 3 minutes and then stopped to talk to Sir W. for about 15 minutes.—It was a very conspicuous affair and noted by every one present— Sir W. naturally was pleased to death. He will have to exercise great tact to forestall jealousy on the part of his associates.[31]

Another witness, Arthur Willert, remembered the meeting this way:

[29] Wiseman to Drummond, July 3, 1917, WWP 42: "The root difficulty is the United States government's rather unreasonable prejudice against Morgan's, and their mistaken idea that our officials here are guided too much by Morgan's. I think, and House agrees, that I should explain verbally to you situation which has arisen since you left." On the received copy of this cable Drummond minuted to Balfour that Wiseman's work was "most useful." Private Secretary's Archives, A. J. Balfour 1917-24, FO 800/200. In reply Balfour approved Wiseman's trip home and said he highly appreciated all Wiseman was doing. Balfour to Wiseman, July 5 [?], 1917, copy in House Diary, July 6, 1917.

[30] House Diary, June 23, 26, 1917; House to Wilson, June 27, 1917, HP 49:8.

[31] Auchincloss Diary, July 22, 1917, Auchincloss Papers, Yale University Library.

. . . Wiseman was presented to the President by Gordon Auchincloss. . . . Instead of treating him to the perfunctory sentence or two usual to such introductions, the President talked with him for nearly half an hour, and then desisted only because he was pried loose by his entourage. Onlookers were astonished and mystified. Who was this unknown young man, obviously English, whom the President had singled out for his attentions? . . . The Diplomatic Corps in Washington was shaken to its gossipy foundations. . . .[32]

Wilson apparently enjoyed his conversation with Wiseman, for two weeks later he invited him to dinner at the White House. By that time House had told Wilson that Wiseman was the de facto ambassador and was going home to "lay the actual situation" before the British government.[33] Wilson doubtless knew that House overstated Wiseman's position, but he probably did not know that Wiseman was still barely known in London. Wiseman's impending trip, in any case, presented a means of communicating with the British government. After dinner Wilson took Wiseman into his study for an hour-long discussion. Among other things, Wilson said that the financial controversy could be solved and proceeded to indicate how.

He urged strongly that more information, both as to actual financial needs and general policy of the Allies must be given to the U.S.G. He pointed out that there was much confusion and some competition in the demands of the various Allies. Specifically, as far as the British are concerned, he pointed out that there was no one who could speak with sufficient financial authority to discuss the whole situation, both financial and political, with the Secretary of the Treasury. All these things should be remedied as soon as possible. That he was thoroughly in favor of a scheme proposed by the Secretary

[32] Willert, *Road to Safety*, p. 61.
[33] House to Wilson, June 27, 1917, HP 49:8; House Diary, July 11, 1917.

of the Treasury for a Council in Paris. This council, composed of representatives of the Allies, should determine what was needed in the way of supplies and money from America. It should also determine the urgency of each requisition, and give proper priority. I suggested that such a council should be composed of the Naval and Military commanders, or their representatives, and that the U.S. should be represented on it. The President did not seem to have any objection, but thought it would be unnecessary for the U.S. to be represented on it until they had their own portion of the front to look after and a large force in Europe.[34]

Wiseman was to revert again to the question of American participation in an Allied military council. He would in fact powerfully influence the President's decision in the matter.[35] But for the moment finance was the burning issue. Wilson confirmed the opinion already formed by Wiseman and House: McAdoo's desire to deal with a "big man" with financial knowledge and political sensitivity would have to be satisfied. Northcliffe selflessly agreed.[36]

Meeting at House's summer home at Magnolia, Massachusetts, Wiseman, Northcliffe, and House chose a candi-

[34] Wiseman, "Notes on Interview with the President Friday, July 13th," 1917, WWP 129; House Diary, July 14, 1917: "Sir William is in the seventh Heaven of pleasurable excitement [because of his reception at the White House]."
One of the matters Wilson discussed with Wiseman was House's suggestion for a secret naval alliance between the United States and England, effective during and after the war. House wanted to assure the American navy use of British capital ships in exchange for its concentrated building of destroyers. Foreign Office officials studied the proposal carefully and concluded that while such an arrangement would not technically violate the Anglo-Japanese alliance, it might nonetheless so offend Japan as to drive her over to Germany's side in the war. Wilson, however, did not ever seriously contemplate approving House's proposal, and so nothing came of it. See Balfour to Prime Minister, Apr. 26, 1917, with attached minutes, and Cecil to Spring Rice, June 4, 1917, FO 371/3119. Also see Lloyd George, *War Memoirs*, Vol. 3, pp. 1,678-80, and Seymour, *Intimate Papers*, Vol. 3, pp. 65-74.
[35] See below, Chap. 4, pp. 80ff.   [36] House Diary, July 16, 1917.

date for McAdoo's "big man." He should be Lord Reading, the Lord Chief Justice of England. Reading, who had demonstrated his financial sagacity during his 1915 mission to New York for private loans, was an English version of an Horatio Alger hero. Born Rufus Isaacs, he overcame the twin handicaps of Jewishness and the lack of university training to become a leading member of the English bar. He rose to prominence in the Liberal party and was appointed by Asquith first to the position of law officer of the crown and then lord chief justice. (In the latter capacity he delivered the death sentence upon Sir Roger Casement, the Irish revolutionary.) In the December 1916 cabinet crisis he backed Lloyd George and was now, while still chief justice, one of Lloyd George's closest advisers. He was, Northcliffe told House, the Colonel House of the British government.[37]

Armed with notes on his interview with the President and with letters of introduction from House and Northcliffe, Wiseman sailed from New York on July 21. Eleven days later he landed in London. There a cable awaited him from Arthur Willert saying that conditions in Washington were not improving—so good a friend of Britain as Frank Polk was complaining of "the number of cooks stirring the British broth." Willert warned that the French, with their Washington operations efficiently organized under special commissioner André Tardieu, were fast overtaking any advantage the British had in influence in American government offices. Willert believed that Britain's ranking as a financial power was endangered by McAdoo's plan for a council of the Allies to determine priority among the requests for loans. As just another member of this council Britain stood to lose face with the other Allies, direct contact with the United States Treasury, and probably some

[37] House Diary, July 16, 1917; Northcliffe to Lloyd George, July 17, 1917, FO 371/3115: "I suggested [Reginald] McKenna or [Walter] Runciman but House, evidently after consultation with President, named Reading and said he was in every way best qualified." Details on Reading may be found in Reading, *Rufus Isaacs*, and H. Montgomery Hyde, *Lord Reading*, New York, 1967.

loans as well. These forebodings, coming from a North-cliffe lieutenant and passed on to the editor of the London *Times*, were just the reinforcements Wiseman needed for his plea for Reading.[38] During the course of his talks in London he wired House and Northcliffe for similar reinforcements.[39]

With support from Willert, House, and Northcliffe, Wiseman made a strong case in London. He found the Treasury fully alive to its dependence on American loans but mistaken as to how to get them—"I do not think the Treasury yet realizes that we cannot get money from America by any form of pressure but only by the frankest appeal to assist us in the common cause." Bonar Law, burdened by his duties as leader of the Commons as well as minister of finance, seemed unconscious of how gingerly McAdoo had to be treated. Wiseman cautioned him that his dispatches to Washington contained the quality of arrogance which on an earlier occasion caused the Boston Tea Party. Not unnaturally, Law and others in the British government wondered how sending yet another envoy would simplify representation at Washington. They were also reluctant to risk the wrath of Northcliffe by suggesting that Reading replace him.[40] Whether or not Wiseman revealed his hope of making Northcliffe feel redundant by bringing over Reading, he did dispel the government's fear of offending Northcliffe by securing the latter's endorsement of, even insistence on, a visit by Reading. House, too, sent a cable asking for Reading or "someone of like distinction."[41]

[38] House Diary, July 21, 1917; Wiseman to House, Aug. 1, 1917, WWP 27; Willert to Wiseman, July 31, 1917, WWP 4. Willert's and Wiseman's suspicion that McAdoo wanted to put Britain financially on a par with the other Allies was well founded. See McAdoo to Wilson, May 16, 1917, McAdoo Papers, Box 522.

[39] Wiseman to House, Aug. 7, 1917, WWP 27; Wiseman to Northcliffe, Aug. 11, 1917, WWP 27.

[40] Wiseman to House, Aug. 7, 1917, WWP 27; Wiseman to Northcliffe, Aug. 16, 1917, WWP 27; House Diary, Sept. 18, 1917.

[41] Northcliffe to C. J. Phillips for Bonar Law, Aug. 21, 1917, WWP 91; Northcliffe to Wiseman, Aug. 24, 1917, WWP 91; House to Wiseman, Aug. 11, 1917, HP 20:45.

At last on August 23 Bonar Law agreed to ask Reading to undertake the mission. Wiseman, in announcing the news, flattered Northcliffe by saying that Reading was sure to agree with Northcliffe's views and would see to it that Spring Rice was recalled. Northcliffe, in turn, urged Reading to accept the assignment and suggested he prepare for it by consulting with Wiseman, who, Northcliffe said, was "well named" and intimately familiar with American politics. Reading did accept.[42] On September 12 he arrived in New York, accompanied by Wiseman and a Treasury adviser, John Maynard Keynes.[43]

Wiseman found that the financial situation had somewhat eased during his absence. Conciliatory gestures toward McAdoo by Northcliffe and House were primarily responsible for this development. Northcliffe, under great pressure from McAdoo, had committed Britain to participate in the Allied Purchasing Commission which McAdoo organized as a cooperating unit of the War Industries Board in Washington. Now purchases by the United States and Allied governments would be conducted through one central office. Northcliffe also indicated that Britain was willing to join McAdoo's proposed finance council of the Allies in Europe.[44] House's gesture had been that of sympathetic listener and counselor. After conceding to McAdoo the necessity for the purchasing commission and finance council, he pointed out the relative importance of Britain over the other Allies. There was, he told McAdoo, the possibility that England and America would be left alone to

[42] Wiseman to Northcliffe, Aug. 11 and 23, 1917, WWP 91; Northcliffe to Wiseman, Aug. 26, 1917, WWP 26; Northcliffe to Reading, Aug. 26, 1917, WWP 26: "I urge you see Wiseman now in London who to the best of my knowledge is only person, English or American, who has access at any time to the President or House, and who understands the American situation." Northcliffe to Reading, Sept. 1, 1917, WWP 91.

[43] House Diary, Sept. 12, 1917; Reading, *Rufus Isaacs*, Vol. 2, p. 59.

[44] Northcliffe to Wiseman, Aug. 24, 1917, WWP 91; Northcliffe to C. J. Phillips, Aug. 22, 1917, WWP 91. Wiseman had advised Northcliffe to hold off signing agreements of this sort until Reading arrived. Wiseman to Northcliffe, Aug. 11, 1917, WWP 27.

fight Germany. Harmony with and loans to Britain were therefore essential, and the latter might as well be extended pleasantly. Besides, a legacy of good feelings would make the loans more easily collectible after the war.[45]

House deduced from his talk with McAdoo that the question of an exchange was the root cause of the Treasury's trouble with Britain. He believed that McAdoo and his assistants wished to take advantage of the present weakness of the pound to substitute the dollar for it as the world's standard of value. House instructed Wiseman to alert Reading to this aspect of the problem.[46]

Well briefed by Wiseman on the details of the financial problem and on the peculiarities of McAdoo and Washington, Reading made a quick and very nearly complete success. A great part of his success could be attributed to his affability. Lansing found him to be unusually frank and pleasant. McAdoo, his *amour propre* at last propitiated, entered into a relationship of "complete candor and confidence" with Reading.[47] The rewards to Britain from this relationship were immediate and lasting. Reading persuaded McAdoo of the necessity virtually to take over Britain's expenses in the United States. He talked McAdoo and Crosby into supporting British exchange, both in New York and elsewhere. Beyond that, he secured an advance of $50,000,000 to pay for British purchases, primarily wheat, in Canada.[48] In return, he heeded McAdoo's suggestion that Britain attempt to raise funds in neutral countries, to reduce her complete reliance on the United

[45] House Diary, Aug. 7, 1917; Northcliffe to C. J. Phillips for Prime Minister and Cabinet, Aug. 15, 1917. This 1500-word cable related what Northcliffe understood House to have told McAdoo. Wiseman reported to House, however, that Northcliffe was attributing to House opinions which Wiseman thought in some cases were not altogether accurate. Wiseman to House, Aug. 18, 1917, WWP 27.

[46] House to Wiseman, Aug. 25, 1917, WWP 26.

[47] Lansing, "Rufus, Earl of Reading," April 1918, Lansing Private Diaries, Box 1; McAdoo, *Crowded Years*, p. 396.

[48] Crosby to Reading, Sept. 27, 1917, and Crosby to Wilson, Oct. 24, 1917, Country File, Box 117, GB 132.1.

States. Also he helped organize in Canada a large war bond campaign, again partly to diminish the strain on American credit.[49]

These efforts at conciliation convinced McAdoo of Britain's reasonableness and made him more willing to help out in the problem of the Morgan overdraft. Indeed, McAdoo had already realized it was to his advantage to make some arrangement for carrying the overdraft, for otherwise Morgan's, tired of being "a target for every peccant politician in Congress,"[50] might wash its hands of the whole affair by selling on the open market the collateral which secured the overdraft. Such a sale might disrupt the stock market. Certainly it would absorb a great deal of capital that McAdoo would prefer to see invested in war bonds. Consequently McAdoo and Crosby began discussion with Morgan's and the British in August in an effort to contain the overdraft. McAdoo recommended two stopgap measures which were accepted. First, Morgan's began a gradual sale of collateral. Second, the British Treasury issued 90-day notes to cover approximately one quarter of the overdraft.[51]

Upon arriving in Washington, Reading learned from McAdoo that the proposed requisition by the American government of British ships under construction in American yards would yield Britain something like $85,000,000. McAdoo suggested this money might be applied to the overdraft. While the British government strongly resented

[49] Crosby, "Report of the Representative of the Treasury Department," Dec. 6, 1917, *Foreign Relations 1917*, Sup. 2, Vol. 1, pp. 392, 399. See also McAdoo to Lansing, Nov. 13, 1917, McAdoo Papers, Box 496, letterbook 55; and Crosby to McAdoo, Nov. 14, 1917, *Foreign Relations 1917*, Sup. 2, Vol. 1, p. 578. Reading, *Rufus Isaacs*, Vol. 2, pp. 64-65.

[50] Northcliffe to Balfour for War Cabinet, Aug. 29, 1917, WWP 91.

[51] Crosby to McAdoo, Aug. 20, 1917, Country File, Box 116, GB 132.4; Reading, *Rufus Isaacs*, Vol. 2, p. 60. See also Lever to Bonar Law, Aug. 1, 1917, FO 371/3116, which describes the contact between McAdoo and Morgan's and which quotes J. P. Morgan as saying "that if there were a fair prospect of reducing the amount to one hundred and fifty million dollars by December 31st he would be fully satisfied and that balance need cause no worry."

the ship requisition, Reading welcomed the opportunity to further reduce the overdraft. Understandably, however, he did not welcome a condition which McAdoo wished to attach to the transaction. The latter was not content merely to hand over the ship money to the British and let them pay off their debt to Morgan's. He demanded that his department be "subrogated" to the rights of the collateral which the ship money would free. In plain language, McAdoo wanted to attach this collateral which could be taken over in case the British government eventually defaulted on its debts to the American government. The British on this occasion refused to submit to McAdoo's demand. But in February 1918 Bonar Law finally acceded to McAdoo's insistence upon a lien on blocs of collateral upon which maturing private debts in the United States were based. Law provided McAdoo with lists of the relevant securities, and this gesture, this submission in principle, apparently satisfied McAdoo. After Reading returned to Washington in February 1918 as ambassador he consulted closely with McAdoo on the use of British-owned collateral, and the latter refrained from taking actual possession of the securities. Meanwhile, through a series of financial maneuvers, all based indirectly on American backing of British credit and currency, the overdraft was gradually reduced. It was finally paid off in July 1919.[52]

THE VALUE OF the patient negotiations among Reading, McAdoo, and the Morgan firm can hardly be overemphasized. A highly explosive issue, which McAdoo undoubtedly could have exploited to his political advantage, was defused and gently dismantled. Wiseman's part in the prevention of an explosion was inconspicuous but crucial. Like officials in the British Treasury he realized the profound

[52] Reading, *Rufus Isaacs*, Vol. 2, pp. 60-62, 65-67, 129-33; McAdoo to Crosby, Dec. 4, 1917, *Foreign Relations, 1917*, Sup. 2, Vol. 1, p. 587; McAdoo to Crosby, Jan. 23, 1918, Polk Papers. On the status of British Treasury obligations to the American Treasury following the Armistice, see Crosby to McAdoo, Nov. 30, 1918, and McAdoo to Crosby, Dec. 4, 1918, SD 841.51/136.

importance of American loans, but in advance of those officials he perceived also the utter reliance of Britain on the good will of McAdoo. The State Department, the President, and later the press of other duties reined in McAdoo's ambition to dictate foreign policy. But McAdoo lessened his distrust of the British and enlarged his respect for their importance to the American war effort through a process of education. That process owed much to Wiseman, who through Strong, Northcliffe, and House, and by bringing over Reading, steadily broke down McAdoo's hostility. Wiseman's early initiative, a stitch in time, prevented a financial rent in the Anglo-American war partnership.

CHAPTER FOUR

READING'S ASSIGNMENT,
WISEMAN'S ACCOMPLISHMENT

> No one excepting Reading, Wiseman, the President and myself really know[s] what Reading's mission to this country is.
>
> House Diary, September 22, 1917

THE ANNOUNCED object of Lord Reading's visit was to untangle the financial snarl. The Lord Chief Justice had an unannounced task as well: to instigate a revision, on the political level, of Allied military strategy. Wiseman could have hardly expected such a result from his journey to London. His chief aim was to put Anglo-American relations on a plane intimate enough to ensure close cooperation. He reasoned that the presence in Washington of a fully empowered, patient, and technically competent negotiatior would hasten the mobilization of American money, supplies, and armed forces. In addition, a visiting observer could report to the War Cabinet on the ridiculous split of British authority in America into Northcliffe and Spring Rice factions. When the British government finally agreed to Wiseman's proposal, Lloyd George perceived a further service the special envoy could perform. He could coax the Americans into backing Lloyd George's design to revamp Allied strategy by lifting it from the control of "westerners," those who continued to believe that victory would come from ceaselessly battering the German line in France. This additional assignment became what House chose to call the real purpose of Reading's mission.

The discussions which resulted in Reading's two-fold mission consumed the entire month of August. Shortly after Wiseman's arrival in London he handed to the Foreign Office a memorandum entitled "Anglo-American Relations, August 1917."[1] The nine-page document, printed for

[1] Wiseman, "Memorandum on Anglo-American Relations, August

61

circulation to the War Cabinet, admirably delineated the conditions that governed cooperation with the American government. At root, Wiseman wrote, two questions faced the British: (1) How to assist and encourage the United States to bring the full might of its power to bear upon the struggle as quickly and as effectively as possible; and (2) How to promote a full agreement between the two countries on war aims and terms of peace. The first was an immediate problem, the second long range. Wiseman emphasized the inseparability of the two and warned against any expedients that might solve the first but jeopardize the second.

Britain, Wiseman reminded the War Cabinet, possessed no means for pressuring the United States into delivering the enormous quantities of supplies required for the war. Nor was there any necessity for trying to pressure the American government, for, he asserted, "The Administration are ready to assist us to the limits of the resources of their country; but it is necessary for them to educate Congress and the nation to appreciate the actual meaning of these gigantic figures. It is not sufficient for us to assure them that without these supplies the war will be lost. For the public ear we must translate dollars and tonnage into the efforts and achievements of the Fleets and the Armies. We must impress upon them the fighting value of their money."[2]

This was a plausible argument, one politicians could appreciate. But Wiseman attributed to the Administration a greater willingness to help Britain than he knew to be the case. He knew that a recalcitrant Congress was not solely or even largely responsible for the slow pace of American mobilization. Congress had shown its readiness to back the Administration by passing in relatively quick order the huge Liberty Loan act and the conscription act. Con-

---

1917," WWP 4. Copy printed for War Cabinet in Balfour Private Papers, FO 800/200.
    [2] Wiseman, "Memorandum . . . ," *ibid.*

gress, after some grumbling, would pass another loan act in September, and the Senate was so keen on waging war that in January 1918 it called the War Department to task for alleged malingering.[3] In any case, Congress's power in wartime declined in comparison to the President's, and Wiseman realized this. He told C. P. Scott, editor of the *Manchester Guardian,* that Wilson's power was practically supreme, that "there were in effect only two powers in the State—the President and the Press."[4] These two, and especially the first, were the parties Wiseman wished to educate. He made no proposals for educating the press. He knew that overt attempts in this direction or a conspicuous propaganda program in the United States would irritate Wilson, just as the coming of Northcliffe the publicist had. Consequently, he resorted to propaganda by indirection. He worked to get censorship restrictions on American reporters lifted, and he proposed to House that a few prominent Americans make speaking tours in Britain.[5] They and American reporters could then broadcast to Americans the sacrifices and needs of the British. Better for Americans to

[3] The Liberty Loan acts that McAdoo drafted for Congress passed speedily on April 24 and September 24. In October Congress passed a new tax act which pushed income tax up to the unprecedented maximum rate of 67 percent. The Selective Service Act aroused some bitter debate but became law on May 18, after only a handful of Congressmen and Senators voted against it. See Frederic L. Paxson, *America at War, 1917-1918,* Boston, 1939, pp. 5-18; McAdoo, *Crowded Years,* pp. 379-91, 408; Paul, *Taxation in the United States,* pp. 112-16.

See Paxson, *America at War,* p. 211, on the Senate investigation of the War Department. Concerning public support for war measures, Paxson, p. 117, says: "No aspect of the process . . . is more interesting than the way in which the people crowded the Government." See also Daniel R. Beaver, *Newton D. Baker and the American War Effort, 1917-1919,* Lincoln, Neb., 1966, Chaps. 3 and 4; and Seward W. Livermore, *Politics is Adjourned,* Middletown, Conn., 1966, pp. 39, 59, 72-100.

[4] Entry in Scott's Diary for August 24, 1917, quoted in J. L. Hammond, *C. P. Scott of the Manchester Guardian,* London, 1934, p. 234.

[5] For instance, Wiseman worked at the request of the Administration from June 1917 to the spring of 1918 to get the Allied Embargo against William R. Hearst's International News Service lifted. Success came in May 1918. See WWP 63. Wiseman to House, August 23, 1917, WWP 27.

propagandize themselves than for British speakers to do so, as Northcliffe desired.[6]

Public indoctrination of any sort, however, was of secondary importance to Wiseman.[7] He considered that the real need was for effective communication on the official level. As he told the War Cabinet,

> The main remedy for the present state of affairs is to see that the Administration better understand the real state of affairs in Europe, and realise the exact and practical significance of the information which is sent to them from the Allied Governments.

> There is a feeling among the British authorities that the President ought to send expert missions to Europe for the purpose of ascertaining the facts and advising him as to the best steps to be taken. Possibly this would be the most practical method, but it is not one which is likely to be adopted. America, and especially the Democratic Party, lacks public men who can leave their personal affairs to look after themselves while they travel abroad,

[6] For Wiseman's worry over Northcliffe's propensity to propagandize, see Wiseman to Drummond, Oct. 4, 1917, WWP 42. Northcliffe wrote articles for newspapers and magazines, which, according to Wiseman, gave some offense to Wilson. See William Denman (Chairman, Shipping Board) to Lansing, Aug. 24, 1917, SD 841.85/30, for a complaint about Northcliffe's resort to publicity.

[7] In March 1919 Wiseman wrote, in response to a request from the Foreign Office, a long letter on propaganda in the United States. His views then matched his attitude in 1917:

... There are two methods of propaganda. ... The first might be called the method of aggressive and the second the method of unobtrusive propaganda. ... Many people ... believe the aggressive method is the only effective one and would like to see Anglo-American societies organized all over the United States, with public demonstrations and meetings, and even go so far as to recommend a big advertising campaign through the Press, posters, and leaflets ... I can only say that I consider such a method would be disastrous and produce exactly the reverse effect to that which its advocates contemplate. I am sure that any kind of artificial demonstrations must have a corresponding reaction, apart from the fact that this method is undignified and offends good-taste in both countries.

Wiseman to Sir William Tyrrell, Mar. 4, 1919, WWP 4.

even though the call be one of public duty. It can be taken as certain that the only way to settle any important negotiations with the States is by sending highly-placed and highly-competent envoys to Washington.[8]

Wiseman had several reasons for referring to the inability of Democratic public men to travel. First, as compared to Republicans, it was true, and Wiseman was still (as he had been in January and March) trying to impress on his government that the Democratic party was in power; British friendship with Republicans was little help and could in fact be disadvantageous. Second, by describing them as untravelled Wiseman indicated Democrats were inexperienced in foreign affairs and not rich enough individually to journey to Europe. However invalid part of this assertion—Democrats like Cleveland Dodge, Breckinridge Long, and Bernard Baruch could have certainly afforded to travel—it did put across a characteristic of the Democratic party that Wiseman and Northcliffe constantly emphasized: the Democratic party had a domestic orientation and on questions of economics and class was "radical," in the British usage of that word. This did not mean, Wiseman pointed out, that Wilson was a socialist or laborite. But it did mean that the Administration was "bitterly antagonistic to what they imagine to be 'Tory England'; and in nine questions out of ten they would be in complete agreement with our advanced Radical party."[9] That being the case, Wiseman's argument had the final purpose of disabusing the War Cabinet of the idea that Wilson himself ought to come to London for negotiations.[10] "Radical" Wilson could, in Wiseman's view, have little in common with the majority of a War Cabinet composed of Lloyd George, Sir Edward Carson, Lord Milner, Lord Curzon, and Bonar Law.

[8] Wiseman, "Memorandum on Anglo-American Relations, August 1917," WWP 4.

[9] *Ibid.* See also Northcliffe to Phillips for Reading, Aug. 26, 1917, and Northcliffe to Winston Churchill, Aug. 29, 1917, both in WWP 26.

[10] Wiseman to Northcliffe, Aug. 23, 1917, WWP 27.

Wiseman was amazed that the British government expected Wilson to come to London, somewhat after the manner of the prime ministers of the British Dominions. "Americans," he declared, "consider that Washington has become the diplomatic centre of the world."[11] The steady stream of Allied missions to Washington made this contention credible, and Wiseman believed the progress of the war would inevitably shift the headquarters of the western coalition to Washington. Most of Europe was already exhausted. Only Germany, Britain, and the United States remained strong, and of these three only the United States would emerge from the war with enhanced, indeed overwhelming, power. She would be the mightiest nation in the world, and it was obviously in Britain's interest to court her favor— more specially to court the favor of the Wilson Administration. For unlike parliamentary governments, the Wilson regime could not be turned out of office on the spur of the moment. Wiseman appreciated, as some in the British government seemed not to, that Wilson would be in office until March 1921 and that he was most unlikely to share his power with Republicans in some sort of coalition war cabinet. In fact, Wiseman prophesied, Wilson, barred by precedent from a third term, would not feel the necessity to defer to pressures even from his own party.[12]

In short, Wilson was, legally and temperamentally, "executively almost an autocrat" and would be so for the next three and a half years. If during those years Britain made a friend of Wilson she could satisfy her present needs and safeguard her future security. For the United States, Wiseman maintained, was on the threshold of a diplomatic revolution.

America is for the first time keenly interested in European problems. . . . The American people, however, have no great knowledge of European problems, or any

[11] *Ibid.*; Wiseman, "Memorandum on Anglo-American Relations, August 1917," WWP 4.

[12] This paragraph is based on *ibid.* and on Wiseman's memo, "Some Notes on the Position in August 1917," HP 20:45.

fixed ideas as to their settlement. Certain interested groups in America are actively engaged in furthering their own particular cause, but America as a whole has only the vaguest notions of the problems which would face a Peace Conference. America would never for a moment admit that she is prepared to follow the lead of England; but it is nevertheless true that unconsciously she is holding on to British traditions and would more readily accept the British than any other point-of-view, always provided no suggestion escaped that England was guiding or leading the foreign policy of the United States. It is no exaggeration to say that the foreign policy of America for many years to come is now in process of formation, and very much depends on the full sympathetic exchange of views between the leaders of the British and American people.[13]

If Wiseman's advice, by concentrating on the importance of courting Wilson, and therefore House, implied greater stature for himself as persona grata to House and Wilson, it also had the virtue of espousing a method of communication that was quiet, straightforward, and genuine. Besides being honorable, this method was eminently sound. Ballyhoo, hustling, and consorting with Wilson's critics might bring pressure to bear on the President but would do nothing for amity between the two governments. Spring Rice was a consorter and Northcliffe an incorrigible propagandist; therefore both must be removed for the good of Anglo-American relations.

Their removal would also end the petty feuding which needlessly complicated the immediate objective of Britain in America, the procurement of supplies and money. Wiseman concisely stated the impossibility of drawing a line between the work of the embassy and the British War Mission when he wrote, "Nowadays most diplomatic questions at Washington concern supplies, and all questions of

[13] Wiseman, "Memorandum on Anglo-American Relations, August 1917," WWP 4.

supplies when other than mere routine become matters for diplomatic negotiation." The reaction of "some people," probably Lloyd George, to this argument was to propose that Northcliffe take charge of both embassy and the War Mission. Although this would have produced the desired consolidation, Wiseman objected on the ground that a man of Northcliffe's temperament was "always danger-ous."[14] Reluctant to recall Northcliffe, Lloyd George was willing to have Reading survey the whole of British repre-sentation in the United States and submit his findings to the War Cabinet.[15]

Wiseman was sanguine about the reportorial aspect of Reading's mission and had in fact urged it. As he told Spring Rice in a cable designed to soften this fresh blow to the ambassador's authority, a financial mission by Read-ing "would have further advantage that he could explain to Prime Minister (with whom he has much influence) other aspects of general political situation and difficulties at Washington, which cannot be too clearly explained to our War Cabinet." More directly put, Wiseman expected Read-ing to make the same assessment as he had of the British muddle in America. Reading might conclude, as he had, that Lord Grey, because of his high esteem in the eyes of Wilson and House, would be the obvious choice to sup-plant Northcliffe and Spring Rice. The government paid no heed when Wiseman suggested Grey. Reading's recom-

[14] Wiseman, draft of a cable addressed but not sent to Drummond, c. Sept. 15, 1917, WWP 43. In the draft Wiseman says he is repeat-ing what he told Drummond in London. Wiseman to House, Aug. 11, 1917, WWP 27. Lord Rothermere to Northcliffe, Aug. 9, 1917, said that Lloyd George hesitated to appoint Reading for fear of "a revival of the Marconi allegations." Quoted in Pound and Harmsworth, *Northcliffe*, p. 570. Rothermere here referred to the allegations of 1913 that Reading, then attorney general, speculated in the shares of the Marconi Company, which held a large government contract. *Ibid.*, pp. 440-41.

[15] The breadth of Reading's instructions, his closeness to Lloyd George, and the events following his visit sustain this assertion.

mendations, which Wiseman immediately set out to influence, would carry more weight.[16]

When Lloyd George and Bonar Law decided to ask
Reading to go to Washington, the Foreign Office finally
came to grips with the question of diplomatic organization
in America. Lord Robert Cecil, Acting Foreign Secretary,
took the extraordinary step of asking Colonel House what
form the organization should take. His cable revealed an
administrator's perplexity over a situation which seemed
to be becoming intolerably complicated.

It is proposed to ask Lord Reading to go to Washington in connection with financial situation. I gather you
approve of this suggestion and in itself it seems excellent.
But I am fearful lest it should complicate still further our
representation in the U.S. unless indeed it were part of
some general rearrangement. It is on this point that I
should greatly value your advice. A complete understanding between our two countries is of such vital importance to both of them and even to the whole world
that I am venturing to hope that you may feel able
to tell me quite candidly and fully what you think. May
I ask you bluntly whether you think our present Ambassador with all his great merits exactly the right man
for the post. Does he command the complete confidence of the President for after all that is the essential
point. If not is there anyone else barring Balfour . . . who
would do better. Then about Northcliffe. Should he
remain and if so in what position. Lastly what powers
should Reading have and how should they be made to
fit in with the position of the Ambassador and Northcliffe if he remains. I know I have no right to ask you for
this service but I also know that whether you feel able
to advise me or not you will forgive me in view of the
vast importance of the interests at stake. I realize that

[16] Wiseman to Spring Rice, Aug. 20, 1917, WWP 27; Wiseman to
House, Aug. 23, 1917, WWP 27; Wiseman to Northcliffe, Aug. 23,
1917, WWP 27.

you were kind enough to express your views very fully on these matters to Mr. Balfour, Drummond and Wiseman, but circumstances have so much changed that I have ventured to ask you for a fresh expression of them.[17]

On the heels of Cecil's cable came one from Wiseman, saying that the British government had reached a crisis in its relations with the United States. "I have told them to recall Spring Rice for conference leaving Barclay [chargé d'affaires] in charge. Send Reading immediately for finance, keep Northcliffe for other supplies, and as soon as possible send Grey as regular Ambassador." Wiseman said that Lloyd George, Balfour, and all except a minority in the government were willing to follow his suggestions. Cecil needed a direct message from House in order to get unanimous consent for the proposal. House's response endorsed Wiseman's proposal and candidly discredited Spring Rice.[18] With an opinion from so near the President, the War Cabinet decided to enact Wiseman's proposal.

In notifying Balfour of the War Cabinet's decision, Cecil quoted the formula under which Reading would operate. He would have full authority to decide on behalf of the British government any question which might be raised. Without this power to overrule both Northcliffe and Spring Rice, Reading refused to undertake the mission, for (according to Cecil) "though he hoped and believed no such

[17] Cecil to House, Aug. 25, 1917, HP 4:38. Seymour, *Intimate Papers*, Vol. 3, p. 119, prints part of this cable but omits the significant questions about Spring Rice and Northcliffe.

[18] Wiseman to House, Aug. 25, 1917, WWP 27. Seymour, *Intimate Papers*, Vol. 3, p. 120, quotes part of House's Aug. 26 reply to Cecil but not the following: "Matters were running along quite well here until Northcliffe came, as the Ambassador seemed willing to permit Wiseman, Crawford and others *to help* do the work ordinarily done by an ambassador. The Ambassador with all his great qualifications is temperamentally unfit to cope with such complex and disturbed conditions. Northcliffe's coming precipitated an impossible situation, since the Ambassador was unwilling to work with him and for reasons he believes sufficient." HP 4:38. The words here italicized were penned in, as if in afterthought, by House after the message was typed.

exercise of authority would be necessary, yet, if he had not it as an ultimate resource, he might be put in an impossible position. He is . . . insistent on his dignities as Lord Chief Justice, both because of what is due to the Office itself, and even more because he regards as his main asset in America, the fact that he is officially a great British 'swell.' "[19]

Perhaps Cecil did not know fully why Reading needed such wide power, for one task that Lloyd George assigned to Reading had not yet been cleared with the War Cabinet. Frustrated by the prospect of stalemate on the Western Front, the Prime Minister yearned to attack the enemy where he was more vulnerable, in Austria or Turkey. But he could expect no support for such a departure from Generals Sir William Robertson and Sir Douglas Haig, respectively the Chief of the Imperial General Staff and the Commander-in-Chief of the British Expeditionary Force; nor was he likely to find unanimous support in the War Cabinet. There was, however, the possibility of enlisting American backing for this new course, and Lloyd George entrusted to Reading the responsibility of explaining the idea to Wilson. To Wiseman the Prime Minister assigned the duty of proselyting House. Lloyd George hoped that the Reading-Wiseman mission would result in House's attending a conference of the co-belligerents and presenting as American the plan for attacking Austria or Turkey. No one seemed to consider it a difficulty that the United States was not at war with Austria and Turkey.[20]

[19] Cecil to Balfour, Aug. 29, 1917, Balfour Papers, 49738, British Museum, and "Formula" dated Aug. 28, 1917. Lord Robert Cecil's Private Papers 1917-1924, FO 800/190.

[20] Lord Hankey, *The Supreme Command, 1914-1918*, 2 vols., London, 1961, Vol. 2, pp. 694-96; House Diary, Sept. 16, 1917; Lloyd George, *War Memoirs*, Vol. IV, pp. 2,333-48. Trask, *United States in the Supreme War Council*, pp. 13-14.

A paper in WWP 101 entitled "Military Position," probably drafted by Lloyd George's secretariat, outlines Lloyd George's plan for taking Allied political action to overcome military opposition to attacking the enemy "at their weakest point," i.e., Austria. The paper contains these significant paragraphs:

71

Theoretically Lloyd George's maneuver stood a fair chance of success. Wilson demonstrated in December that he was willing to go to war with Austria without an immediate casus belli. Though inclined to make its stand on the Western Front, the American army was still in early enough stage of formation in September that it might establish itself on another front. Wilson, if reluctant to intervene in matters of military strategy, was nonetheless eager to bring the war to a conclusion and was amenable to new ideas which promised that end. On August 11 he gave a pep talk to officers of the Atlantic fleet, urging them to "throw traditions to the winds" and condemning the unimaginativeness of the British navy. An enthusiastic and well reasoned presentation of the innovation Lloyd George proposed might have secured Wilson's endorsement.[21] Reading probably attempted such a presentation. Wiseman, however, accompanied his presentation with numerous reservations, and it was on the basis of Wiseman's exposition, not Reading's, that Wilson made his decision.

Reading and Wiseman disembarked at New York on September 12, and each headed toward the man he was charged to influence. Reading carried a letter from Lloyd

---

In view of the fact that the military are certain to object to this scheme, the political difficulties in England and France would be very great if civilian authorities tried to enforce their views. These difficulties would, however, disappear to a large extent if these suggestions were put forward or supported by the United States.

It might, in some way, be semi-officially announced that the Allies wanted the advantage of American opinion on important strategic problems.

Below these remarks, Wiseman penciled: "Send H. for short trip. U.S. *must* take part in strategical comd."
Lloyd George considered sending General Sir Henry Wilson over to lay the new strategy before President Wilson. General Wilson refused because he was told he would be under the authority of Northcliffe. C. E. Callwell, *Field-Marshal Sir Henry Wilson*, 2 vols., London, 1927, Vol. 2, p. 11.

[21] Victor S. Mamatey, *The United States and East Central Europe 1914-1918*, Princeton, 1957, pp. 157-60; Trask, *United States in the Supreme War Council*, p. 15; Ray Stannard Baker, *Woodrow Wilson Life & Letters*, 8 vols., New York, 1927-39, Vol. 7, pp. 211-12.

George to the President. Not delivered until September 20, it asked for American representation on an Allied military council and advocated in general terms an offensive against Germany's southeastern allies. In a shorter letter to House Lloyd George wrote that Wiseman would "explain to you what I think about the present situation . . . [and] tell you why I believe that a representative of the United States could render invaluable service to the Allied cause." So Wiseman did. For three days—at Magnolia, during an automobile trip to New London, and on the train to New York—he discussed with House the desirability of coordinating American and Allied military strategy. He explained Lloyd George's project of laying siege to Austria and forcing her into a separate peace. Wiseman believed the plan had merit militarily but he did not think Lloyd George had sufficiently considered the political consequences of a separate peace with Austria. What disposition was to be made of the Austrian Slavs and Poles, whose chief foe was the Hapsburg regime and whose welfare the British had promised to protect? Wiseman, so he told House, wanted the Allies and America, in consultation with Polish, Czech, and Yugoslav leaders, to reach an accord on the future of the Hapsburg Empire before pressing for a separate peace. And, Wiseman cautioned, this was just one of the political questions which should be considered along with deliberations on military strategy.[22]

More damaging than Wiseman's criticism of Lloyd George's project as not adequately thought through was

[22] House Diary, Sept. 12, 1917, Sept. 16, 1917; Lloyd George to Wilson, Sept. 3, 1917, printed in Lloyd George, *War Memoirs*, Vol. 4, pp. 2,348-57.

Lloyd George to House, Sept. 4, 1917, HP 12:32. Apparently Lloyd George at first intended to write only Wilson. See Geoffrey Dawson to Lloyd George, Sept. 1, 1917, Lloyd George Papers F/41/7/18, Beaverbrook Library, for indication of how Wiseman maneuvered to secure a letter to House also.

The substance of Wiseman's remarks to House was later included in the memo, "Some Notes on the Position in August 1917," HP 20:45. See Wiseman to House, Sept. 26, 1917, WWP 64.

his warning that Lloyd George was "anything but progressive" and devious as well. Just as he earlier warned the War Cabinet that the United States government was radical, now he was telling House that the British government was "honeycombed with reactionaries." Why did Wiseman emphasize to each of the governments their contrasting philosophical inclinations? Again Wiseman's policy of candor provides the answer. There should be no illusions by either as to the other's objectives. He knew that Wilson was fighting to vindicate certain moral and legal principles, such as the establishment of democracy in Germany, whereas the British were aiming for a specific territorial arrangement for the stabilization of European peace. However much he may have personally preferred the British objectives—and while evidence on his own beliefs is scant there is no reason to believe he was a fervent democrat—Wiseman also recognized that the United States potentially had the power to insist on her objectives. This meant that Britain, in order to share in and benefit from American power, must by and large acquiesce in American objectives. It also meant that the friendship of House for England must not be jeopardized by implicating him in a British Cabinet struggle. And, Wiseman explained to House, Lloyd George's purpose in inviting him to London would do just that—Lloyd George wanted to use House to foil Haig and Robertson. House, previously no particularly warm admirer of Lloyd George, now peevishly recorded that "Lloyd George's methods and purposes are not always of the highest. . . . It is not pleasant when one is unable to receive statements of policy at their face value."[23]

On September 16 House reported his conversations with Wiseman to the President who was aboard his yacht in

[23] House Diary, Sept. 16, 1917; C. P. Scott's diary entry for August 24, 1917, quoted in Hammond, *Scott*, pp. 233-34. House Diary, Oct. 13, 1917: Wiseman "thought Lloyd George was making a distinct effort to use me to further his plans" to overrule Haig and Robertson. Wiseman undoubtedly said something similar during his talks with House Sept. 13-16.

New York Harbor. Wilson's reaction to Lloyd George's proposals was noncommital, apparently both as to the military council and the scheme to attack Austria. He did agree that something different should be tried in the conduct of the war, and upon returning to Washington he ordered an evaluation by the War Department of the "eastern" strategy.[24] On September 18 he received a cautioning message from House: "After thinking the matter over I find myself not altogether trusting Lloyd George's plan which Reading is to present to you. The English naturally want the road to Egypt and India blocked, and Lloyd George is not above using us to further this plan. He is not of the Grey-Balfour type and in dealing with him it is well to bear this in mind."[25] Thus Wilson was in possession of the essence of Lloyd George's proposals as well as of House's and Wiseman's forewarnings before Reading officially presented the proposals on September 20. On that occasion the President responded courteously but guardedly.[26] It was three weeks before he made a decision in the matter.

During those weeks Wiseman moved into an apartment at 115 East 53rd Street, the building in Manhattan where House lived.[27] There the two men overhauled and reworked Lloyd George's proposals. They agreed on the necessity of a conference to map the strategy of the war and on the necessity for the United States to participate in it. But they neglected to campaign for the "eastern" strategy or to urge the President to send House to the strategy conference. As to the former, Wiseman believed that a decision should be made by military experts at the conference itself, not in advance. As to a visit by House, he found the Colonel reluctant to

[24] House Diary, Sept. 16, 1917; Trask, *United States in the Supreme War Council*, pp. 14, 183-84, note 33. Wilson sent Baker a memo by Major H. H. Sargent endorsing the "eastern strategy" on Sept. 22. There is no reason to think Sargent's memo was in any way related to Lloyd George's proposal, but the latter probably prompted Wilson to seek the War Department's evaluation.

[25] House to Wilson, Sept. 18, 1917, HP 49:9.

[26] Reading to War Cabinet, Sept. 21, 1917, FO 371/3112.

[27] Wiseman to Arthur Murray, Oct. 3, 1917, WWP 85.

become involved in military logistics and strategy. House had just accepted the President's appointment to begin studies for the eventual peace conference and preferred to let Secretaries Baker and McAdoo, the men directly responsible for waging the war, attend such a war conference as Lloyd George proposed.[28]

Furthermore, Wiseman seemed to delay carrying out Lloyd George's instructions until he could be sure that the British government as a whole desired a war conference and House's presence at it, until he could be sure that the scheme was more than just a vehicle for Lloyd George to overcome opposition in his own cabinet. In a cable which indicated that the Foreign Office did not know what Lloyd George had in mind, Wiseman asked, as if making a brand new proposal, whether Balfour would desire a visit to Europe by House.[29] Balfour in reply stated that from the standpoint of usefulness to the Allies, House's presence was more valuable in the United States, therefore a visit by McAdoo or Baker was preferable. The War Cabinet, however, overruled Balfour and requested House as "the only suitable person."[30]

Delay by Wiseman—or rather his abstention from interfering in the delay by Wilson and House—did not mean he opposed a conference on strategy. Quite the contrary. In a

[28] Wiseman, "Some Notes on the Position in August 1917," HP 20:45. House to Wilson, Sept. 24, 1917, HP 49:9; House to Lloyd George, Sept. 24, 1917, HP 12:32. House was appointed to gather materials for the peace conference on September 2. Seymour, *Intimate Papers*, Vol. 3, p. 169.

[29] If the Foreign Office had been conversant with Lloyd George's scheme, Wiseman needed not have worded his inquiry this way: "For your private information only, I believe it would be possible to persuade the President to send House or Baker, War Minister, on official visit to London and Paris to confer. Do you think this would be desirable?" Wiseman to Drummond, Sept. 20, 1917, WWP 42.

While stalling, Wiseman advised Reading that "we must not be surprised" if the first attempt at joint consultation "opens rather slowly." Wiseman to Reading, Sept. 26, 1917, WWP 107.

[30] Drummond to Wiseman, Sept. 26, 1917, WWP 42; *ibid.*, Sept. 30, 1917.

memorandum[31] for House, which House described as "what we thought should be the war policy of the Allies,"[32] Wiseman pressed for immediate agreement between the United States and Britain on their military and political objectives. His views, he said, were the result of talks with dozens of people in London, with the King, all the members of the War Cabinet, naval and military leaders, French and Italian liaison officers, labor leaders, journalists, and "pacifists" like Sidney Webb. From these talks Wiseman concluded that all the Western powers except Britain and America were exhausted. The problem was to bridge the three thousand miles that separated London and Washington, the geographical condition that was Germany's chief advantage. If Britain and America, the "controlling" Western powers, could agree on a course of action, the other Allies would undoubtedly go along. British and American officials should therefore enter into frank discussions, arrive at a policy, and solicit the endorsement of it by the other co-belligerents.

Agreement would be required on more than military plans, Wiseman continued. An attempt should be made to reconcile the several co-belligerents' war aims. "If alterations are necessary in the plans of the Allies, both military and political, now is the right time for them to be made." Answering Wilson's objection that the United States should abstain from advising on strategy until her army was in the field, Wiseman noted "that military plans should be discussed, and indeed decided, from six months to a year before they can come into full swing. Political plans may take even longer to mature."

Wiseman chose the Austro-Hungarian Empire, Bulgaria, and Russia, to illustrate the importance of joining political and military planning. Concerning Lloyd George's ambition to make a separate peace with Austria, he cautioned

---

[31] Wiseman, "Some Notes on the Position in August 1917," and the covering letter, Wiseman to House, Sept. 26, 1917, both in HP 20:45.

[32] House Diary, Sept. 26, 1917.

that the nationalist aspirations within the empire raised grave complications. Perhaps the appeal should be made to the national minorities rather than to Austria. "It would seem that, if these people were really roused and concentrated on any tangible project, they could break up the Central Empires from inside. . . . Any suggestion of a separate peace with Austria inevitably arouses anger and dismay among them, and might even drive them to some policy which would be fatal to the Allied cause." In other words, the Czechs, Yugoslavs, and Poles if they sensed that they were being deserted by the Allies might extract such concessions as they could get from their present rulers and then support the latter against the Allies. On the other hand, Bulgaria, in Wiseman's opinion, had little in common with Germany and might for a price be lured into a separate peace.

In the case of Russia Wiseman declared that Germany's enemies must not permit the situation to drift. At present the Germans were so little challenged on the Eastern Front that they were able to shift troops from that theatre to the Western Front. Nor was the political chaos in Russia of merely temporary or military use to the Germans.

> If the Russian situation does not improve, the Germans will obtain political control of the country, and will begin moulding sections of political opinion which they can use to their own advantage when peace terms are discussed. . . . I believe the Russian Republic will be influenced by a foreign power, and I think the only question is whether that power will be Germany or the United States. You ought to consider the idea of sending an American army to Russia. It would become a rallying point for all decent citizens and a menace to German influence.[33]

Obviously Wiseman's agenda for an Allied conference was a formidable one. It aimed for the ideal, an understand-

[33] Wiseman, "Some Notes on the Position in August 1917," HP 20:45.

ing on political objectives throughout Europe and on the means of accomplishing them. Defining the desirable, while a step in the right direction, was relatively simple; achieving it enormously complicated. How could House or any other mortal control all the strands of military and political activity in a war involving over half the world? Wiseman, who of course wanted House to control as much as possible, appeared to desire something like the following approach:

(1) Let McAdoo, Baker, or Lansing (or some combination of them) meet with Allied officials to discuss the myriad details of supply, finance, manpower, and military/naval strategy.

(2) Let Wilson and House judge, on the basis of long-range political consequences and with knowledge of British desires, the conclusions and recommendations of such discussions.

(3) In case American policy decisions then differed from British, House, using Wiseman as liaison, could mediate a settlement.

In such a comprehensive system of control Lloyd George's proposed war conference became just one of a series of continuing consultations on the operational level. Grand strategy would be ordered by a directorate consisting of the President (closely advised by House) and the British War Cabinet, with Wiseman the link between the sectors of the directorate.

President Wilson turned to consideration of the proposed war council on October 10. Two days earlier he wrote House saying that Mrs. Wilson's bout with grippe was over and that House could now come to the White House for talks on Lloyd George's proposition.[34] By this time Wiseman had given to House his views on what an Allied conference or war council should do and had expressed his opposition to House's participating in such a meeting. At

[34] Wilson to House, Oct. 8, 1917, HP 49:18.

House's request he accompanied the Colonel to Washington. Because of Reading's objection he did not meet with the President personally, but he was in constant touch with House who transmitted Wiseman's thoughts on American-Allied cooperation to Wilson.[35]

The outcome of three days of deliberations among Wilson, House, Reading, and Lansing was the President's decision to have House represent the United States at the war council. Wilson at one point was on the verge of sending House to Europe for an extended stay. Then House read him a statement by Wiseman, which read in part,

I believe that if you will go over and attend the war council and stay in Europe to the end of the war you cannot avoid dealing with all the problems that arise after they have reached a certain point of importance. It would seem to me better to face the situation from the outset and realize that your government is taking a very important step. In my opinion it is no less than shifting the center of gravity of the war from Washington to London and Paris. It would be a bad thing for American prestige to have American representatives in Europe who are not able to give decisions, and apart from that, such representatives would not be able to help things along and might as well not be there. From the point of view of carrying on the war most effectively I have no doubt that it would be best to send a permanent American Commission with offices in both London and Paris. . . . This, in my opinion, is the only practicable and

[35] House Diary, Oct. 9, 1917; Auchincloss Diary, Oct. 10, 11, 12, 1917; Wiseman to Drummond, Oct. 13, 1917, WWP 42. William Phillips, Third Assistant Secretary of State, recorded in his diary on October 12: "Last night the President spoke to me on the telephone and asked me to see Lord Reading and Sir William Weisman [sic] and ask them to come to see him and Col. House tomorrow at twelve. Called upon Lord Reading at nine o'clock and was warmly received until I suggested that Weisman would accompany him, whereupon a most extraordinary frost occurred. Arrangements were made during the morning so that Lord Reading went alone to see the President. Weisman did not call, and everything was happy, apparently." William Phillips Papers, Harvard University Library.

effective way of getting proper cooperation, but there remain the two difficulties to be overcome. In the first place you must contemplate delegating an important part of the authority of the American Government to the Commission; and secondly, you must consider if you go as head of the Commission, it would be impossible for you to keep clear of the many vital problems which arise almost daily in the cooperation of the Allies and devote sufficient time to those problems which are really the most important and which you have made your particularly study.

According to House, Wiseman's statement "shook the President because he has no intention of loosening his hold on the situation." Instead, Wilson determined that House would make only a short visit and that the temporary delegation of "an important part" of the authority of the American government would expire at the end of House's visit.[36] For the remainder of the war, until armistice negotiations, Wilson jealously guarded against delegating power to representatives in Europe. Despite McAdoo's entreaties, he would not even grant the Treasury's chief representative, whose duties were extremely important, the title of "high commissioner."[37]

As soon as the President made his decision, Reading informed London, and the Allies then officially invited the United States to attend their next conference.[38] It appeared that the "real purpose" of Reading's mission was achieved: House was coming to Europe. But what of the other parts of Lloyd George's proposal, the "eastern" strategy and American membership in the joint war council?

[36] House Diary, Oct. 13, 1917. Wiseman's statement, in a letter to House, is dated Oct. 10, 1917. HP 20:45 and WWP 64.

[37] McAdoo to Wilson, Jan. 14, 1918, McAdoo Papers, Box 524; McAdoo to Wilson, May 27, 1918; Lansing to Wilson, May 31, 1918; Wilson to McAdoo, June 1, 1918, all in Wilson Papers, File 6, Box 587, folder 4488. Wilson finally permitted Crosby the constricting title of "Special United States Commissioner of Finance in Europe."

[38] Reading to Wilson, Oct. 15, 1917, HP 16:30.

The War Department vetoed the first.[39] Wiseman, by persuading Wilson and House against a long-term stay by House in Europe, diluted American participation in the war council. House, the only person Wilson would let represent him, would attend only two of the council's sessions, one in December and the other the last session in October and November 1918. Wiseman's advice in effect undermined the Supreme War Council before it was established.

Wiseman of course did not indicate to London the advice he gave House. He told his superiors that House's reluctance to come to Europe stemmed from his greater interest in peace terms than in war measures. House would only come, Wiseman said, if the Allied conference scheduled for October 15 and designed to discuss overall war plans could be postponed to November, the earliest date House could arrive. Otherwise a second conference would have to be arranged at which general strategic and political plans could be discussed. "In a word, there must be some reason other than the discussion of finance and supplies in order to persuade House to come." Since Wilson had already decided that House would go to Europe, this last statement may be read as meaning that unless the Allies postponed their general discussions Wiseman would dissuade House from coming.[40]

When House accepted the President's charge to go to Europe, he insisted that Wiseman accompany him. In telling London of this Wiseman said, "I do not exactly know what he thinks I can do for him. I think he would like to have me about as a sort of A.-D.-C. while he is in London."[41] Actually Wiseman had become House's chief ad-

[39] Trask, *United States in the Supreme War Council*, pp. 15, 184 and note 36.

[40] Wiseman to Drummond, Oct. 14, 1917, WWP 43.

[41] *Ibid.* Wiseman to [Secret Service Department], Oct. 14, 1917, WWP 64: "House insists that . . . I must come with him. I think this may make the position a little difficult for me in London, but I daresay I can keep out of sight, and naturally I want to meet his wishes in every way I can."

viser on American-Allied cooperation. Neither House nor Wilson was certain as to what precisely was expected of the United States in an Allied conference. Lloyd George's letters to them were vague concerning how the much desired coordination of efforts was to be accomplished, and whatever Reading may have told the President, the latter remained confused regarding the several inter-Allied councils being proposed.[42] For the information of House and Wilson, Wiseman composed a paper describing three councils which the United States should join, and it was these three that the United States did join.[43]

Wiseman described the three councils in advance of their actual formation. His description was of considerable importance in determining House's and Wilson's conception of the responsibilities of the councils. The war council, he said, was the most important of the lot, the one on which House would sit. Its members—prime ministers in the case of the Allies—would "have supreme authority from their Governments to discuss the political aims of the Allies and the various military objectives which may help us realize these aims." Though Wiseman noted that the first order of business for this council was determination of the military strategy to be employed in 1918, he did not think of this council as one which could be called into session at almost any time to alter strategy, as Lloyd George wished it to. The council Lloyd George had in mind, what was to become the Supreme War Council, ideally would superintend the execution as well as the formation of strategy and would be prepared to overrule military commanders. The council Wiseman described was identical with the infrequent and not very effective (mili-

[42] Wiseman to Drummond, Oct. 13, 1917, WWP 42: "It was evident . . . that there was some confusion in the President's mind regarding these various proposed councils. . . ."

[43] Wiseman, Memorandum dated Oct. 10, 1917, HP 20:45. House's notation on the memo: "Mem. written by Sir Wm. W. for the President's information and mine in order to guide us in the decision we are making as to my going to Europe now. EMH. Oct. 10/17." The memorandum is printed in Seymour, *Intimate Papers*, Vol. 3, pp. 199-200.

tarily) conferences the Allied prime ministers had held throughout the war. Thus there was considerable difference between the war council Wilson and House thought House would be attending and the one Lloyd George and his advisers (particularly General Sir Henry Wilson) were hoping to establish.[44]

The other two councils Wiseman described for House and Wilson would be, he noted, permanent and specialized. The first, the one desired by McAdoo, would regulate the distribution of American money and supplies to the Allies. The second, proposed by the British, would coordinate joint negotiations with neutral countries on trade. Its task, as Wiseman felicitously phrased it, would be to ensure that "British blockade measures would not clash with the policy of the American Government."[45]

These descriptions of the proposed councils by Wiseman were unofficial and written on his own initiative. Nonetheless they formed the basis of House's thoughts on American participation in Allied bodies, and the President left it to House to determine the nature of that participation. At first Wilson wanted House to go alone to confer with the Allies. Then he approved House's request to be accompanied by military and naval advisers. A few days later House asked that Vance McCormick, Chairman of the War Trade Board, go with him to study Britain's embargo methods. Finally, on October 23, Wilson authorized House to take army, navy, munitions, food, finance, shipping, and embargo representatives with him. These seven categories were precisely those suggested by Wiseman, and it is significant that House referred, as did Wiseman, to "Munitions" and "Embargo" departments—not to the War Industries Board or the War Trade Board, as the munitions and embargo authorities in the United States were called.[46]

[44] Wiseman, Memorandum dated Oct. 10, 1917, HP 20:46. See Callwell, *Henry Wilson*, Vol. 2, p. 10.
[45] Wiseman, Memorandum dated Oct. 10, 1917, HP 20:46.
[46] House Diary, Oct. 13, 23, 1917; House to Wilson, Oct. 16, 1917,

In listing the seven categories for House, Wiseman acted on his own. He wrote that "disappointment—even dismay" would be felt in Europe if House's party did not include experts from the seven named agencies. But he made these suggestions before receiving a set of instructions from the War Cabinet which enumerated the questions, virtually all military, which the British wished to discuss with House. Wiseman's own list touched lightly on military and naval plans and concentrated on the areas in which he forsaw difficulty: shipping, munitions, food, finance, and embargo. He obviously believed streamlining the flow of American goods to Europe could be one of the best results of the House mission.[47]

Wiseman was not, however, as pessimistic as Reading about the future. On September 27 Reading reported to Lloyd George a growing lack of coordination between the American and Allied war programs. He spoke of domestic opposition to Wilson, suspicion of the purposes of the Allies, disorganization in the Administration, nervousness and "oppression" in the Treasury, and the probable inability of the United States sufficiently to supply war materials to the Allies. In case of shortage of either money or supplies, he thought the Administration would look to its own needs first. Reading's message reached London by way of the Wiseman channel—not, however, before Wiseman and House studied it and decided that Wiseman should send a commentary on it to the Foreign Office.[48]

Wiseman muted all of Reading's warnings, noting that Reading had dealt with only the Treasury Department, which contained an anti-British element. The political situation, which underpinned all other questions, was, Wise-

---

in Seymour, *Intimate Papers*, Vol. 3, p. 204. Wiseman's suggestions are contained in a memorandum, "America's Part in the War," c. Oct. 15, 1917, WWP 4.

[47] *Ibid.*; Drummond to Wiseman, Oct. 20, 1917, WWP 43; Wiseman to Drummond, Oct. 21, 1917, WWP 43.

[48] Reading to Prime Minister, Chancellor of Exchequer, and Balfour, Sept. 21, 1917, WWP 107; House Diary, Sept. 29, 1917.

man thought, more hopeful than Reading reported. The "best elements" of the Republican party were wholeheartedly supporting the President, whose authority had "increased enormously during the past six months, with the result that all opposition has been practically cleared away and reduced to noisy criticism on the part of the Roosevelt wing, of the Administration's past inaction." There was in fact in the United States "a unanimity probably unequalled in any other belligerent country."[49]

Wiseman agreed with Reading that Britain would more likely be embarrassed by a shortage of supplies than of money from America. And in time of shortage Americans would naturally take the attitude described by the term "America first."

> But this must not be interpreted as an undervaluation of the Allies, or a misconception of their part, nor does it imply the slightest hostility towards them. America's own requirements will come first, but there is no reason to fear that the American programme will interfere with those of the Allies to the common detriment, provided we also have a clear-cut programme and can tell the Americans clearly what our needs are.[50]

This recognition of the need for a clear-cut program and the effective communication of it underlay Wiseman's recommendations for the composition of House's mission staff. In the summer there had been the financial crisis, now subdued but still alive. By September the British wished to talk more definitely of a matter which Balfour hesitantly broached in April—American blockade and embargo policy. An ironic consequence of American participation in the war was the vigorous application of embargo measures. Indeed the United States seemed prepared to take a sterner line than Britain's against the Scandinavian neutrals. The British feared that unless their policy conformed with America's, the neutrals would find it easier to defy both.

[49] Wiseman to Drummond, Oct. 4, 1917, WWP 42.
[50] *Ibid.*

Cecil, in charge of the blockade ministry, proposed a joint council and, on the advice of the British embassy, appealed to House for American concurrence.[51]

Wiseman gave Cecil's proposal to House, along with a confidential War Cabinet memorandum on Britain's embargo policy. The memorandum indicated concern that Sweden or Norway might join the war on Germany's side if pressed too closely by the Allies. House used this argument in urging caution on Vance McCormick, whose War Trade Board was on the verge of applying "final pressure" to stop shipments of Swedish ore to Germany. Wiseman cabled McCormick's attitude to Balfour who replied that Sweden should be dealt with by bargaining, not by ultimatum. He renewed the request for American representation on a joint blockade board in London.[52]

A week later, Secretary of State Lansing, perhaps not privy to the arrangements being discussed between House and Balfour, cabled Ambassador Page that the Administration was being urged to cut off entirely Norwegian fish exports and Swedish iron ore exports to Germany. Lansing stated that the British seemed to desire such a complete embargo but were hesitant to recommend it. Page in reply said, "The British Government are confident that complete demands can now be made without risk of driving any

[51] Balfour to House, Sept. 15, 1917, HP 2:22; Wiseman to Drummond, Sept. 20, 1917, WWP 42; Drummond to Wiseman, Sept. 27, 1917, WWP 42; Wiseman to Colville Barclay, Sept. 28, 1917, WWP 46; Colville Barclay to Wiseman, Sept. 20, 1917, WWP 46; House Diary, Sept. 29, 1917. Also see Thomas A. Bailey, *The Policy of the United States toward the Neutrals, 1917-1918*, Baltimore, 1942, pp. 186-92, 98-101.

[52] Wiseman to Drummond, Sept. 29, 1917, WWP 42; House to Wilson, Oct. 3, 1917, HP 49:9; Balfour to Wiseman, Oct. 2, 1917, WWP 42. Wiseman to Secret Service Department, Oct. 7, 1917, WWP 64: "McCormick . . . is in favor of the policy of driving all neutrals to declare against Germany. He wants to cut off all supplies from the northern neutrals, and the position now is that our Foreign Office is trying to restrain Washington from treating the neutrals too harshly in the matter of blockade. I knew very well that this would happen as soon as the States came in. A little later on we may easily find the European Allies anxious for peace while the Americans insist on carrying the war onto German soil."

87

border neutral into the war on the side of Germany." This appeared to contradict what Balfour had told Wiseman, and House so informed the President. Wiseman asked clarification from the Foreign Office. Drummond replied that the British now favored full demands being brought to bear on the neutrals, who probably would then seek to bargain.[53] Clearly, as Balfour noted, closer consultation than that possible by telegram was needed.

Maritime tonnage, without which American power could not be exerted in Europe, became a topic of even greater anxiety to the British in October. A confidential War Cabinet study, which Wiseman caused to be sent to the Administration in August, revealed how successful the German submarine campaign of 1917 was.[54] In a long cable dispatched to Wiseman on October 11, and forwarded by House to Wilson, Lloyd George rehearsed the British losses and suggested that the United States undertake to offset the losses by building ships at the rate of six million tons per year. Lloyd George could not, he said, "lay too great a stress on the grave possibility that the superior efforts being made by all the Allies in various other directions may be set at naught by inadequate provision for making good the loss of tonnage."[55] While Wilson did not, as House suggested, make a reply to Lloyd George through Wiseman, the cable undoubtedly made him more receptive to the proposal to include a shipping expert on the House mission. Certainly the cable prompted Wiseman to suggest the inclusion.[56]

[53] Lansing to Page, Oct. 9, 1917, *Foreign Relations, 1917*, Sup. 2, Vol. 1, p. 962; Page to Lansing, Oct. 13, 1917, *ibid.*, pp. 970-71; House to Wilson, Oct. 17, 1917, HP 49:9; Wiseman to Drummond, Oct. 17, 1917, WWP 43; Drummond to Wiseman, Oct. 20, 1917, WWP 43.

[54] Wiseman to House, Aug. 2, 1917, WWP 27.

[55] Drummond to Wiseman, Oct. 11, 1917, WWP 43. The cable is printed in Seymour, *Intimate Papers*, Vol. 3, pp. 190-93, as being from Balfour to House, but the original in WWP indicates it was from Lloyd George to Wilson.

[56] House to Wilson, Oct. 14, 1917, HP 49:9. Wiseman refers to the cable in his recommendations to House concerning the composition

At the time Wiseman was advising House on an agenda and staff for his mission, there existed no acute problem involving food or supplies. A certain amount of coherence had been introduced into the supply program when Northcliffe and other Allied representatives signed an agreement to place their orders through the United States War Purchase Board. But Wiseman believed food and supplies to be intimately bound up with questions of tonnage and military planning. He foresaw the possibility of "a dangerous interval, possibly next summer, between the time when we run short of necessary supplies, owing to [the] American programme, and the time when the U.S. Army is ready to take a big part on the Western Front." He hoped arrangements could be made during the House visit to prevent or at least shorten such an interval.[57]

Having prescribed the kind of staff House should take with him, Wiseman went on to nominate individual members. He suggested Robert S. Lovett, whom Northcliffe admired, for supplies; Oscar T. Crosby, whom Wiseman thought anti-British but who had handled loans to the Allies, for the Treasury; and, significantly, Benjamin Strong, Britain's friend in the financial crisis, also for the Treasury. Of these, only Crosby was chosen. House prudently asked the agencies involved to name their representatives.[58]

With the appointment of House's staff made, House and Wiseman spent the remaining days of October in frequent consultation about and preparation for the trip. Wiseman

---

of House's mission. Wiseman, "America's Part in the War," WWP 4. Wilson did give House a memo on shipping to take to London for Lloyd George's information. Wilson to House, Oct. 26, 1917, HP 49:18.

[57] Northcliffe to Wiseman, Aug. 24, 1917, WWP 91; Wiseman to Drummond, Oct. 14, 1917, WWP 42.

[58] Wiseman, "America's Part in the War," WWP 4. The staff as chosen by House and the relevant agencies: Rear Admiral W. S. Benson, General Tasker H. Bliss, Oscar T. Crosby (Treasury), Vance C. McCormick (War Trade Board), Bainbridge Colby (Shipping Board), Dr. Alonzo R. Taylor (Food Controller), and Thomas N. Perkins (War Industries Board). Seymour, *Intimate Papers*, Vol. 3, pp. 207-208.

had already asked the Foreign Office to take extra care to ensure the Americans' comfort, pointing out that House was frail and that Americans liked heated rooms. He now asked that the dates and names of the mission not be revealed because the American government had not yet made them known to Page. But the elaborate secrecy surrounding the plans for the trip must have seemed insufficient when a cable from Ambassador Francis in Petrograd came asking, "Where is House? Understand *en route* Europe."[59]

Wiseman, assigned by Balfour to be at House's disposal during the visit, left New York two days earlier than House. He did so in order to prevent offense to the other Allies and "much" to House's inconvenience. On the day before he sailed he witnessed, along with the Attorney General of the United States and the president of the College of the City of New York, the drawing up of House's will.[60] When his ship, the *New York*, weighed anchor at noon on October 27, one of his fellow passengers was Edgar Sisson, a man who like Wiseman would later be telling the American government what to do in Russia.[61]

[59] Wiseman to Drummond, Oct. 14, 1917, WWP 43; Wiseman to Drummond, Oct. 25, 1917, WWP 43. Page was informed the next day. Lansing to Page, Oct, 26, 1917, *Foreign Relations, 1917*, Sup. 2, Vol. 1, p. 278. Francis to Lansing, Oct. 15, 1917, *ibid.*, p. 254.

[60] Balfour to House, Oct. 26, 1917, WWP 43; Auchincloss Diary, Oct. 24, 1917; House Diary, Oct. 26, 1917.

[61] Edgar Sisson, *One Hundred Red Days*, New Haven, 1931, p. 12, describes Sisson's encounter with Wiseman on the ship: "Among the passengers was Capt. Sir William Wiseman, the slight, cool, and canny man whom I knew to be David Lloyd George's confidential messenger between London and Washington. Captain Wiseman knew also that I was on mission from President Wilson, and my destination. In London he speeded up requests to the British Government for transportation onward. On board ship he was an amusing companion. Invalided after passing through the hell of the defensive fighting of Kitchener's proud-named Contemptibles, he glossed satire over reality and so kept life palatable. He was wearied, too, of all slogans, including that of Democracy. 'I would be willing,' he said, 'to pass the rest of my life on a desert island, if I were sure that there I would never hear the word again.' On this sentiment he and I disagreed whimsically."

THE PLANNING of House's trip eclipsed other transactions conducted by Wiseman in the period of August through October. These other transactions occupied much of his time and by their diversity illustrated the range of matters which impinged on Anglo-American relations and the care which Wiseman took to please the Administration.

On the eve of his departure from London at the beginning of September, Wiseman cabled House that British intelligence had intercepted some German messages, the "most important disclosures since Zimmermann note." The disclosures became known as the Luxberg telegrams and involved neutral Sweden's disingenuous transmission of Germany military orders. American newspapers shrieked indignation at the revelation, and credited the State Department, which released the news earlier than Wiseman planned, with intercepting the messages. To leave no doubt of authenticity, Wiseman brought to Wilson and House documentary confirmation of Sweden's unneutral behavior. The episode was significant chiefly as another instance of Wiseman's courting the Administration.[62] Later, in October, acting upon what he interpreted to be House's wishes, he urged the British to release some Swedish mailbags they had seized. The Foreign Office replied, "in deference to President's wishes we are going to hand back Swedish mail bags unopened."[63]

Two peace probes were made in this period. The first came from Pope Benedict XV addressed to the belligerent governments. On August 10, six days before the American government, which had no representative at the Vatican, received the appeal, Wiseman alerted House from London that such an appeal was on its way. He remarked how care-

[62] Wiseman to House, Aug. 31, 1917, WWP 27. Page to Lansing for Wilson, Aug. 31, 1917, SD 763.72111/7336, told the President that the Luxberg documents would be delivered to him "by a trustworthy messenger personally known to you." For an account of the disclosure, see the New York *World*, Sept. 5, 1917. House Diary, Sept. 12, 17, 1917; Lansing Desk Diary, Sept. 18, 1917.

[63] Wiseman to Drummond, Oct. 17, 1917, WWP 43; Drummond to Wiseman, Oct. 20, 1917, WWP 43.

fully an answer should be considered and asked whether Wilson might privately foreshadow his views to Balfour. Wilson, to whom House forwarded Wiseman's cable, informed Balfour that if he did answer the Pope he would make the argument that it was futile to accept pledges from the "morally bankrupt" German government. Balfour replied that the British would, in effect, stall until the President made his move. Wiseman then cabled that in case the President did reply to the Pope, he would "urge the British Government to make no answer excepting to state they entirely agree with what the President has to say."[64]

The result could have been a statement of war aims by the President, similar to his later Fourteen Points. Acting Foreign Secretary Lord Robert Cecil realized this and declined to endorse Wilson's answer prior to seeing it. As it happened, Wilson's answer to the Pope did not specify war aims. He had "not thought it wise to say more or to be more specific because it might provoke dissenting voices from France or Italy if I should, —if I should say, for example, that their territorial claims did not interest us." Wilson was, however, eager to announce a set of war aims, both for the United States and the Allies: "we should speak at the earliest possible moment now, and I hope with all my heart that the British and other associated governments will adopt Sir William Wiseman's suggestions and say ditto to us."[65]

[64] Wiseman to House, Aug. 10, 1917, WWP 27. The State Department officially received the Pope's message on Aug. 16. Page to Lansing, Aug. 15, 1917, *Foreign Relations, 1917*, Sup. 2, Vol. 1, pp. 161-64. House to Balfour, Aug. 18, 1917, Seymour, *Intimate Papers*, Vol. 3, pp. 154-55. Wiseman to House, Aug. 22, 1917, HP 20:45. See also Wiseman's remarks to C. P. Scott on Aug. 24, Hammond, *Scott*, pp. 233-34.

[65] Cecil to House, Aug. 27, 1917, Seymour, *Intimate Papers*, Vol. 3, p. 167; Wilson to House, Aug. 22, 1917, HP 49:18. Wilson's message to the Pope was sent August 27 via Page and the Foreign Office, and is printed in *Foreign Relations, 1917*, Sup. 2, Vol. 1, pp. 177-79. The French and Russian ambassadors at Washington, like Balfour, hoped Wilson would consult the Allies before answering. The Italian prime minister was content to let the American response precede those of the Allies. See French Ambassador to Lansing, Aug. 18, 1917; Lansing

This episode gave Wilson a chance to appreciate that Wiseman was on his side. It also pointed up the value of the Wiseman-House-Balfour channel of communications for Anglo-American relations. Because of it Wilson if he did not give the British an advance copy of his reply to the Pope did adumbrate to them what he would say. That was more than he did toward the other Allies.

News of another peace proposal, this time a sounding from Germany through the Spanish government to Balfour, also reached Wilson through the Wiseman channel. The President authorized a reply, drafted by Wiseman and House, suggesting that Balfour refrain from any discussions unless a definite proposal was made. Wilson's attitude pleased the Foreign Office. The method by which it was related delighted Wiseman. Proudly he cited the instance to Balfour as "a remarkable example of the prompt assistance House extends to us in urgent matters and the confidential relations between House and Wilson." The Foreign Office thanked Wiseman for his service but also, in an indication of some unease at conducting official business unofficially, asked for confirmation of the American position through the American Embassy.[66]

Correspondence between American and European Zionists proceeded via Wiseman's cable facilities.[67] So did American and British consultation concerning a national home for Jews. On September 3 Cecil asked House if he could ascertain whether the President favored a declaration of sympathy with the Zionist movement. House replied on the 10th that Wilson thought "the time is not opportune for any definite statement further perhaps than one of sym-

---

to President, Aug. 21, 1917; Chargé in Italy to Lansing, Aug. 21, 1917; all in *ibid.*, pp. 165-67.

[66] House to Wilson, Oct. 5, 1917, forwarding Balfour's cable to Wiseman of the same date, HP 49:9. House Diary, Oct. 5, 1917; Wilson to House, Oct. 7, 1917 (copy), WWP 64; Wiseman to Balfour, Oct. 7, 1917, WWP 42; C. J. Phillips to Wiseman, Oct. 8, 1917, WWP 42.

[67] House Diary, Sept. 22, 1917. Two file folders of cables exchanged by the Zionists are in WWP.

pathy provided it can be made without conveying any real commitment." A month later Balfour cabled that because of reports that the German government was trying to capture the Zionist movement the cabinet had again considered the question and was contemplating issuing a statement promising "best endeavours" to establish a Jewish national state. How would the President react to a declaration to this effect? Wiseman answered that Wilson approved the formula "but asks that no mention of his approval shall be made when H.M.G. makes formula public, as he has arranged that American Jews shall then ask him for his approval which he will give publicly here."[68] When the British statement, the Balfour Declaration, was released on November 2, little space was given it in the American press. Nor did the President make a public endorsement until the following summer. Even his private approval was apparently not conveyed to Lansing, for the latter on December 15 instructed Page to find out the cause of the Balfour Declaration.[69]

By discreet transmittal of information Wiseman set in motion a reciprocity of confidences between leaders of the American and British governments. He worked hard at his job. In London he made known Wilson's concern over the unrest in Ireland and returned with copies of Sir Horace Plunkett's confidential report on the Irish Convention for Wilson and House. He arranged for the Foreign Office to send collations of political information to House. He for-

[68] Cecil to House, Sept. 3, 1917, HP 20:45; House to Cecil, Sept. 10, 1917, HP 4:38; Balfour to House, Oct. 6, 1917, WWP 42; Wiseman to Drummond, Oct. 16, 1917, WWP 43. Wilson's approval of the Balfour draft declaration is given in Wilson to House, Oct. 13, 1917, HP 49:18. For the formulation of the Balfour Declaration, see Leonard Stein, *The Balfour Declaration*, London, 1961.

[69] First announcement of the Balfour Declaration by the *New York Times* came on Nov. 9, 1917. Wilson to Rabbi Stephen S. Wise, Aug. 31, 1918, expressed satisfaction with the Balfour Declaration. Baker, *Wilson Life & Letters*, Vol. 8, pp. 372-73. Lansing to Page, Dec. 15, 1917, *Foreign Relations, 1917*, Sup. 2, Vol. 1, p. 473. Page asked Lansing on Nov. 23 what the President thought of the Balfour Declaration; *ibid.*, p. 317.

warded intelligence reports from Russia to the President. He also passed on to officials in the State Department observations he himself made in Europe.[70] By the fall of 1917 his contacts were excellent, and with his most important contact his influence was even greater than in July when House had written to Balfour: "As you know, Sir William has my confidence. . . . With matters as they are I regard him as invaluable to you here, and I hope he will return soon strengthened in authority."[71]

In a few weeks Wiseman's authority would be clothed in an official title. It was already recognized.

[70] Wiseman to House, Aug. 10, 1917, WWP 27; Drummond to Wiseman, Oct. 2, 1917, WWP 42; Drummond to Wiseman, Aug. 24, 1917, WWP 42; House to Wilson, Oct. 15, 1917, HP 49:9. In addition to using House's private telephone line to the State Department, Wiseman occasionally visited Polk and Auchincloss at the Department, and in 1918 he began visiting Lansing as well. For dates of some of his visits during the period under discussion, see Polk Confidential Diary, Apr. 6, 7, June 5, 6, 1917; Auchincloss Diary, Sept. 24, Oct. 10, 11, 12, 23, 1917.

[71] House to Balfour, July 15, 1917, HP 2:22.

CHAPTER FIVE

ATTEMPTS AT UNITY

> Naturally the Americans would not be prepared to agree to any important change in their methods of co-operation without consulting the French and possibly other Governments, but they would be very willing to discuss the matter with their British colleagues and arrive at proposals which can be put before the Allies. . . .
>
> Wiseman, 14 November 1917

HOUSE's company of experts, nicknamed the "House Party," remained on European soil exactly one month. Its schedule covered three sets of meetings: consultations with the British (November 8-22), with the French (November 23-28), and participation in the 18-nation Inter-Allied Conference at Paris (November 29-December 3). Spurning almost all entertainments and ceremony, mission members busied themselves with collecting data and advice from their more experienced partners in war. Except in private interviews conducted by House, the topic of peace did not arise. The Americans and the European Allies were, Secretary Lansing told the public, holding "a War Conference and nothing else."[1]

During the Paris conference House and Gen. Tasker Bliss attended the second gathering of the Supreme War Council at Versailles. The council had been created at Rapallo by Britain, France, and Italy on November 7 and symbolized the sense of urgency which the events of November imposed on the Allies. That fateful month began with the crumbling of the Italian lines at Caporetto. Then the Bolsheviks took power in Russia and promised to end their fight against the Central Powers. The French ministry of Painlevé fell on November 13. The same day Lloyd George returned from Rapallo and Paris to face a possible

[1] *New York Times*, Nov. 8, 1917. Pershing, *My Experiences*, Vol. 1, p. 248, tells of the "House Party" nickname.

vote of censure for his support of the Supreme War Council and his implied distrust of the British military command. The month closed with the failure of the British tank offensive at Cambrai. Gordon Auchincloss's reaction probably typified that of the visiting Americans: "We have certainly come at a critical time and have found things in a terrible mess: governments falling right and left, and general panic prevailing."[2]

In Britain the atmosphere of crisis did not interfere with the Foreign Office's solicitous attitude toward House. Wiseman met the Americans when they landed at Plymouth on the evening of November 7. He ushered them onto a special train to London where Balfour and other dignitaries lined the Paddington Station platform to extend a midnight welcome. Then House, his wife, and personal attendants retired to the spacious splendor of Chesterfield House, made available to them by the British government. Wiseman and his wife also stayed at Chesterfield House, while House's American staff resided at Claridge's Hotel.[3]

For the next two weeks Wiseman was a combination adviser, host and troubleshooter for House. He accompanied House on visits to the King, the Prime Minister, and other officials. He arranged press releases, scheduled meetings between the British and American experts, and looked after the personal comfort of the visitors, especially House and Auchincloss. If superficially Wiseman appeared to be a sort of tourguide, close inspection revealed that he was as active in policy as in protocol. He had a hand in all the great issues between Britain and the United States which emerged during House's visit and which persisted through 1918. Those issues were manpower, policy in Russia, war aims and peace plans, and, encompassing the former three, machinery for cooperation between the unofficial allies.

[2] Seymour, *Intimate Papers*, Vol. 3, pp. 210-17; Cyril Falls, *The Great War*, New York, 1959, pp. 282-315. House's report on the mission outlining the situation in Europe, is printed in *Foreign Relations, 1917*, Sup. 2, Vol. 1, pp. 334-57. Auchincloss Diary, Nov. 14, 1917, Auchincloss Papers.
[3] House Diary, Nov. 8, 1917; Auchincloss Diary, Nov. 7, 1917.

97

House initially planned to leave London for Paris on November 14, but soon after his arrival he acceded to Balfour's request that the Paris conference be postponed from November 16 to November 22. In view of the rapidly changing conditions in France and Italy a postponement seemed reasonable. On the fifteenth, however, a rumor reached House that Lloyd George himself had decided not to attend the conference. House reacted angrily, saying that "George, upon the impulse of the moment, has created the Supreme War Council and now he does not think it necessary to have the main conference. He is mistaken, and I shall insist upon it going through as scheduled, not indeed, for what it may do in its deliberations, but for its moral effect." He might have added that Lloyd George wanted to get parliamentary approval of his acts at the last international conference—Rapallo—before embarking so soon on another.[4] Ironically, the Prime Minister's September fervor for a full meeting of the co-belligerents had become his November aversion to such a meeting.

House and Wiseman decided "to read the riot act to Mr. Lloyd George." Wiseman telephoned Northcliffe and told him that if Lloyd George did not attend the Paris conference, neither would House. Northcliffe agreed with House's position and eagerly volunteered to set the Prime Minister right. With Wiseman in tow, he went to 10 Downing Street. There they found, in addition to Lloyd George, Gen. Jan Smuts and Lord Milner. The result of this group's discussion, and of one among Reading, Smuts, and Milner later in the afternoon, was Lloyd George's decision to pay a personal call on House. Such a visit by the Prime Minister was, Wiseman told House, unprecedented and had caused Lloyd George's secretaries to be "struck dumb."[5]

[4] American Embassy, London, to American Embassy, Paris, Nov. 8, 1917, HP 35:33B. House Diary, Nov. 9, 15, 1917. Lloyd George, *War Memoirs*, Vol. 4, pp. 2,396, 2,402.

[5] House Diary, Nov. 15, 1917; Milner Diary, Nov. 15, 1917, Milner Papers.

Reading preceded Lloyd George to Chesterfield House in order to explain why Lloyd George opposed an early meeting of the Allies. Lloyd George wished to await a stabilization in the French government and on the Italian front. House was unmoved. He called the conference essential and reproved Lloyd George for announcing the formation of the Supreme War Council before the conference had met. Had Lloyd George waited, House argued, there would have been no criticism of the Council,"because everyone would have thought it had been decided upon by common agreement, and that the United States was largely responsible." Then in a deftly shielded threat, House remarked that if the British government would cooperate with him, it could not be overthrown. In other words, House offered to give American support to Lloyd George's defense of the Supreme War Council if Lloyd George would go ahead with the Paris conference. As the President's trusted agent, with Northcliffe as his ally, and with Parliament restive, House was perhaps not exaggerating his power over the British ministry. 153581

As Reading and House talked, the Prime Minister and Wiseman arrived. If Wiseman had coached his superior in the art of dealing with House, it was to little avail, for to House, Lloyd George's performance was a patent farce. He began by remarking what a pleasant coincidence it was that Reading, whom he had in fact sent to set the stage, should be present. Reading could, he hoped, help House appreciate his position, which he proceeded to expound along the lines already stated by Reading. Lloyd George's lengthy plea achieved only a shadow of success. House finally agreed to delay the conference to November 29, a concession of one week.[6] Believing that he had won a victory over Lloyd George, House reported to the President:

> Northcliffe has been splendid. He holds a club over the P.M. and threatens to use it unless he does as desired. . . . Wiseman heard him tell George that he did not

[6] House Diary, Nov. 15, 1917.

propose to relinquish the right to criticize when he thought it necessary.

We are using Reading to button things up after decisions are made. With this combination of Wiseman, Reading and Northcliffe, things are now being accomplished with more rapidity than I have ever experienced here.[7]

Lloyd George also profited from appeasing House. With America's endorsement of the Supreme War Council he was able to put down his parliamentary critics, who took their cue from General Robertson. The American endorsement was never really in doubt. House had recommended to Wilson that the United States be represented on the council ("because of the moral effect it will have here") prior to his confrontation with Lloyd George over the question of the Paris conference. His threat to embarrass the British government was thus partially bluff. But even after Lloyd George agreed to go ahead with the conference, House did not give as firm support to the council as Wilson authorized. Wilson instructed House to "take the position that we not only approve a continuance of the plan for a war council but insist on it." The statement that House released on November 18, the day before Parliament debated the Supreme War Council, stated that "unity of plan and control between all the Allies and the United States is essential in order to achieve a just and permanent peace." House so phrased his statement because he did not wish to approve specifically Lloyd George's plan. That would have caused Robertson's supporters to think that House and Lloyd George were "playing together." And before House issued the statement at all he secured a pledge that the Supreme War Council would meet in conjunction with the Paris conference.[8]

[7] House to Wilson, Nov. 16, 1917, HP 49:9.

[8] House to Wilson, Nov. 13, 1917, in Seymour, *Intimate Papers*, Vol. 3, p. 219. House to Wilson, Nov. 16, 1917, HP 49:9. London *Times*, Nov. 19, 1917; House Diary, Nov. 18, 1917.

For a discussion of British public and parliamentary attitudes toward

House's reluctance to endorse fully the Supreme War Council did not stem from any petty desire to best Lloyd George. In fact, had times not been so grave for the Allies generally and for the British ministry particularly, House may well not have endorsed the Supreme War Council at all. He and Wiseman agreed that as planned, the council would not work. Their chief objection was to its composition of heads of government, with a subordinate and advisory panel of military attachés. That is, the Supreme War Council placed over-all conduct of strategy in political rather than in military hands and provided no supreme commander or military executive. But Lloyd George had no hope of persuading Parliament to accept an Allied generalissimo; he had already gone the limit, for the time being, in hobbling Haig and Robertson.[9] From House's and Wiseman's viewpoint, the best plan was to accept what Lloyd George had begun and attempt reforms later. Wiseman, in a *Times* leader which he helped Geoffrey Dawson, the editor, compose, generally approved the council. But he had reservations, too: "The Wilson endorsement does emphasize unmistakably the central principle for which Mr. Lloyd George is standing at this moment—that 'unity of plan and control' which received partial recognition at Rapallo. We say partial recognition because it is clear enough from the President's message . . . that the work begun at Rapallo is still very far from being complete to competent observers. Unity of war aims is at least as essential to victory as unity of strategy, and it comes first in order of achievement. Unity of strategy depends in turn upon unity of resources and supply. All three call for urgent attention."[10]

The article was labelled "excellent" by House,[11] and it

the Supreme War Council, see Paul Guinn, *British Strategy and Politics, 1914 to 1918*, Oxford, 1965, pp. 259-69.

[9] House Diary, Nov. 27, 1917. Lloyd George later explained why he concentrated on unity of strategy rather than unity of command in *War Memoirs*, Vol. 4, pp. 2,409-10.

[10] House Diary, Nov. 18, 1917; London *Times*, Nov. 19, 1917.

[11] House Diary, Nov. 19, 1917.

was fair warning to any who knew its inspiration that the United States would be unwilling to delegate any political decisions to the Supreme War Council until unity of war aims was achieved. Later events showed that President Wilson, although he authorized House (and Bliss, as military representative) to sit on the council, did not recognize any capacity on the part of the council to bind the United States to any diplomatic or political position. A Washington reporter for the *New York Herald* had reliable information when he wrote: "The fact of the matter is that neither Colonel House nor General Bliss is expected to do more than listen to the discussions around the council table, and to inform themselves upon the details of the military situation so that they may report the fact to President Wilson. They are expected to make no suggestions nor to give any advice. Upon being asked to have a representative at the conference the President immediately decided that he would accept because it would offer him an excellent channel of getting first hand information upon every phase of the war. That was his sole purpose."[12]

In Paris, House and Bliss attempted to revise the Supreme War Council. With French support, Bliss drafted a plan for a "purely military council" consisting of the national chiefs of staff and the commanders-in-chief of the armies. On November 27 House thought he had convinced Lloyd George to drop the "civil end" of the council, but early the next morning Wiseman reported that someone "had had Lloyd George's ear" and that he again wanted the civil end. Probably Wiseman and House were mistaken in ever thinking that Lloyd George would accept Bliss's revision, for that would have meant putting Haig and Robertson on the council, and Lloyd George had devised the council specifically to bypass those two. Lloyd George unquestionably agreed with Gen. Henry Wilson, his military representative on the council and later Robertson's successor, that it was "intolerable if arrangements come to at Rapallo one week can be upset the next." Far from enter-

[12] *New York Herald*, Nov. 24, 1917.

taining the proposed revision, Lloyd George threatened to leave Paris if the Rapallo agreement was not honored.[13]

The Prime Minister had his way. When the Supreme War Council convened on December 1 it did so under the provisions of the Rapallo convention. The formal session was brief. Lloyd George and Clemenceau, the new French premier, urged a careful study of the military situation to be faced in 1918. The council assigned this task to the Permanent Military Representatives. The council also empowered itself to receive intelligence from departments of the component governments, establish a secretariat for the Permanent Military Representatives, and instructed the Permanent Military Representatives to investigate the status of the Italian front, transport arrangements, the possible use of the Belgian army, and the military situation in the Balkans. The *procès-verbal* of the meeting did not record a single word by House. He thought it best to remain in the background and listen.[14]

The plenary sessions of the Inter-Allied Conference made no important decisions, or ringing declarations either. House was disappointed that the British and French, with all their experience, offered no definite proposals for action. How, then did he justify his opinion that the conference might well be considered the turning point in the war? First, there was the boost in morale which came from the American presence. More concretely, there was the considerable progress made in coordinating the resources of the co-belligerents.[15] The experts representing the major

[13] Trask, *United States in the Supreme War Council*, p. 33. See also the transcript of the November 25 conversation between House, Bliss, Clemenceau, and Pétain, in HP 35:35. House Diary, Nov. 27, 28, 1917. Callwell, *Sir Henry Wilson*, Vol. 2, p. 32.
Lloyd George may have thought that House's suggested revision was inspired by Robertson. Sir Maurice (Lord) Hankey, War Cabinet Secretary, on November 15 asked, "Why does Robertson cut the War Cabinet and see House and the Leader of the Opposition? Was it in order to intrigue against the Council?" Hankey, *The Supreme Command, 1914-1918*, London, 1961, Vol. 2, p. 728.

[14] A copy of the *procès-verbal* is in HP 35:42. House Diary, Dec. 1, 1917.

[15] House Diary, Dec. 1, 11, 12, 1917.

powers exchanged information on topics ranging from manpower to wheat and organized committees for further consultation. Thanks to Wiseman, the problems requiring immediate attention had been agreed upon in London by the British and Americans.

Because of the postponement of the Paris conference, House's party had an additional week to tarry in London. Upon Wiseman's initiative, the British government used that time well. From the second day of the Americans' arrival Wiseman deprecated the haphazard way in which consultations were progressing. While he in New York had suggested topics for discussion and drawn up a list of British leaders House should interview, the Foreign Office had failed to arrange an agenda for discussions between the visitors and their British counterparts. As the result, each American arranged his own interviews. Presuming to speak for House, Wiseman gave Balfour a "wigging" about the lack of a coherent agenda.[16] In a memorandum on the subject he predicted: "It will be a misfortune amounting to disaster if the Mission returns to America without having been told by the Allies what they want the United States to do, and without having agreed upon some machinery to work out satisfactory co-operation between America and the Allies. . . . If the Mission returns to the States with the impression that the Allies do not know what they want America to do, it must have a bad effect, not only on the American Government, but with popular opinion, and the result would certainly be halfhearted co-operation on the part of the States."[17]

At the same time, Wiseman took his grievance to Lord Milner, the powerful member of the War Cabinet who later headed the War Office. The Americans had com-

[16] Wiseman, "Suggested List of Important People to be Seen," no date, HP 20:46. Wiseman, "Memorandum Regarding American Mission," Nov. 14, 1917, WWP 2. House Diary, Nov. 9, 1917. House expressed impatience at the manner of consultations in his cable to Wilson, Nov. 11, 1917, HP 49:9.

[17] Wiseman, "Memorandum Regarding American Mission," Nov. 14, 1917, WWP 2.

plained, according to Wiseman, that they had been unable to grasp the really vital questions because any matter of policy involved several departments of the British government. He proposed a joint meeting of the Americans and their British opposites under the presidency of a member of the War Cabinet. Prior to the meeting, both sides should decide what were the important large questions confronting the two nations.[18]

Milner spent part of the next five days arranging an implementation of Wiseman's proposal. Once again the behavior of Lord Northcliffe prodded the government to action. In a public letter, the main purpose of which was to decline a government post already occupied and which Lloyd George maintained he never offered, Northcliffe warned the Prime Minister that "unless there is swift improvement in our methods here, the United States will rightly take into its own hands the entire management of a great part of the war." Wiseman, who conferred with Northcliffe on the day the letter was written, probably planted the seed which became Northcliffe's warning, although he may not have recommended that the warning be published in the newspapers. The British government took the point. Lloyd George invited the American mission to meet on November 20 with the full War Cabinet at 10 Downing Street.[19]

Assembled in the same room where Lord North had directed attempts to put down the American Revolution, the American delegation (minus House) faced the Prime Minister, the War Cabinet, and the heads of all departments engaged in making war. Each side had concluded, inde-

[18] *Ibid.* Milner Diary, Nov. 14, 1917. In another memorandum Wiseman suggested the establishment of a ministry for American affairs. Wiseman, "Confidential Memorandum," Nov. 18, 1917, WWP 2.

[19] Milner Diary, Nov. 15, 17, 19, 20, 1917. Northcliffe's letter, dated Nov. 15 and published in the London *Times* on Nov. 16, is printed in Lloyd George, *War Memoirs*, Vol. 4, pp. 1,871-74. See also Lord Beaverbrook, *Men and Power, 1917-1918*, New York, 1956, pp. 83-84. Lloyd George, *War Memoirs*, Vol. 5, p. 3,004.

pendently, in advance what problems required top priority. For the Americans these were the shipping shortage and the military plans for 1918 and 1919; for the British, manpower and shipping. Lloyd George did most of the talking, stressing the need for men and ships and asking also for steel, guns, planes, and food. Admiral Benson responded, declaring America's willingness to help and forecasting a schedule of production, which, at least in the case of ships and planes, in the event proved to be too optimistic. The session ended where it began, on the question of how to get more ships to bring more American men to Europe. In the end, a special subcommittee was appointed to devise ways of sharing and increasing tonnage, with particular attention to be paid to the use of dormant neutral ships sheltered in the United States.[20]

In Paris the Americans heard similar descriptions of what the Allies needed: more men and materiel and some way of getting them to Europe. General Bliss committed the United States to send 24 divisions to France by June 30, 1918. An Allied Maritime Transport Council, located in London and largely an Anglo-American organ, was established to maximize shipping efficiency. The Allies acceded to Oscar Crosby's plans for determining priority in finance and supply, and the Inter-Allied Council on War Purchases and Finance was in operation by mid-December. Councils on petroleum, food, and munitions also grew out of the Paris conference. When the conference was over, Vance McCormick, chairman of the War Trade Board, concluded that "There remain only questions of policy, which change with the progress of the war, and under these circumstances, future negotiations ought to be greatly simplified as compared to those of the past."[21]

[20] *Ibid.* Auchincloss Diary, Nov. 15, 1917. Minutes of the Anglo-American meeting are printed in *Foreign Relations, 1917*, Sup. 2, Vol. 1, pp. 366-84.

[21] Bliss to Acting Chief of Staff, cable no. 10 [c. Dec. 1, 1917], Bliss Papers, Box 66. Seymour, *Intimate Papers*, Vol. 3, p. 297. McCormick's statement is taken from his report to House, *Foreign*

The unification of an over-all policy, however, had not been achieved by the Allies and the United States. Bainbridge Colby, Shipping Board representative, doubted that coordination by agreement was possible. He accurately predicted that the evolution of the kind of policy "which has authority and can exact compliance" would come only during a grave crisis in the war or at the point when a solitarily strong United States could coerce the Allies.[22]

THE PARIS meeting of the co-belligerents produced no agreement in two important related areas of policy, the treatment of Russia and the publication of war aims. Wiseman and House strove to coordinate at least the British and American positions in these areas, but in the main their governments chose to take independent if occasionally parallel courses.

House contrived to keep official discussion of Russia off the agenda of the Inter-Allied Conference, thinking that the topic was explosive. In private conversations and in sessions concerning war aims, however, the Russian situation formed the basis of much anxious discussion. All feared that Bolshevik Russia, which had already signed a truce with Germany, was on the verge of making a separate peace. House attempted to get the Allies to woo the Bolsheviks by issuing a statement of war aims similar to the Bolshevik chant of "no annexations, no indemnities." The Allies refused. Italy and France also turned down a British proposal to release the Russians from their alliance obligations and thereby rob the Bolsheviks of their charge that the Allies were driving Russian soldiers to slaughter for imperialist aims. House, on the other hand, refused to commit the United States to a more militant proposal for open support to the Cossack General Kaledin's anti-Bolshevik forces. The four powers quit Paris without coordinating

---

Relations, 1917, Sup. 2, Vol. 1, p. 408. For all reports by the mission members, see *Foreign Relations, 1917*, Sup. 2, Vol. 1, pp. 366ff.

[22] *Ibid.*, p. 419.

their plans concerning Russia. Each nation retained a free hand to form its own policy.[23]

Both Lansing and House concluded that the American policy should be one of doing nothing.[24] This proved to be as potent a policy as the previous one of propaganda, applied while Russia was under the nominal rule of the Provisional Government. Because of the great distance and America's lack of war preparation, propaganda—if financial and technical aid be excepted—was virtually the only weapon the United States had in 1917 Russia. The weapon was seized eagerly, in large part because of the widespread opinion that Russian pacifism and Bolshevism were the products of German propaganda and intrigue. Elihu Root, head of the special American mission to Russia and generally considered a realist, placed high hopes on the efficacy of propaganda and insisted that Washington counter the "tremendous German propaganda" which he observed. As a result, the Committee on Public Information, headed by George Creel, appointed Edgar Sisson, former editor of *Cosmopolitan Magazine*, to inaugurate an ambitious publicity campaign in Petrograd. Sisson left New York on October 27, 10 days before the Bolshevik coup, and arrived in Petrograd on November 25. If Sisson was too late to assist the Provisional Government and keep Russia in the war, other Americans were there in time and made similar attempts. William B. Thompson and Raymond Robins and their associates in the American Red Cross Commission from early August up to the November Revolution spent large sums, mostly from Thompson's own pocket, on propaganda.[25]

Yet another publicity venture, which has remained barely

[23] House Diary, Nov. 16, 28, 1917; Richard H. Ullman, *Intervention and the War*, Princeton, 1961, pp. 26-27.

[24] House Diary, Jan. 2, 1918; Lansing, "Memorandum on the Russian Situation December 7, 1917," Lansing Private Diaries, Box 1, Vol. 2.

[25] George F. Kennan, *Russia Leaves the War*, Princeton, 1956, pp. 23, 46, 50, 55-58; Root to Lansing, June 17, 1917, *Foreign Relations, 1918, Russia*, Vol. 1, pp. 120-22.

known and which culminated at the time of House's mission to Europe, was the one organized and directed by Wiseman. As unsuccessful as the others, it differed from them in its bi-national, furtive, and, now amusingly amateurish aspects. At the time, however, the venture was taken seriously by those few, including the President, who knew about it.

Wiseman began to think of a propaganda expedition to Russia soon after the United States declared war. He was impelled to do so by an April 7 cablegram from Balfour which related "alarming news from Petrograd." According to Balfour there was "real danger of revolutionary pacifists obtaining the upper hand and occupying position of provisional government." To counteract this danger, Balfour requested, as a matter of the "highest importance," the dispatch to Russia of "messages from labour leaders, from Russian Americans, and from prominent men in U.S. emphasising necessity of continuing the war in order to secure triumph of principles of freedom and democracy. . . ."[26] Shortly afterward, a cable from the British Secret Service identified the "revolutionary pacifists" as Jews. Wiseman was directed, therefore, to contact Richard Gottheil, Professor of Semitic Languages at Columbia University and a Zionist spokesman, and secure from him a statement by leading American Jews which would encourage their Russian brethren to continue the fight against Germany. Gottheil got Justice Louis Brandeis, former Ambassador Oscar Straus, and Rabbi Stephen Wise to sign with him such a statement for public release in Petrograd. Wiseman and Gottheil in addition arranged similar appeals to individuals —for example, one from Jacob Schiff to a banker in Petrograd, and another from representatives of anarchist revolutionary societies in New York to Madame Breshkovskaya, the "Little Grandmother of the Revolution." In relaying these communications over Secret Service cables,

[26] Balfour to Spring Rice, Apr. 7, 1917, FO 115/2317. Other documents in this file indicate that Spring Rice delegated to Wiseman the responsibility of meeting Balfour's request.

Wiseman warned that "Reds in Petrograd" must not learn by whom the messages had been instigated. And he declined the suggestion from London that a statement be solicited from Samuel Gompers. "Gompers," Wiseman noted, "is not trusted by advanced Socialists and Reds, consequently cable from him would do harm."[27]

The cables that *were* sent apparently did little good. They were offset by events in Russia and perhaps by a continuing migration of "anarchists" and "syndicalists" of Russian (and often Jewish) background from the United States to Russia. Professor Gottheil was distressed to find that some of his Russian-connected colleagues at Columbia favored Russia's withdrawal from the war. He concluded that such sentiments were anti-British, anti-American, pro-German, and, in part, the result of work by German secret agents. Wiseman echoed Gottheil in a memorandum addressed to Colonel House:

> . . . the Germans are counting on their propaganda to bring about a separate peace with Russia; but the details of their intrigue are not so well-known.
>
> We have reliable information that the Germans are organizing from every neutral country parties of Russian refugees, largely Jewish socialists. These parties are sent to Petrograd where they are organized by German agents posing as advanced Socialists. . . . The Germans have been able to make the Russian people somewhat suspicious of the aims of the French and English. . . .
>
> German agents have already been at work in the United States, and are sending Russian-Jewish Socialists

[27] A memorandum by Wiseman, Apr. 16, 1917, FO 115/2317, reports his contact with Gottheil and encloses copies of the cablegrams here described. See also Wiseman to Gottheil, June 30, 1917, WWP 112. There are in the Wiseman Papers numerous messages from American Zionists which were wired via Wiseman's office to European Zionists. Sir Arthur Willert told me (Sept. 4, 1964) that he used to call on Brandeis twice weekly to collect such messages for dispatch.

For a description of Gottheil see George Alexander Kohut, "Professor Gottheil—An Appraisal at Seventy," *Columbia University Quarterly*, Vol. 25, June 1933, pp. 137-45.

back to Petrograd who are either knowingly or unknowingly working in the German cause.[28]

When writing this, Wiseman undoubtedly had in mind Leon Trotsky, who left New York in April bound for Russia and who was interned at Halifax, Nova Scotia, by the British, possibly on a tip from Wiseman. It is not clear whether he had information more definite than Gottheil's generalized fears concerning other "Russian-Jewish-Socialists." He might have had firmer evidence from German defectors or from Emanuel V. Voska, a ubiquitous Bohemian-American who was expending his modest fortune thwarting Germany and Austria in the hope of making Czechoslovakia independent.[29] Still the suspicion remains that Wiseman inflated the danger posed by exiles returning to Russia. For, as we shall see, he perceived the combatting of Russian pacifism as an opportunity to make himself useful to the Administration and thereby improve the prospects for Anglo-American cooperation in other more important matters. For the moment, however, he was obliged both to represent the Russian situation as serious and to propose a method of dealing with it.

The method proposed was essentially one of canceling out the influence of the returning exiles who were allegedly serving the German cause. Wiseman wanted to send to Russia pro-Ally refugees as well as Russian workingmen "who have come to this country and made good," leaders from Czech, Slovak, and Polish secret societies in America, an unnamed "Nihilist" leader, and a demagogic, anti-German Russian monk named Illiador. These "lecturers and propagandists" were to be sent to Petrograd in six or seven different missions, each entirely unknown to the other. They would not interfere in Russian domestic affairs and would appear to have "been sent to Russia by different philanthropic Americans who were anxious to assist the New Russian Republic. They would carry with them details of

[28] Wiseman, "Russia" [May 15, 1917], WWP 112; House Diary, May 15, 1917.
[29] Willert, *Road to Safety*, pp. 23-24.

111

the German intrigues in America, and warn their Russian comrades against similar traps. They would emphasize the necessity for the two great republics working together for the freedom of the World, and, above all, they would seek to warn the Russian people of the plot to enslave them again which is being carried out by the combined efforts of the old reactionary Government and the Military Party in Germany."

Behind the philanthropic guise would be Wiseman, disbursing Anglo-American money and giving over-all direction. His goal would be "first, to expose present German intrigues and their undoubted connection with the late reactionary [i.e., Czarist] Government. Secondly, to persuade the Russians to attack the Germans with all their might and thus accomplish the overthrow of the Hohenzollern dynasty and autocracy in Berlin."[30]

It was an ambitious and fervently worded plan. House approved it, no doubt in part because Wiseman asserted that it was based on reliable British intelligence data. Wiseman also led his superiors in the British Secret Service to believe he was proceeding on information gathered by the American government. He represented American authorities as believing "that the Germans are using Russian exiles in the United States and other countries as their agents, sometimes consciously and sometimes unconsciously. A great deal of this work is done by Jewish-Socialists, in the guise of pacifists. The United States Government feel that the United States is perhaps the best country from which to organize a counter-propaganda. In the first place, propaganda from the United States is not regarded in Russia with the same suspicion as propaganda from England; and in the second place, there are in this country very large numbers of intelligent Russians who could be used for this purpose."[31] This was the same argument, with appropriate

[30] Wiseman, "Russia" [May 15, 1918], WWP 112; House Diary, May 15, 18, 1917.
[31] Wiseman, "Russian Affairs," May 26, 1917, WWP 112. Internal evidence indicates this memo was addressed to Secret Service head-

alterations regarding the source of facts, earlier used on House. It was in fact a Wiseman argument, presented to House as an authoritative British one and to the British as an authoritative American one.

The Foreign Office, already spending large sums on propaganda in Russia, approved Wiseman's scheme in principle but preferred to have the American government handle it alone.[32] Wiseman replied that the Americans were not likely to undertake the project singlehandedly because they had no means of dealing with the Slavic societies, upon whose help the project depended, except through himself. He also reported that the President had become particularly interested in the matter since receiving messages from Root in Russia. Then in a sentence calculated to rouse the Foreign Office he noted: "It is possible that by acting practically as a confidential agent for the United States Government I might strengthen the understanding with House so that in future he will keep us informed of steps taken by the United States Government in their foreign affairs, which would ordinarily not be a matter of common knowledge to the Governments of the two countries." The Foreign Office got the point, agreed to co-sponsor the venture, and placed $75,000 to Wiseman's credit at J. P. Morgan and Company.[33] Several days later

---

quarters in London. See also Wiseman to Drummond, memorandum, May 23, 1917, Private Secretary Archives, 1917-1924, A. J. Balfour, FO 800/197.

[32] Drummond to Wiseman, June 19, 1917, WWP 42. On the received copy of Wiseman's cable CXP 189, June 16, 1917, WWP 42, Drummond minuted (18 June): "I had already told Col. House that I thought the U.S. Govt. had better deal with the scheme alone, but they are evidently anxious for our cooperation & to employ Sir W. Wiseman." Private Secretary Archives, 1917-1924, A. J. Balfour, FO 800/197.

[33] Wiseman to Drummond, June 20, 1917, WWP 42; Drummond to Wiseman, June 26, 1917, WWP 42. The Foreign Office gave as its reason for approval, "the fact that the scheme seems to afford sound measure for checking German pacifist propaganda in Russia, and that President is interested in it. . . ." *Ibid.*, and Drummond's minute on Wiseman's cable of June 20, 1917, Private Secretary Archives, 1917-1924, A. J. Balfour, FO 800/197.

the President allocated a like amount as the American contribution. Wilson had seen Wiseman's memorandum and had apparently agreed with Secretary Lansing that "no stone should be left unturned to counteract the German propaganda which is being carried on there."[34]

Wiseman chose as his top agent in Petrograd the English author Somerset Maugham. Maugham earlier in the war had worked as a secret agent in Switzerland. He turned up in the United States, but apparently not by pre-arrangement, just as Wiseman was completing plans for his scheme. He had no particular knowledge of Russia, but his former exerience, his relation by marriage to Wiseman, and the excuse which his profession as a writer would offer for his presence in Russia all recommended Maugham for the job. Financial independence also made Maugham an attractive choice. He told Wiseman that he did not need a salary but pointed out that his earlier refusal of pay in Switzerland had not caused him to be regarded as "patriotic or generous but merely as damned foolish."[35]

[34] Lansing to Wilson, June 8, 1917, SD 861.00/423-1/2A. This letter forwarded Wiseman's "Russia" [May 15, 1917] to the President as "a memorandum . . . handed to Mr. Polk by one of the British representatives, and which contains suggestions which appeal very strongly to me." These handwritten notes appear on the margin of the letter: "Approved by Pres[iden]t orally 6/15/17 R[obert] L[ansing]" and "$75000 allotted & advanced by Polk to W[iseman] F[rank] P[olk]"; Polk to McAdoo, July 16, 1917, Polk Papers, enclosed the President's approval of $75,000 "for expenses of a confidential nature to be done by this [State] Department."

[35] Wiseman to Gottheil, June 30, 1917, WWP 112; Maugham to Wiseman, July 7, 1917, WWP 112. Concerning his Russian assignment Maugham later wrote: "I was diffident of accepting the post, which seemed to demand capacities that I did not think I possessed; but there seemed to be no one more competent available at the moment and my being a writer was very good 'cover' for what I was asked to do. I was not very well. . . . But I could not miss the opportunity of spending certainly a considerable time in the country of Tolstoi, Dostoievski, and Chekov; I had a notion that in the intervals of the work I was being sent to do I could get something for myself that would be of value; so I set my foot hard on the loud pedal of patriotism and persuaded the physician I consulted that under the tragic circumstances of the moment I was taking no undue risk. I set off in high spirits with unlimited money at my disposal and four

To prepare for his mission Maugham consulted with Rabbi Wise, several Russian Jews, and Voska. He had letters of introduction to Justice Brandeis and to Charles R. Crane and Professor Samuel Harper, respectively patron and teacher of Russian studies at the University of Chicago, but it is not clear that Maugham ever saw these men. On July 28, with a voucher from Wiseman for $21,000, he sailed from the West Coast for Tokyo, thence to Siberia and an overland trip to Petrograd. He was subsequently joined by Voska and three of the latter's colleagues—the Reverend Alois Koikol, a Presbyterian pastor from New York City; Joseph Martinek, editor of a Czech-language newspaper; and Dr. Vac Svarc, attorney for the Slovak League.[36]

Assembled at the Hotel Europa in Petrograd by early September, Maugham's group made contact with the future president of Czechoslovakia, Professor Thomas Masaryk,

---

devoted Czecks to act as Liaison officers between me and Professor Masaryk who had under his control in various parts of Russia something like sixty thousand of his compatriots. I was exhilerated by the responsibility of my position. I went as a private agent, who could be disavowed if necessary, with instructions to get in touch with parties hostile to the government and devise a scheme that would keep Russia in the war and prevent the Bolsheviks, supported by the Central Powers, from seizing power." Maugham, *The Summing Up*, London, 1938, pp. 203-204.

[36] Gottheil to Wiseman, July 2, 1917, WWP 112; Maugham to Wiseman, July 14, 1917, WWP 112; Maugham to Norman Thwaites (Wiseman's assistant), July 16, 1917, WWP 112. Maugham's signed receipt for $21,000 is in WWP 112, along with two receipts for a total of $4,000 signed by Voska. Voska and Will Irwin, *Spy and Counter-Spy*, London, 1941, p. 187, identify Voska's three companions. They give this version of Voska's instructions: " 'Go to Petrograd. Establish there a branch of the Slav Press Bureau. Organize the Czechs and Slovaks of the Empire to keep Russia in the war. You may take three other men with you. We will stand any reasonable expense. So far as we are concerned, you may have the greatest freedom of action. But you must co-operate with the Inter-Allied Committee at Petrograd. Above all—hurry!' "

Victor S. Mamatey, *The United States and East Central Europe, 1914-1918*, Princeton, 1957, authoritatively treats Czech and Slovak activities during the First World War but does not mention Voska or Wiseman's propaganda scheme.

who had previously met Wiseman in England.[37] Masaryk helped Voska establish a Slav press bureau which was to make use of a Czech organization consisting of 1,200 branches and 70,000 men to disseminate anti-German propaganda. As to the Russian political situation, Masaryk thought there was little likelihood of the Provisional Government's signing a separate peace and urged that a Japanese army of at least 300,000 be sent to the Eastern Front to restore the morale of the Russian troops. Maugham himself somewhat contradicted Masaryk's views, in a report of them, by pointing out that the Allies, presumably including the Japanese, were not popular in Russia and suggesting that the Allied ambassadors show more sympathy to Russian radicals. He warned, on about September 23, that Kerensky's government was losing favor and probably could not last.[38]

In early November Maugham, on Wiseman's instructions, left Russia in order to report personally to the British and American officials gathering in London. He brought with him the transcript of an interview of October 30 with Alexander Kerensky, head of the Provisional Government. Ke-

[37] Voska and Irwin, *Spy and Counter-Spy*, p. 191, say that Voska arrived in early August. This is unlikely, since he was in New York on July 21 (the day he signed the receipt for money from Wiseman) and traveled from there via Vancouver, Tokyo, and Vladivostok to Petrograd; *ibid.*, pp. 187-88. Maugham left Tokyo for Petrograd on August 27. Drummond to Wiseman, August 29, 1917, WWP 42; Masaryk, *The Making of a State*, London, 1927, pp. 135, 223.

[38] Wiseman, "Summary of Reports received from Agent in Petrograd, under date of September 11, 1917," HP 20:45; Maugham to Wiseman, Sept. 14, 1917, WWP 112; Wiseman to Drummond, Sept. 24, 1917, WWP 42. In *Ashenden, or the British Agent*, New York, 1927, pp. 293-95, the fictionalized account of his escapade in Petrograd, Maugham writes that Ashenden (Maugham) "was promised all the money he needed. Ashenden knew he could do nothing unless the Provisional Government remained in power for another three months; but winter was at hand and food was getting scarcer every day. The army was mutinous. The people clamoured for peace. Every morning at the Europa Ashenden drank a cup of chocolate with Professor Z [Masaryk] and discussed with him how best to make use of his devoted Czechs. . . . Kerensky ran hither and thither like a frightened hen."

116

rensky condemned Allied diplomacy and asked Maugham to tell Lloyd George that with Germany offering peace and the cold weather coming on he did not believe his government could continue, as, indeed, it did not. On November 7 it was toppled by the Bolsheviks, who immediately sued for peace. Kerensky's message became, in the words of Sir Eric Drummond, "of only historical interest now." Maugham's efforts had not kept Russia in the war, but he retained the belief that he had been on the right track and that if he had begun his work six months earlier he might well have succeeded.[39]

In London Wiseman, after consulting with Maugham and a Polish nationalist, Jan Horodyski, recommended bold action in Russia. The Allies must decide at once if they needed the Eastern Front in order to achieve victory. If they decided affirmatively, the only way to save the situation was to support General Kaledin's Cossacks, the only body that seemed to have the force and will to restore order and continue the war. Backed by Allied money, Kaledin should assume a dictatorship and command an army of his Cossacks, 100,000 men to be furnished by the Allies, and the Polish and Czech corps (estimated at 80,000 each) already in Russia. B. V. Savinkov, an anti-Bolshevik leftist who had impressed Maugham, should be recognized as Kaledin's political adviser. Assuming that Kaledin would attract loyal regiments from other parts of Russia, he could be expected to put together a total force of about a million men.[40]

[39] Wiseman, "Intelligence & Propaganda Work in Russia July to December 1917," Jan. 19, 1918, WWP 113. A copy of Maugham's report of the Kerensky interview is in Private Secretary Archives, 1917-1924, A. J. Balfour, FO 800/197, with this notation by Drummond: "Communicated by Sir W. Wiseman who had received document from Mr. Maugham who has just returned from Petrograd. ED 18-11-17." Also see Maugham, *Summing Up*, p. 205.

[40] These suggestions are contained in a memorandum dated Nov. 19, 1917, WWP 112, across the top of which is written: "As a result of Maugham's report W wrote to House." In view of this note and the inclusion in the memo of recommendations concerning both the Czechs

Here was the germ of the proposal—that the Allies should offer their support to Kaledin—which Balfour pressed on House on November 21. House had already heard of the proposal from Auchincloss. The latter was present at a November 20 meeting when Wiseman, Maugham, and Horodyski discussed the plan with Sir Edward Carson, member of the War Cabinet, and General Sir George Mc-Donough, director of British military intelligence. Auchincloss told Carson that the United States was not likely to give open support to Kaledin but might send aid to Romania which could in turn sustain Kaledin.[41] House, briefed by Auchincloss, repeated this view to Balfour and cabled Lansing that so far as the Kaledin scheme was concerned, he had committed the United States only financially. On December 22, after House had left Europe, France and Britain, relying on American assistance, agreed to underwrite Kaledin. But no American money was ever paid over to Kaledin, who, weakened by desertions and Bolshevik attacks, committed suicide in early February 1918.[42] Both Wiseman's propaganda scheme and the successor plan he recommended were now dead.

DEVELOPMENTS in Russia continued, however, to influence the foreign policies of Britain and America. On January 23, 1918 President Wilson told Wiseman that it had been the Bolshevik publication of Russia's secret treaties with the Allies that had necessitated his and Lloyd George's recent statements of war aims.[43] Actually the President's state-

---

and Poles, it would appear that Auchincloss's diary was mistaken in attributing the memo to Horodyski. Auchincloss Diary, Nov. 20, 1917. Most likely, Wiseman wrote the memo from Maugham's and Horodyski's reports. Maugham, *A Writer's Notebook*, New York, 1949, p. 185, gives high praise to Savinkov.

[41] Auchincloss Diary, Nov. 20, 1917; House Diary, Nov. 20, 1917.

[42] Ullman, *Intervention and the War*, pp. 42-43; House Diary, Nov. 21, 1917; House to Lansing, Dec. 1, 1917, HP 12:12; Kennan, *Russia Leaves the War*, pp. 177-78, 183; Phillips Diary, Dec. 26, 1917.

[43] Wiseman, "Notes on Interview with the President January 23rd, 1918," WWP 43.

ment on January 8th, containing the famous Fourteen Points, was the realization of a desire he harbored well in advance of the Bolshevik Revolution. Convinced that the United States was not in the war for the same ends as the Allies, he had been tempted to outline war aims in his August response to the Pope. Shortly afterward he appointed House to prepare plans for a peace settlement. When the Allies at Paris declined to approve even the vaguely progressive war aims that House proposed, Wilson decided it was time for the United States to make a unilateral declaration.[44]

Beginning on December 18, and using memoranda drawn up by House's peace "Inquiry," Wilson and House drafted the Fourteen Points speech. Right away, House suggested that Wiseman, still in England, be sent for "in order to have the benefit of his advice regarding the way England would receive what we have in mind to say." This was a remarkable request for House, who only days before had consulted all the important British leaders. It showed how solicitous he was for Britain's position as well as the extent to which he relied on Wiseman's counsel. Wilson demurred, thinking it better to consult no one, but later he agreed to summon Wiseman to see if anything in the draft might offend the British.[45]

Wiseman, although summoned, failed to arrive in Washington before Wilson delivered the speech.[46] Had he arrived in time, his representation of British war aims would have probably been very similar to that contained in a

[44] Wilson to House, Aug. 22, 1917, HP 49:18; Seymour, *Intimate Papers*, Vol. 3, pp. 168-69, 281-86, 317. Almost from the United States' entry into the war House agitated for a declaration of "liberal" war aims. See his letters of May 20 and 30, 1917 to Wilson, HP 49:18.

[45] Seymour, *Intimate Papers*, Vol. 3, pp. 316-48; House Diary, Dec. 18, 1917.

[46] Wiseman may not have known the exact reason for his being summoned. House's cable merely stated, "It is important that you come over immediately for consultation and that you reach New York before January first." He did know, however, that House and Wilson were planning a war aims statement. House to Wiseman, Dec. 19, 1917 and Wiseman to House, Dec. 20, 22, 1917, HP 20:46.

memorandum on the subject which he wrote for House the preceding September. At that time, apparently after consulting Philip Kerr (later Lord Lothian), Lloyd George's secretary, Wiseman attempted to speak for "the average Britisher." That abstract figure's principal war aim, according to Wiseman, was to "do the right thing" by Belgium. After that he would want to protect the British Empire, satisfy the demands of the Dominions, return Alsace-Lorraine to France, and see Germany compensate—at least in principle—for the war damage to Belgium and France. For the future he would favor strong defense of the British Isles, international limitation on the manufacture of arms, limitation of navies in ratio to the size of merchant marines, no secret treaties, and a league of peace. The latter, Wiseman expected, would find its greatest support among political thinkers and the better educated working classes.[47]

In this memorandum Wiseman alluded delicately to what the Allies subsequently found unsatisfactory in the Wilson peace program: the prohibition of reparations and the threat to Britain's naval supremacy. Had he been in Washington during the drafting of the Fourteen Points he might have corrected House's wrong impression that the British might accept the phrasing of the point concerning "freedom of the seas." But he probably could not have prevented the declaration of the point. His request that any statement of war aims be postponed until after his arrival ("as I am collecting information which may be useful") went unheeded.[48]

Wiseman wanted Wilson to hold off stating war aims because he brought with him a new draft of British war aims, far more progressive than any previously issued by the British. The draft Wiseman carried was composed by Lord

[47] Wiseman, "Some Thoughts on War-Aims and Peace—September 1917," HP 20:45. A paper initialed by Kerr discussed the "War Aims of the Average Britisher" in terms similar to Wiseman's. "Some Suggestions for a Letter," Lothian [Kerr] Papers, Box 139, Scottish Record Office.
[48] Wiseman to House, Dec. 22, 1917, WWP 4.

Robert Cecil on January 3, the day before Wiseman embarked for New York. On January 5 Lloyd George delivered his war aims speech, which almost bodily incorporated the Cecil draft.[49] Wiseman did not know the speech was to be made, and his ignorance of the Prime Minister's plans strikingly illustrated the difference in stature which he and House, whatever their other similarities were, each enjoyed within his own government. Wiseman landed in New York on January 15 (after an unusually long voyage marked by submarine threats and a snow storm). He was surprised to learn that while he was at sea both Lloyd George and Wilson had made their war aims speeches.[50]

The closeness of the dates of the two speeches was remarkable but merely coincidental. Wilson, hoping to stir world opinion, feared that Lloyd George's speech, preceding his own by three days, had stolen his thunder. For a moment he considered not making the speech.[51] But the greater enthusiasm which met his speech justified House's advice to go ahead with it. If the similarity of Lloyd George's statement to his own hurt Wilson's pride as an innovator—and both speeches, in different language, advocated self-determination, arms limitation, and an international organization of nations[52]—then the news that Wiseman brought helped salve the hurt. For, as House quickly reported to Wilson, Lloyd George had little to do with the composition of the speech. And the basis of the speech, Cecil's memorandum, was drafted after several conferences

[49] A copy of the Cecil memorandum is in WWP 101. Lloyd George's speech is printed in his *War Memoirs*, Vol. 5, pp. 2,515-27. See note 57 below.

[50] Wiseman to [Secret Service] "Chief," Jan. 18, 1918, WWP 7; House Diary, Jan. 19, 1918.

[51] Wilson to House, Jan. 2, 1918, HP 49:19; Seymour, *Intimate Papers*, Vol. 3, pp. 338-41.

[52] Wilson's speech is printed in Baker and Dodd, *The Public Papers of Woodrow Wilson*, Vol. 5, pp. 155-62. A detailed comparison of Lloyd George's and Wilson's speeches is made by Arno J. Mayer, *Political Origins of the New Diplomacy, 1917-1918*, New Haven, 1959, Chapters 8 and 9, esp. pp. 353-67.

between Cecil and Wiseman, who was able to put forward House's and Wilson's views. Therefore, House seemed to imply, the speech was almost of American origin.[53]

When Wiseman next saw the President, he found him curious to learn the background of Lloyd George's speech.

> . . . he was anxious to know the genesis of the speech—which he said was often as interesting as a speech itself. I told him of the discussions in London at the time of the House Mission; also of the pressure by the Labour party, which obviously interested him. He was delighted to find George's speech coincided so closely with his own views, which he earnestly believed were also the views of the American people. It was important that the British and American world-policies should run on similar lines. He was glad to believe that was so at present.
>
> . . . George's speech—the liberal note, the policy of self-determination, and the absence of annexationist ideas would, he said, be duly appreciated in America.[54]

Wiseman undoubtedly encouraged whatever tendency Wilson had to feel responsible for the liberal nature of Lloyd George's statement.

It would have been wrong, however, to see Lloyd George's speech as a result solely, or even chiefly, of American influence. The Prime Minister was at the time chiefly concerned over the manpower shortage and the possibility that Bolshevik pacifism would attract a following among English workingmen.[55] His speech was designed to renew

[53] House wrote Wilson that Wiseman brought news of Lloyd George's speech "which will amuse you. It is just as I thought, it was not his speech at all." House to Wilson, Jan. 20, 1918, HP 49:10. In his diary House recorded that neither the style nor substance of the speech was Lloyd George's. And in a broad hint to future historians he noted: "Knowing the inside of matters as I do, it makes me wonder where the credit really lies for the great things that have been done in the world." House Diary, Jan. 19, 1918.

[54] Wiseman, "Notes on Interview with the President January 23rd, 1918," WWP 43.

[55] Wiseman reported on December 22: "Man-power problem absorbs public attention at the moment." Wiseman to House, Dec. 22, 1917, WWP 4. Lloyd George, *War Memoirs*, Vol. 5, pp. 2,483-85.

the loyalty of labor which had adopted the advanced views of the British left, especially those of the Union of Democratic Control.[56] Cecil's contribution to the speech—of the speech's 34 paragraphs, 21 (12 of them verbatim) came wholly or principally from the Cecil memorandum—was that of a Tory minister who wanted desperately to end the war. He wrote his memorandum as a response to the Austrian foreign minister's peace terms of December 25 and undoubtedly hoped to appeal to liberal sentiment in the Central empires. That same sentiment was in the forethought of the other contributors to the speech, Smuts and Lloyd George.[57]

WHEN Wiseman returned to the United States (January 15) he came with a new designation. He was, by appointment of the Prime Minister, "liaison officer between the War Cabinet and any special representative they might send out to represent them in the United States." House more accurately described him as "liaison officer between me personally and the British Government."[58] Both House and the President expressed great pleasure at his return. House had become quite attached to Wiseman and freely arrogated to

[56] Mayer, *Political Origins of New Diplomacy*, p. 318. Mayer's analysis makes no mention of the Cecil memorandum. A.J.P. Taylor, *The Trouble Makers*, London, 1957, p. 156, concludes that Lloyd George's speech indicated that "the U.D.C. was dictating foreign policy, through the agency of the Labour movement. . . ."

[57] Cecil wrote of the speech: "It was composed as to two-fifths by Smuts, one-fifth by the Prime Minister himself, and two-fifths by me." Cecil to Balfour, Jan. 8, 1918, Balfour Papers 49738, British Museum. Quantitatively, if not otherwise, Cecil was too modest. A comparison of his memo with the speech shows that 12 of the speech's 34 paragraphs are verbatim Cecil, seven are almost verbatim, and two are paraphrases. Cecil phrased the concluding summation of Britain's war aims—"sanctity of treaties," "territorial settlement . . . based on the right of self-determination," and "international organisation to limit the burden of armaments and diminish the probability of war." For Cecil's early advocacy of a league of nations, see Cecil, *The Great Experiment*, London, 1941, Chap. 2, and Henry R. Winkler, *The League of Nations Movement in Great Britain, 1914-1919*, New Brunswick, N.J., 1952, pp. 111, 230-31, 242-50, 261.

[58] Balfour to Wiseman, Dec. 19, 1917, WWP 7; House Diary, Dec. 18, 1917.

himself credit for Wiseman's new eminence: "I have given Wiseman an immense leverage by putting him in touch with the President and with the leaders of his own country. They do not quite understand why I have done this, but it is because of his ability, loyalty and trustworthiness. He has qualities which are rarely met with in one man."[59]

House was essentially right. In London he had told Balfour, in a statement which "touched" the latter, of his absolute confidence in Wiseman. He described Wiseman to the King as "one of the most efficient men of his age I had ever met" and later sent the King a farewell note (and oral response to the King's question as to Northcliffe and Robertson's influence in the British government) by Wiseman.[60] Certainly without boosts of this sort Wiseman would have remained just an efficient intelligence officer. But credit had also to be given to Wiseman's enterprise and ingenuity. He skillfully cultivated the confidence of influential men— House, Balfour, Northcliffe, and Reading—and then exploited that confidence to promote his own program for the achievement of an Anglo-American entente. As 1918 opened he was in a very strong position to pursue his program.

Reading was to become Wiseman's chief ally. In January 1918 the British government at last recalled Ambassador Spring Rice and named Reading as his successor with the title of Ambassador and High Commissioner.[61] The Brit-

[59] Wiseman to [Secret Service] "Chief," Jan. 18, 1918, WWP 7; Wiseman, "Notes on Interview with the President January 23rd, 1918," WWP 43; House Diary, Feb. 2, 1918.

[60] House Diary, Nov. 10, 20, 27, 1917; Auchincloss Diary, Nov. 22, 1917.

[61] Although Spring Rice expected to be replaced, he was greatly upset by the actual recall. Wiseman to [secret service] "Chief," Jan. 18, 1918, WWP 7. He retired to Ottawa and there died on February 14, 1918. A few days earlier he philosophically wrote Frank Polk that "it is obvious that the U S being what it is now in the world's drama requires someone to represent the Belligerents who is more than a mere trained diplomatist." Spring Rice to Polk, Feb. 1, 1918, Polk Papers, 73:112. He also wrote a pleasant farewell to Wiseman,

ish thereby embittered Spring Rice and his Republican friends but pleased the Administration and succeeded in bringing all British agencies in America under one head (as Wiseman had recommended). Northcliffe's position as nominal head of the British War Mission prevented complete tidiness on the organizational chart. House, eager to make use of the press lord, encouraged Lloyd George to send Northcliffe back to America. The decision was apparently up to Northcliffe himself. On December 14 he told Balfour that he had not yet decided whether to return. On January 3, however, he wrote a friend that Reading would go to America as high commissioner while he himself would remain in London for two or three months to organize the British end of the War Mission. In February he answered Lloyd George's call to direct propaganda in enemy countries, and thereafter, although he clung to his title of Chairman of the British War Mission, he took no active part in Anglo-American diplomacy.[62]

Reading appeared to refuse to undertake his assignment in America until it was clear that Northcliffe would not be returning also. He did not arrive in Washington until Feb-

---

wishing him well in his "interesting career." Spring Rice to Wiseman, Jan. 31, 1918, WWP 121.

Sen. Henry Cabot Lodge, a close friend of Spring Rice, attributed Spring Rice's recall to intrigue on the part of Reading but could not see any legitimate reason for Reading to desire the ambassadorship. Lodge to Dr. W. S. Bigelow, Jan. 10, 1918, Lodge Papers, Massachusetts Historical Society.

[62] House Diary, Dec. 1, 1917; Northcliffe to Balfour, Dec. 14, 1917, Private Secretary Archives, 1917-1924, A. J. Balfour, FO 800/200. Lloyd George assured Austen Chamberlain, the British delegate to the Inter-Allied Council on War Purchases and Finance, that Northcliffe would have nothing to do with the Council or British procurement in America. Lloyd George to Chamberlain, Jan. 7, 1918, Chamberlain Papers, Box AC 12. Pound and Harmsworth, *Northcliffe*, pp. 607, 612-13. See also Northcliffe to House, Jan. 12, 1918, HP 14:63. In May 1918 Arthur Murray, a specialist on American affairs in the Foreign Office, in response to Reading's inquiry as to Northcliffe's War Mission duties stated that Northcliffe had no official activities other than enemy propaganda. Murray to Reading, May 15, 1918, Lord Reading's Private Papers, FO 800/210.

ruary 10. Up to that time Wiseman served, in House's words, as acting ambassador. The President twice called him in for reports on the European situation and expressed an intention to summon him again from time to time.[63] Wiseman, in reporting to the Foreign Office, said that he would not continue going to the White House once Reading arrived, for Reading's *amour propre* might be offended. On the received copy of Wiseman's cable Drummond noted, ". . . it may be necessary that he should still have conversations as much publicity will attach to every visit paid by Lord Reading to the President & our Allies are very jealous." Balfour marked "Concur" on the cable and sent it to Lloyd George.[64] In the months ahead both the British and Americans found Wiseman's nonambassadorial status to be one of his most valuable attributes.

[63] House Diary, Feb. 10, 1918; House to Wilson, Jan. 20, 1918, HP 49:10. Wiseman's account of the interviews, Jan. 23 and Feb. 3, are in WWP 43 and 129. Both interviews were noted in the log of the White House usher. Irwin H. Hoover MSS, Box 4, Library of Congress.

[64] Wiseman to Drummond, CXP 522, 523, Feb. 4, 1918, WWP 129. The received copy with endorsements is in Balfour Papers, 49741, British Museum.

CHAPTER SIX

AMERICAN MANPOWER: SOURCE OF
STRENGTH AND DIVISION

". . . victory for us depends on squeezing the last ounce of
proper use out of the American Army."

Jan C. Smuts to Lloyd George,
8 June 1918

SHORTLY after Wiseman returned to the United States in
January 1918, President Wilson invited him to call at the
White House. Their conversation—Wilson called it a "bully
talk"—ranged freely over several aspects of the war and
the future peace, although Wilson seemed chiefly interested
in what Wiseman could tell him of the genesis of Lloyd
George's war aims speech. Considering himself unusually
complimented by the hour-long conversation, Wiseman
was taken by surprise when a few days later the President
again invited him to the White House. "Wilson has just sent
for me," he cabled the Foreign Office, "Don't know what
for." Nor did House know, although he assumed Wilson
wanted to discuss the recent British proposal to send Japanese troops into Siberia. Wilson did want to discuss troops
and a British proposal for their use, but the troops were
American and the location was France.[1] For just as Britain
had turned to the United States six months earlier for financial relief, now she was asking the United States to
save her from a bankruptcy of manpower. In the earlier
case Wilson's Secretary of the Treasury drove a hard bargain and eagerly sought to dictate policy toward Britain.
Now Wilson's commander in the field, General John J.
Pershing, would drive an even harder bargain with greater
skill. In both cases Britain received more sympathetic treat-

[1] Wiseman, "Notes on Interview with the President Jan. 23rd, 1918,"
WWP 43; Wiseman to Drummond, Feb. 2, 1918, WWP 43; House
to Wilson, Feb. 2, 1918, HP 49:10; Wiseman to Balfour, Feb. 3,
1918, WWP 129.

ment from the United States because of the efforts of Wiseman.

In answer to the President's invitation, Wiseman appeared for lunch at the White House on February 3, a Sunday. Secretary of War Newton D. Baker was there too and appeared somewhat shaken. The President was outwardly calm but disturbed enough to break his Calvinist Sabbath for mundane business. The reason for the discomfiture of Baker and Wilson, Wiseman found, was the possibility that the flames of criticism against the War Department which they had almost brought under control would be fanned afresh by expected proposals of Lloyd George and the Supreme War Council. Six days earlier Baker's testimony before the Senate Committee on Military Affairs allayed senatorial fears that the War Department was incapable of fielding an army in Europe. Now those fears might be resurrected, for the British were asking that American battalions be incorporated into the British and French divisions.[2] With rare unanimity, Lloyd George, Haig, and Robertson insisted that "There was only one way in which the American army could really participate in the operation of 1918, and that was by amalgamation with the British and French armies."[3] Would not this attitude confirm critics of the Administration in their belief that the American army, hobbled by Washington's blunders, was incapable of fighting on its own?

The British proposal for amalgamation signified more the weakening of the Allies' armies than the ineptness of the War Department. Wastage, that unfeeling shorthand for slaughter and maiming in battle, threatened to become a

[2] Wiseman to Drummond and Balfour, Feb. 4, 1918, WWP 129; Frederick Palmer, *Newton D. Baker*, 2 vols., New York, 1931, Vol. 2, pp. 61-80; Baker, *Wilson Life & Letters*, Vol. 7, p. 511.

[3] Statement by Haig as recorded in the minutes of the third session of the Supreme War Council, Jan. 30, 1918, printed in United States Department of the Army (Historical Division), *United States Army in the World War, 1917-1919*, 17 vols. Washington, D.C., 1948, Vol. 2, p. 187 (hereafter cited as *U.S. Army in the World War*). Lloyd George and Robertson expressed the same opinion.

word of literal descriptiveness to the British in early 1918. After three and a half years of fighting and hundreds of thousands of entries under the category "wastage," defeat seemed all too real a possibility. With Russia out of the war Germany would obviously make a supreme effort to overwhelm the Allies on the Western Front before the Americans arrived. The prospect of such a German attack would have been frightening in any year. In 1918 Britain faced a troop deficit of 250,000 men by March, when the German attack could be expected. There was, according to the experts in London, no British source from which this deficit could be made good.[4] During December and January rumors circulated of drastic new measures to conscript previously exempt youths, older men, and workers in industries vital to defense. Lloyd George's war aims speech to the Trade Unions Congress had the immediate purpose of making another "comb-out" less odious to labor, and in Parliament the Minister of National Service felt obliged, in the interest of national morale, to deliberately understate the acuteness of the manpower shortage.[5] But "even with freedom from liability for Government pledges to Trade Unions" the government had no hopes of providing more than 100,000 men for the army.[6]

Given these gloomy forecasts, the temptation to rely on American replacements for the British army was irresistible. The United States, with a population of 100 million, to Britain's 48 million (excluding the approximately 350 million of the Commonwealth and colonies), had been in the war nine months but still did not have an army ready to take over part of the front.[7] Starting nearly from scratch, the

---

[4] Sir James Edward Edmonds, *Military Operations, France and Belgium, 1918* [*History of the Great War Based on Official Documents*], 5 vols. and a volume of appendices, London, 1935-47, appendices, pp. 17-19, 30-34.

[5] Lloyd George, *War Memoirs*, Vol. 5, pp. 2,483-84; Auckland C. Geddes (Baron Geddes), *The Forging of a Family*, London, 1952, pp. 317-18. Geddes was Minister of National Service in 1918.

[6] Edmonds, *Military Operations*, appendices, p. 31.

[7] The American Expeditionary Force numbered 165,080 men and 9,804 officers on December 31, 1917. Although a few Americans

American army had to be recruited, trained (in the United States), transported, and supplied. Because of the gross inadequacy of American shipping and French ports, Allied and American authorities feared it would be 1919 before the weight of the American army, organized under its own commanders, could be felt. Could not, the British asked, the process be speeded up by feeding small units of the American army into British divisions where by virtue of a common language officers and men might train quickly under actual war conditions and, not incidentally, keep the British army up to strength?[8] This question obsessed the British and hounded the Americans throughout the first half of 1918.

Amalgamation was not a new proposal in January 1918. Gen. Tom Bridges, the military member of Balfour's mission, had urged it the preceding April as the quickest way to throw American soldiers into the battle. Although recognizing the force of Bridges' argument, Secretary of War Baker decided to form an autonomous army under its own commander.[9] Pershing unswervingly followed that plan, and the British dropped talk of amalgamation until after the Caporetto disaster and the Bolshevik revolution. As they were digesting the meaning of these two setbacks, the British learned from General Bliss, during House's visit to Paris, that only 24 divisions, or approximately 600,000 men could be transported to France by the end of June 1918. General Robertson, the British Chief of the Imperial General Staff, reopened the idea of amalgamation in a doleful

---

experienced combat, for purposes of training, from October 1917 onward, and one division entered a quiet part of the line in January, it was not until May that an American division undertook independent action. Pershing assigned two divisions to the French for combat in March. Pershing, *My Experiences*, Vol. 1, pp. 201, 213, 369; Vol. 2, pp. 17, 59. See also Hanson W. Baldwin, *World War I*, New York, 1962, pp. 112, 143-44.

[8] Frederick Palmer, *Bliss, Peacemaker*, New York, 1934, pp. 209, 216; Pershing, *My Experiences*, Vol. 1, pp. 249-56.

[9] Baker to Wilson, May 2, 1917, Newton D. Baker Papers, Box 4, Library of Congress.

memorandum to Lloyd George, which the latter sent to Colonel House with the plea that amalgamation be approved. Despite Wiseman's efforts, already noted, to get the British to state their needs fully and directly to the House mission, this most pressing need of all was presented to House as a sort of footnote to his consultations with the British Cabinet and the Supreme War Council. House received the Robertson memorandum from the hands of Lord Reading on the eve of his departure from Europe.[10] The British thereby lost their best chance to impress forcefully the amalgamation scheme on their best friend in the American hierarchy.

Routinely presented, the amalgamation request got routine consideration. House reported it to the President but failed to urge its adoption. He was well aware of the War Department's opposition to the scheme and of their standard argument that it was unthinkable to ask American soldiers to surrender national identity when Canadians and Australians had refused to do so. Just as House was filing his report,[11] however, a cable from Wiseman (still in London) revealed that the British were quite anxious for him to secure the President's approval of amalgamation: "The most urgent problem at present [Wiseman's cable read] is man-power to secure our Western line against formidable German attacks which may be expected through the winter. . . . It is vitally important that the United States come to the assistance of the Allies with man-power immediately; that U.S. troops now in France should take their place by companies in the line with our men, as sug-

[10] Bliss to Acting Chief of Staff, Dec. 4, 1917, Bliss Papers, Box 66, Library of Congress. Robertson's memorandum and a covering note by Lloyd George to Reading (Dec. 2, 1917) instructing the latter to beg House to consider amalgamation favorably, are printed in *U.S. Army in the World War*, Vol. 3, p. 4. Reading delivered the memorandum and note to House on December 4. House Diary, Dec. 4, 1917.

[11] House's report, Dec. 15, 1917, *Foreign Relations, 1917*, Sup. 2, Vol. 1, p. 356. Canadians and Australians were organized in their own national corps but were under the over-all command of the British commander-in-chief.

gested to you in Paris, and also that reinforcements should be hurried from America at all costs. The next few months will be critical."[12]

This appeal produced results—or so it seemed. House replied to Wiseman that he had "worked out something" and that instructions were on their way to Pershing. Pershing's instructions, a copy of which went to the British government, were vague enough, however, both to permit the British to believe that Wilson had accepted their position and to confirm Pershing in his understanding that the power to dispose of American troops was his alone. The President, according to the instructions to Pershing, did "not desire loss of identity of our forces, but regards that as secondary to the meeting of any critical situation by the most helpful use possible" of Pershing's troops. Wilson gave Pershing "full authority" and "entire freedom" in the use of his men but hoped he would do so in consultation with the French and British commanders-in-chief. Considering the subsequent complications in this question, it is important to note that Wilson made no mention of amalgamation nor of the Supreme War Council. Pershing was specifically ordered to make his own arrangements with the British and French commanders. There was good reason, therefore, for his later insistence that the Supreme War Council had no jurisdiction over the assignment of his troops.[13]

Interpreting the President's instructions as an endorsement of amalgamation, both the British and French besieged Pershing with requests for men. Pershing conceived of their requests as a device to draw on the American Expeditionary Force as a manpower pool for the other armies. He bitterly resented that the British had appealed over his head to House. He was in fact enraged that the Allies had discussed military matters at all with House. He dressed

---

[12] Wiseman to House, Dec. 14, 1917, WWP 64.

[13] House to Wiseman, Dec. 18, 1917, WWP 64; Baker to Pershing, Dec. 18, 1917, HP 2:17. The instructions, received by Pershing on December 25, are printed in Pershing, *My Experiences*, Vol. 1, pp. 271-72. See also *U.S. Army in the World War*, Vol. 2, pp. 123-24.

down General Pétain for revealing to House the probable sector of the line eventually to be taken over by the American army. Later he recalled, with contrived naïvete, that the "French probably regarded Mr. House as a sort of special ambassador and thought that they might be able to lay the foundation for an approach through him to the question of amalgamation." Of course the French, the British, and Pershing himself knew that House *was* a special ambassador. What the British and French did not realize at the time was that they had made a mistake in appealing to House. Partly to assert his authority and largely because of his unyielding desire to establish a great and separate American force, Pershing rejected the Allies' petitions.[14]

But Pershing, although he had full control over the use of American soldiers, was vulnerable in one area. He did not have nearly enough ships to bring over the components of the large army he wanted to build. The British, but not the French, did have ships, and when they dangled the possibility of a loan of their ships Pershing indicated that he might spare a few troops after all. To him the situation was as simple as horse-trading in his native Missouri: "the British were bargaining for men to fill their ranks and we were trying to get shipping to carry over our armies."[15] Given free rein by his government, Pershing proved to be more than a match in the bargaining with the British. Squabbles among the Allies, the weakness of the Supreme War Council, and the absence of any superior in Europe all strengthened his hand, and he did not hesitate to deal as an equal with the prime ministers when they replaced their commanders in the negotiations with Pershing. For despite his dependence on the Allies for numerous supplies, and particularly on the British for shipping, Pershing controlled the most valuable commodity of all—manpower.

The first stage of the British bargaining with Pershing

[14] *Ibid.*, pp. 105-106, 123; Pershing, *My Experiences*, Vol. 1, pp. 256-57.
[15] *Ibid.*, p. 269.

opened on January 10. General Robertson came over to France with an offer of ships, to be diverted from British traffic in food and supplies, sufficient to transport 150,000 soldiers above and beyond the regular program of troop shipments. These soldiers, 150 battalions, would be transported over a period of about three months and would serve, primarily for training but if necessary for combat as well, with British divisions for what the British considered "a reasonable period of time—say 4 or 5 months." Pershing countered Robertson's proposal by asking that the British bring over complete American divisions instead of the 150 battalions, and he insisted that assignment of troops to British units be temporary and subject to recall whenever he decided. Robertson replied that the British would be taking a great risk in diverting ships from food shipments, necessary to maintain civilian morale, to haul American troops and could do so only if it meant bringing over the largest possible number and that that number be available to the British for a "reasonable" period of time. Pershing did not dispute that more men could be hauled under the battalion plan—complete divisions would include animals, artillery, and other bulky equipment not necessary for detached battalions—but argued that American national sentiment would not permit the fragmentation and loaning of American divisions. Finally he agreed to cable Robertson's plan to Washington with the endorsement that it be given "serious consideration."[16]

Both London and Washington interpreted Pershing's recommendation for serious consideration to mean he approved the battalion plan. Secretary of War Baker therefore authorized General Bliss, in London on his way to Versailles to act as the United States Permanent Military Representative at the Supreme War Council, to make arrangements with the British government to implement the battalion plan. Bliss soon learned from Pershing, however, that he had never approved the project and was instead insisting that six whole divisions be hauled in British bot-

[16] *U.S. Army in the World War,* Vol. 3, pp. 11-14, 17-19.

1. Sir William Wiseman

2. General John J. Pershing

3. William G. McAdoo

4. Frank L. Polk

5. Arthur J. Balfour

6. Lord Robert Cecil

7. Sir Eric Drummond

8. Lord Rufus Isaacs Reading

10. Sir Cecil Spring Rice
and Lord Northcliffe

9. Gordon Auchincloss and
Colonel Edward M. House

11. Douglas Fairbanks, Mary Pickford, Colonel House, and Wiseman (c. 1921),
"Ambassadors All"

toms. Pershing proved so adamant in his position that Bliss decided to give way to him, despite his own preference for the battalion plan. With Bliss now supporting Pershing, the British reluctantly agreed to the American plan, which gave them temporary use of the infantry of the six divisions, a smaller number of men than they would have got from 150 battalions of infantry.[17] Pershing had won, and was confirmed in his opinion that the British if pushed hard enough would produce the shipping that they had available all along.

It was immediately after Lloyd George and his advisers hammered out the six-division agreement with Pershing that the President called in Wiseman to discuss the use of American troops. Since the agreement had already been reached, the question arises why Wilson thought it necessary to discuss the matter further with Wiseman. The answer is that although the British had acceded to the six-division plan, which involved troops not yet in France, they appeared to be on the verge of joining with the Italians and French in a demand for the amalgamation of American troops already in France. Bliss in the same cable reporting the agreement on six divisions, warned that the Allied representatives at the Supreme War Council, whose third session was just getting underway, unanimously agreed that without amalgamation the American army would be of no help in meeting the apprehended German attack. He thought it probable that the three European members of the Supreme War Council would formally demand the amalgamation of all American troops.[18] Such a demand, which did not materialize, would have produced explosive effects, forcing Wilson to disappoint either Pershing or the Supreme War Council. Domestically, the effect of Baker's recent assurances to the Senate committee would be undone. Hence, Wilson called in Wiseman to con-

[17] Lloyd George, *War Memoirs*, Vol. 5, p. 3,025; Trask, *United States in the Supreme War Council*, pp. 77-78; Pershing, *My Experiences*, Vol. 1, pp. 304-305.

[18] Bliss to Baker, Jan. 30, 1918, *U.S. Army in the World War*, Vol. 3, pp. 35-36.

vey to the British that his desire to cooperate in the matter of manpower did not extend to the point of amalgamation.

Wilson, who had earlier formed the suspicion that the British would try to barter shipping for soldiers,[19] told Wiseman that the American people would not understand if the British consented to transport American troops only on the condition that they be used as British reinforcements. Wiseman informed London that Wilson "For political reasons, which in my opinion are sound, . . . feels that public opinion here must be carefully considered in carrying out such a scheme. It must not be said here that, instead of an American army, the Americans are only depot battalions for British troops used thus to avoid trouble the British Government may have with their Labour Party on man-power. If it is done it must be shown as an effort on America's part additional to raising her national army—as an emergency and temporary measure adopted by the American Commander-in-Chief in France."[20] Wilson maintained this position even while admitting the validity of Wiseman's rejoinder that the establishment of an autonomous American army might come too late to be of any use. Wilson thought that any course taken was a gamble but insisted, both for reasons of domestic politics and military soundness, that Pershing was the proper official to decide the use of American troops. "It would not have so bad an effect," he told Wiseman, "if Pershing . . . decided after the men arrived in France that it was necessary to place some of them at the disposal of the British. . . ."[21]

An emergency was not long in materializing. On March 21 the Germans opened their spring offensive, which rolled back the British line fourteen miles in four days. The British Fifth Army suffered extremely heavy casualties, and immediately the British government reopened their cam-

[19] Wilson to Baker, Jan. 20, 1918, Baker Papers, Box 8.
[20] Wiseman to Drummond and Balfour, Feb. 4, 1918, WWP 129.
[21] Wiseman to Balfour, Feb. 3, 1918, WWP 129.

paign for amalgamation. They had reason to hope that the German successes might startle Wilson into a more compliant mood. From Wiseman's office in New York Ambassador Reading reported that as a result of the battle the Administration at last realized that appeals to liberal sentiment in Germany were futile and that force was the only language for communicating with Germany. He predicted a "really important speeding-up of the American effort" and hinted that Wilson might now agree to amalgamation. "We may well take this opportunity of pressing for a settlement of the most essential questions of principle in the joint conduct of the war," he cabled Balfour.[22]

Had the decision been House's to make, American infantry would have been fed into the British divisions, at least for the duration of the March-April emergency. He passed on to Wilson Balfour's request for the exclusive shipping of infantry with the "urgent recommendation" that it be granted. But Wilson was not to be stampeded. Unwilling to make a decision which in his view could be more wisely made in Europe, he ordered Secretary of War Baker, then in London, to return to France to consult with Bliss and Pershing. Whatever plan those three worked out in association with the Supreme War Council would be acceptable to him. In view of Wilson's attitude and of the decisions made by the American military officials in France, House's assurance to Balfour that his request would be met was premature.[23] For Pershing, even in this period of great crisis, still adamantly opposed the use of American infantry as reserves in the Allied armies, and his adamancy

[22] Reading to Balfour, Mar. 27, 1918, WWP 4. Lloyd George, *War Memoirs*, Vol. 5, pp. 3,036-37, and Reading, *Rufus Isaacs*, Vol. 2, pp. 94-95, reproduce the whole of the cable *except*, significantly, the sentence here quoted. Wiseman composed a similar message for the Foreign Office but did not send it, presumably because Reading's made it redundant. See undated draft of a cable to Balfour, WWP 129.

[23] Balfour to House, Mar. 26, 1918, HP 2:23; House to Balfour, Mar. 26, 1918, HP 2:23; Wilson to Auchincloss (for House), Mar. 27, 1918, HP 49:19.

more than offset the inclination of Baker and Bliss to go along with amalgamation.[24]

Bliss indicated his sympathy with temporary amalgamation by endorsing the Permanent Military Representatives' Joint Note 18 (March 28). The note provided that "until otherwise directed by the Supreme War Council, only American infantry and machine gun units . . . be brought to France, and that all agreements or conventions hitherto made in conflict with this decision be modified accordingly."[25] The Permanent Military Representatives, whose project of a common Allied reserve had been torpedoed by Pétain's and Haig's failure to contribute to it,[26] were now claiming jurisdiction over the shipping priorities of American army units. They were, in Pershing's view, subverting his construction of a balanced and complete army and were assuming responsibility for determining when such an army would be born. To take effect, Joint Note 18 had to be approved by the Supreme War Council, that is, by President Wilson as well as the three prime ministers. Wilson approved the note but, on the recommendation of Baker, only in a limited way. Caught between the conflicting advice of Pershing and Bliss, Baker suggested that Wilson affirm the scheme of preferential shipping of infantry and machinegun units while at the same time reiterating the control of Pershing over such units and the determination of the United States to speedily collect its forces into an independent army. The effect of Baker's recommendation and Wilson's approval of it was a victory for Pershing. He retained full control of all American units, and neither he nor Wilson

[24] That Bliss was willing to accept temporary amalgamation is indicated in the next paragraph of the text above. Baker's position was less clear, but from his later actions, his respect for Bliss's opinions, and from the impression he gave Balfour and Lloyd George *at the time*, I believe he would have accepted temporary amalgamation had not Pershing been so vehemently opposed. See Trask, *United States in the Supreme War Council*, pp. 81-82; Lloyd George, *War Memoirs*, Vol. 5, pp. 3,031-32, and Pershing, *My Experiences*, Vol. 1, pp. 358-60.

[25] *U.S. Army in the World War*, Vol. 2, pp. 257-58.

[26] Trask, *United States in the Supreme War Council*, pp. 60-62.

had conceded that the Supreme War Council should determine how long the preferential shipping would continue. Dramatically and adroitly, Pershing signified both his independence from the Supreme War Council and his apparent wish to cooperate with the Allies by offering directly to General Foch, the newly designated generalissimo of the Allied and American armies, whole divisions for use at the front. This offer, of course, in no way supplied the replacements so desperately desired by Britain for her own divisions.[27]

While repeatedly delegating responsibility for the disposition of American troops to Baker and Pershing and approving their decisions, President Wilson underwent a rain of appeals from London for more men and for amalgamation. On the evening of March 27 Reading read to the Lotos Club in New York a message from Lloyd George which by urging America to accelerate the flow of men to Europe implied, at least in Wilson's opinion, laggardness on the part of the Administration.[28] Reading's speech, the sort of appeal to people rather than to government that Wilson himself sometimes employed, outraged the President. He contemplated telling Reading that the speech was sufficient reason to ask for his recall. House, who along

[27] Baker to War Department, Mar. 28, 1918, and Gen. Peyton C. March to Baker, Mar. 29, 1918, *U.S. Army in the World War*, Vol. 2, pp. 261-62, 264, respectively. Pershing, *My Experiences*, Vol. 1, pp. 360-65.

[28] Reading's speech (including Lloyd George's warning, "In War, time is vital. It is impossible to exaggerate the importance of getting American reinforcements across the Atlantic in the shortest possible space of time.") was printed on the front page of the *New York Times*, Mar. 28, 1918. Charles Evans Hughes, Wilson's opponent for the presidency in 1916, also spoke to the Lotos Club. Another speaker, George Harvey, Wilson's ardent enemy, pointedly urged the cessation of "futile attempts to differentiate between Huns who command and Huns who murder." *Ibid*. For full texts of the Lotos Club speeches see *"Across the Flood"*; *Addresses at the Dinner in Honor of the Earl of Reading at the Lotos Club, New York, March 27th, 1918*, New York, 1918.

Reading had asked Lloyd George for a statement that would stimulate the American people and Wilson to draft one million additional men. Reading to Lloyd George, Mar. 25, 1918, FO 800/209.

with Wiseman came to Washington on the 28th, talked Wilson out of the idea, and as a substitute suggested that the British government be asked to state publicly that the Administration had done everything possible to help in the war. Wiseman enthusiastically approved this stratagem because, as he told House, Lloyd George, unless checked in advance, might try to blame the failure in France on Wilson. Wiseman helped Reading compose the request to Lloyd George for a public statement and separately cabled the Foreign Office that House set great store on the issuance of such a statement.[29] Although grumbling that the Americans were in fact responsible for the great crisis by having "fallen egregiously short of their programme," Lloyd George nonetheless authorized a press release lauding the American contribution.[30] Wilson was delighted: "that pockets Mr. Lloyd George for the moment," he said.[31]

Public praise of the American war effort was a small price for what Lloyd George believed he had extracted from Wilson. Before issuing the statement to the press he learned from Reading that the President had agreed to embark 120,000 infantrymen each month during April, May, June, and July, as Lloyd George had requested.[32] The Prime Minister bragged to his associates that he had at last stirred Wilson into action by sending the message Reading read to the Lotos Club.[33] But Lloyd George's jubilation was short-lived. For whereas he interpreted Reading's cable to mean that Wilson would ship a total of 480,000 men to be brigaded with French and British divisions,

[29] House Diary, Mar. 29, 1918; Wiseman to Drummond, Mar. 31, 1918, WWP 4; Reading to Lloyd George, Mar. 31, 1918, Lloyd George Papers F/60/2/50.

[30] Balfour to Reading, Apr. 1, 1918, Reading's Private Papers, FO 800/211. The London *Times* for Apr. 2, 1918 stated that the Prime Minister wanted the British people to know that "President Wilson has shown the greatest anxiety to do everything possible to assist the Allies, and has left nothing undone which could contribute thereto."

[31] House Diary, Apr. 9, 1918.

[32] Reading to Lloyd George, Mar. 30, 1918, WWP 3.

[33] Lord Riddell, *Lord Riddell's War Diary, 1914-1918*, London, 1933, p. 322.

Reading plainly stated that the President approved brigading "provided General Pershing finds it practicable."[34] Because Lloyd George chose to overlook this condition and because Pershing tenaciously resisted all but token and temporary brigading, for training purposes only, the use of American manpower remained a source of ill feeling between the two countries for the remainder of the spring.

On April 3 Lloyd George personally informed Pershing of the President's "pledge" of 480,000 infantrymen and machinegunners. Pershing refused to believe that the President had in effect endorsed the concept of brigading, which the shipment of infantry and machinegun units without the other components of a division meant. Secretary Baker, learning of Pershing's and Lloyd George's conversation, cabled Wilson from France asking what specific commitments he had made to Reading.[35] Wilson replied that he had agreed "upon no details whatever. . . ."[36] In making so definite a statement, Wilson was not being entirely candid. The figure of 120,000 men per month surely was established as a shipping goal, for the United States Shipping Board on April 5 was making plans at the President's direction to transport that number.[37] Apparently, however, neither Wilson nor Reading fully realized that by shipping only infantrymen they would virtually force brigading upon Pershing, for the latter could not construct divisions or an army solely from infantry and machinegunners. In Wilson's defense, it should be said that he was extremely reluctant to make any firm commitments in the absence of his Secretary of War. He attempted to avoid seeing Reading[38] and failing that, stressed to the Ambassador that military details and the extent of brigading must be left to Baker and Per-

[34] Reading to Lloyd George, Mar. 30, 1918, WWP 3.

[35] Baker to Wilson, Apr. 5, 1918, Bliss Papers, Box 75; Pershing, *My Experiences*, Vol. 1, pp. 382-83; Trask, *United States in the Supreme War Council*, p. 83.

[36] Wilson to Baker, Apr. 6, 1918, in Baker, *Wilson Life & Letters*, Vol. 8, p. 77.

[37] Lansing to Page, Apr. 5, 1918, *Foreign Relations, 1918*, Sup. 1, Vol. 1, pp. 198-99.

[38] Lansing Desk Diary, Mar. 30, 1918.

shing to decide. He promised Reading on March 28 that he would do his "damnedst" to help the Allies, but a few days later he also told a group of foreign newsmen that his "instinctive judgment" opposed the feeding of American soldiers into the French and British armies.[39]

Wilson revealed his rather cloudy understanding of the brigading controversy to Wiseman on April 1, a few days prior to Wiseman's leaving for Europe. Wilson confessed that he did not understand the military situation. He was convinced, however, that the result of the war depended on the number of reserves available on either side. If Germany now had larger reserves she might win the war before the Americans arrived, but Wilson refused to believe that would happen. He chided the British for not having revealed to Colonel House during his visit their desperate need for manpower and for not having made shipping available earlier. But regardless of the past, he was now directing that as many men as possible be shipped, and the British, with that assurance, ought to keep calm. He hoped that the British generals were not as "rattled" as British politicians had shown themselves to be by their frenzied calls for American infantry. At no point in his talk with Wiseman did Wilson mention brigading or indicate that he was displeased with Pershing. In fact he dwelt more on America's responsibility to arrange a just conclusion of the war than on the prosecution of it. Wilson, at least, was following his own advice to keep calm.[40]

With a sheaf of shorthand notes from his conversation with Wilson,[41] Wiseman sailed from New York on April 9. He went as a quasi-American observer. As Reading informed Balfour, "Wiseman goes to London because Col House wished it so much & of course I assented. The P[resident] also expressed pleasure that he was about to pay a visit to England and is really anxious to get a report at

[39] Baker, *Wilson Life & Letters*, Vol. 8, pp. 59, 79.
[40] Wiseman, "Notes on Interview with the President—April 1st, 1918, at 5.30 p.m.," Balfour Papers 49741, British Museum. A copy of these notes has now been placed in WWP.
[41] "Miscellaneous Notes," WWP 84.

first hand of all the tremendously important events."[42] Serving Wilson as an observer was an unorthodox and complimentary task for Wiseman of which he naturally was proud, but in later years he exaggerated his position at this time to that of an executive agent for the President. In 1944 he remembered that Wilson asked him to attend the May meeting of the Supreme War Council at Abbeville and there explain to Pershing the President's views on the use of American manpower. When Wiseman, according to his later account, protested that Pershing would surely object to receiving a presidential message from a British officer, Wilson then asked him to brief A. H. Frazier, the American diplomatic observer at the Supreme War Council, who could in turn brief Pershing. This, Wiseman said in 1944, he did.[43] The implication of Wiseman's memory is that Wilson sent him to Europe to instruct Pershing, indirectly, to accede to the Allies' desire for amalgamation. Wiseman did indeed visit Frazier and Pershing and, as we shall see, did play a part in the Abbeville conference, but there is no reason to believe that he delivered directly or indirectly anything like instructions or a reprimand from Wilson to Pershing. Aside from other difficulties with Wiseman's 1944 account, there is the fact that he left the United States prior to Secretary Baker's return from Europe, and Wilson surely would not have vouchsafed any explanations

---

[42] Reading to Balfour, Apr. 5, 1918, Private Secretary Archives, 1917-1924, A. J. Balfour, FO 800/200. House Diary, Apr. 9, 1918: "It has been definitely arranged for Wiseman to go to Europe at once. Reading objected, but the President agrees with me that he should go, and while I cannot use the President's name to the Ambassador, I have pressed it upon him as my desire until Reading was compelled to yield. I had to promise to look out for him during Sir William's absence. . . ."

Reading to Lloyd George, Apr. 5, 1918, Lloyd George Papers F/60/2/53: "Wiseman is really an invaluable person to us and I am most sorry to lose him even temporarily. He supplies the rarely satisfied need of one with whom I can talk and be sure you [sic] will get some suggestion at least well worthy of consideration."

[43] Wiseman to Arthur C. Murray (Lord Elibank), Mar. 17, 1944, printed in Murray's At Close Quarters, A Sidelight on Anglo-American Diplomatic Relations, London, 1946, pp. 20-23. See also Wiseman to Charles Seymour, Jan. 28, 1944, HP 45:13.

to Wiseman for Pershing before he had heard Baker's report on the war situation.

As Baker and Wiseman made their opposite ways across the Atlantic in early April, the question of brigading hung momentarily suspended. But not the course of the war. On April 9 the Germans opened another successful offensive, and the manpower crisis again faced the British with all its original intensity. Since Pershing chose not to believe that Wilson had meant to pledge 120,000 men per month to the British, Lloyd George despaired of dealing with him and hastened a fresh appeal to Wilson. He instructed Reading to tell Wilson that the "difference of opinion between General Pershing . . . and what we conceive to be the President's policy . . . is so fundamental and touches so nearly the issue of the whole war that we are bound to have the matter clearer."[44] Reading once again went to the White House in the hope of an unequivocal answer, but Wilson, still awaiting Baker, declined to discuss the matter. Reading, reflecting Wilson's irritation, warned London that the misunderstanding would have to wait to be cleared up directly by Wilson and Baker. Meantime, the Ambassador secured some help from House. The Colonel wrote Wilson pointing out the difficulties a disaster in France would cause the Administration domestically and questioning whether Pershing's goal of an independent army was worth the risk. The "thing to be done now is to stop the Germans," House wrote, "and to stop them it is evident that we must put in every man that is available." House failed to sway Wilson who still waited for Baker.[45]

On April 19 Wilson cancelled a Cabinet meeting in order to have a long conference with the just-returned Secretary of War. Apparently Baker did sympathize, as Lloyd George insisted he did, with a form of temporary brigading, for

[44] Balfour to Reading, Apr. 8, 1918, Reading's Private Papers, FO 800/211. Balfour said that "broadly speaking" Baker and Bliss sympathized with the British position. The paraphrase of this cable given to Wilson and to House was made much milder in tone. HP 16:30.

[45] Reading to Lloyd George and Balfour, Apr. 10, 1918, WWP 3; House to Wilson, Apr. 9, 1918, HP 49:10.

out of his conference with Wilson came a new presidential decision undertaking to ship 120,000 infantrymen and machinegunners per month during April through July. Assignment of the troops thus shipped would remain, however, in the hands of Pershing, and the American government reserved the right to depart from the policy it now stated should the military situation change. Baker conveyed the results of his and Wilson's conference to Reading in the form of a memorandum, which became known as the Baker-Reading agreement (21 April 1918).[46] Reading, while conceding the loopholes contained in the memorandum, urged his government to accept it without objection, "for I am sure that no better result will be obtained." The British quickly accepted.[47]

Pershing did not. Lord Milner, newly appointed Secretary of State for War, confronted him with the Baker-Reading agreement during Pershing's April 21-24 visit to London. Pershing, in his own words, "declined to consider the information [in the agreement] as conclusive."[48] The British were stunned and angered by Pershing's behavior. Milner, however, kept his head and after consulting Wiseman, who had just arrived in London and who apparently gave Milner no cause to think the Baker-Reading agreement reduced Pershing's authority, proposed an arrangement that Pershing accepted. The Pershing-Milner agreement (24 April 1918) differed from the Baker-Reading agreement by allowing other units beside infantry and machinegunners to be included in the 120,000 quota. Further, it applied only to May, after which a new arrangement would be required.[49] Reading complained stoutly of this modification,

[46] Baker, *Wilson Life & Letters*, Vol. 8, pp. 96-97. Copy of the agreement in *U.S. Army in the World War*, Vol. 2, pp. 336-37. See also Trask, *United States in the Supreme War Council*, p. 85.

[47] Reading to Balfour, Apr. 21, 1918, and Balfour to Reading, Apr. 23, 1918, Reading's Private Papers, FO 800/211.

[48] Pershing, *My Experiences*, Vol. 2, p. 6.

[49] Wiseman to Reading, Apr. 24, 1918. Reading's Private Papers, FO 800/211. Milner talked with Wiseman on the morning of Apr. 23. Milner Diary, Apr. 23, 1918. Text of the Pershing-Milner agreement in *U.S. Army in the World War*, Vol. 3, pp. 91-92.

but Baker was content to let it stand, and Wiseman reported that Milner considered it "fairly satisfactory."[50] Pershing had again escaped the controls the British hoped to impose on him from Washington.

Both the Baker-Reading and Pershing-Milner agreements were of course bilateral. Not surprisingly the French suspected a deal to their disadvantage had been made, and at the Supreme War Council meeting in May they attempted to junk the Pershing-Milner accord in favor of a three-power agreement. Foch and Clemenceau violently condemned the Pershing-Milner agreement because it appeared to loan American soldiers to Britain exclusively. Ironically, Lloyd George was forced to defend the half-loaf he had won from Pershing. He assured the French that no disposition of the troops was to be made prior to their arrival. Foch still wanted the Council to appeal to Wilson for a clearcut approval of brigading, but Lloyd George feared placing Wilson in a position to decide between the council and Pershing. After two days of often uninhibited debating, the French had to submit to an Anglo-American settlement.[51] They, after all, had only the supreme commander, whereas the Americans had the manpower and the British the ships.

The Abbeville agreement—in effect a month-long extension of the Pershing-Milner agreement—provided for the preferential shipping in June of infantry and machine-

[50] Reading to Balfour, Apr. 30, 1918, Reading's Private Papers, FO 800/211. Lloyd George replied (Balfour to Reading, May 4, 1918, *ibid.*), saying he was equally disappointed but explaining, "We have . . . been forced to make best bargain we could with man who is responsible on the spot. General Pershing is an obstinate man."

Baker wrote the President of Reading's disappointment and said, "I told him, however, that I felt he and I were too far from the situation to see this as clearly as those in Europe and that so far as I was concerned I felt it my duty to cooperate to carry out the arrangement which seemed wise to Lord Milner and General Pershing." Baker to Wilson, Apr. 29, 1918, Baker Papers, Box 8. Wiseman to Reading, Apr. 24, 1918, Reading's Private Papers, FO 800/211.

[51] A. H. Frazier, American observer at the Supreme War Council, reported the "acrimonious" French attacks in his cables to Lansing, May 1 and 4, 1918, HP 35:66C and 35:79 respectively. Trask, *United States in the Supreme War Council*, pp. 87-88.

gunners for service with the British or French, as Pershing would determine. In exchange for his concession, Pershing received the council's formal adherence to the principle of the early establishment of an American army.[52] The compromise thus reached was, according to A. H. Frazier, American observer at the council, the result of private negotiations between Pershing and Lloyd George, with Frazier and Wiseman acting as intermediaries.[53] Wiseman's presence as an observer for Wilson and House perhaps increased Pershing's desire to appear cooperative, but chiefly his contribution was that of a conciliator. Frazier wrote that Wiseman's "knack at smoothing over rough places" greatly facilitated the negotiation of the Abbeville agreement.[54]

Having played a part in the Abbeville agreement did not make Wiseman a defender of it. On the contrary, he soon decided that the Allies had erred by giving in to Pershing. They should have, he thought, admitted inability to agree with Pershing, placed Foch's arguments for amalgamation before Wilson, and let him make a decision.[55] Acting on his second thoughts, Wiseman set about undermining Pershing's position before the next discussion of the use of American soldiers came up in June. As soon as the Abbeville meeting broke up he visited Clemenceau and urged him to dispatch Foch's statement criticizing Pershing to Washington. Clemenceau replied that the statement had already gone to Washington as an expression of the sentiments of both the French and British governments.[56] Wiseman cabled the Allies' unhappiness with Abbeville to House and induced Frazier to report similarly to the State Department. To House he characterized Pershing as sus-

[52] The Abbeville agreement is printed in *U.S. Army in the World War*, Vol. 2, pp. 370-71.

[53] Frazier to House, Sept. 25, 1936, HP 8:7: "Willie Wiseman and I repeatedly went from Lloyd George's rooms to Pershing's until a formula was finally agreed on that satisfied both parties."

[54] Frazier to House, May 10, 1918, HP 8:4. Wiseman had an interview with Pershing on May 3. Pershing Diary, May 3, 1918, Pershing Papers, Box 4-5, Library of Congress.

[55] Wiseman to Reading, May 8, 1918, WWP 107.

[56] Frazier to Lansing and House, May 5, 1918, HP 35:79.

picious of the Allies, obsessed with the idea of an autonomous army, and unable to get along with Bliss. Pershing acted, Wiseman said, as if he were a head of government rather than a field commander. Plainly, Wiseman hoped to impress on House and Wilson, who received a copy of the cable, that the Allies signed the Abbeville agreement only because of Pershing's unrestrained power.[57]

Nonetheless, the British by signing the agreement weakened the force of these tardy objections to it. House, although he agreed with Wiseman's preference for Foch's plan and forwarded Wiseman's reports to Wilson,[58] realized that there was little chance of undoing Abbeville. He peevishly compared the British government's panicky requests with what they officially accepted from Pershing. "In the future," he asked Wiseman, "how can we be certain that we are not working uselessly?"[59]

President Wilson, finding the Abbeville agreement "entirely satisfactory," showed no inclination to follow Wiseman's suggestion that he go before the people and explain that America would delay the formation of an independent army in order to enter the fight at once. Wilson agreed with Baker that the Abbeville arrangement had been "arrived at by just the right sort of conference in the right way" and that if it really were inadequate a new agreement should be worked out by Foch and Pershing.[60] No

[57] *Ibid.*; Wiseman to House, May 11, 1918, WWP 64 (copy in Woodrow Wilson Papers, Series 2, Box 167, Library of Congress). This was a 1500-word cable in which Wiseman rehearsed the various stages of the controversy over the use of American manpower and gave his assessment of the military situation. He stated that Pershing and Bliss were not on amicable terms and that Bliss, with the other Permanent Military Representatives, foresaw grave danger unless the Allies somehow received new reserves, i.e., more Americans. He concluded: "I have not shown this cable to any one or consulted them as to suggestions which I have ventured to make just as if I were talking to you."

[58] House to Wilson, May 12, 1918, HP 49:10.

[59] House to Wiseman, May 12, 1918, WWP 64.

[60] Wilson to Baker, May 6, 1918, and Baker to Wilson, May 10, 1918, Baker Papers, Box 8. Wiseman's suggestion was made in Wiseman to House, May 11, 1918, WWP 64. See note 57 above.

doubt Wilson considered the Anglo-French efforts to renege on the Abbeville agreement as but another sign of their rattled vacillation. Beyond directing Pershing to strive for a "constant sympathy" with Foch, the Administration made no effort to curb Pershing until after Wiseman's return from Europe.[61]

Before leaving Paris Wiseman obtained support for his campaign against Pershing from two important Americans. Frazier, as we have seen, repeated Wiseman's objections to the Abbeville agreement to the State Department. He also forwarded to Washington Wiseman's suggestion that some sort of high commissioner be sent to Europe to take charge of the negotiations that Pershing presently conducted directly with heads of government and war ministers.[62] General Bliss, whose position at the Supreme War Council had been completely overshadowed by Pershing, also sent high praise of Wiseman to Washington. "I do not know," he wrote Baker, "of the many men with whom I have been associated here, anyone who is better informed than he [Wiseman] or of cooler and more dispassionate judgment."[63] Such words from Bliss were bound to enhance Wiseman's standing with Baker and Wilson, for both valued highly the opinions of the sagacious old general.[64]

On May 29, four days after Wiseman's return, the Presi-

[61] Pershing to Baker, May 15, 1918, and Baker to Wilson, May 16, 1918, Wilson Papers, Series 2, Box 167.

[62] Frazier to Lansing and House, May 7, 1918, HP 35:66C. Lloyd George apparently had instructed Reading to urge the President to appoint a political representative who could overrule Pershing to the Supreme War Council, but Reading doubted the wisdom of such an attempt. "It is obvious we should try to work with Pershing reconciled to or agreeing with our views, rather than with him discontented and trying to hinder Wilson's plan." Reading to Wiseman, May 9, 1918, WWP 107. Wiseman agreed with Reading and was obviously trying to shift some of Pershing's responsibilities onto a high commissioner who need not necessarily outrank Pershing. Wiseman to Reading, May 10, 1918, WWP 107.

[63] Bliss to Baker, May 11, 1918, Bliss Papers, Box 74.

[64] Wilson to Baker, June 19, 1918, Baker Papers Box 8: "Bliss is a remarkable man. Every word he writes strengthens my impression that he is a real thinking man, who takes the pain to think straight."

149

dent invited him to the White House for an hour-long interview. After listening to Wiseman's exposition of what had
happened at Abbeville (apparently including Pershing's
complaints about the Administration's slowness in providing men and supplies), Wilson remarked that the
dispute seemed somewhat academic because Baker was
shipping all infantry and machinegun units as quickly as
possible. Pershing, Wilson thought, was only asserting the
principle of nonbrigading while in fact loaning his men to
the Allies. But if Pershing really was impairing military
effectiveness, Wilson promised that "he would be ordered
to stand out of the way. . . ." As to Wiseman's suggestion
of a high commissioner in Europe, Wilson could see no advantage in it, for "Pershing had full authority, and the part
America was playing in Europe was purely that of rendering military assistance."[65]

In this remark lay the crux of the brigade problem. Wilson had brought the United States into the Supreme War
Council, a body which Lloyd George devised to assert strategic unity through political means over the various national
commanders. Yet Wilson refused to admit that matters of
military coordination were matters for only the politicians
to decide. So determined was he to steer an independent
course concerning postwar plans, the "political" matters
that really counted to him, that he refused to allow a
permanent delegate to sit on the Supreme War Council,
which, he feared, hoped to commit the United States dip-
lomatically.[66] To Wilson the council was an executive
agency designed to facilitate the actual fighting of the war.
When it agreed on a military policy he was willing to support it. The anomaly of Pershing's debating on an equal
level with Foch and the European political leaders did not
seem to bother Wilson at all. In part this was a result of his

[65] Wiseman to Drummond, May 30, 1918 (CXP 627, 628, 629),
WWP 129.

[66] On February 18 Wilson severely reprimanded the prime ministers
for having issued a political opinion on behalf of the Supreme War
Council without consulting him. See Baker, *Wilson Life & Letters*,
Vol. 7, pp. 519, 549.

own distance from the battlefield and his consequent reluctance to override the man on the spot. Consciously or not, he also seemed to consider the Supreme War Council as an organization of Europeans for dealing with the American army, rather than an organization of which the United States government was one of four components. As a result, the American relation to the council was never that of the Europeans; indeed, the council failed to become as effective as it might have because of the American insistence on standing only partially in it.

Wiseman had told his superiors previously that Wilson's concept of the Supreme War Council was not the same as theirs.[67] Now he told them that Wilson considered the council in combination with Foch to be the supreme military authority. Wiseman therefore advised, in a high priority cable designed to reach Lloyd George before the June council meeting got underway, that any request or recommendation to the President take the form of a formal recommendation by Foch with the endorsement of the council. Then Pershing would be obliged to make his objections, if any, directly to the President rather than in the sessions of the Council. Wiseman also warned that Wilson was sure that America was sending over all the men she could, despite what the Europeans or Pershing thought. That being Wilson's feeling, Wiseman said, "surely we can do no more than record our thanks for the prompt help and urge that their preparations here should be speeded-up so that even more can be sent until the emergency is passed."[68]

Apparently Wiseman's advice, also sent in abbreviated form by Reading to Lloyd George,[69] prompted the June

[67] "Miscellaneous Notes," WWP 84.

[68] Wiseman to Drummond, May 30, 1918 (CXP 624), WWP 129.

[69] There can be no doubt that Reading to Lloyd George, May 29, 1918, WWP 3, was inspired by Wiseman after his talk with the President. Reading said: "The suggestion I wish to convey is that your Supreme Council could pass a resolution affirming General Foch's recommendations as to sending of infantrymen and machine gun units and then communicate it either to Frazier or by the French or British

recommendations of the Supreme War Council to Wilson. Meeting June 1-3 at Versailles, the council immediately reached a stalemate with Pershing. It looked like Abbeville all over again. But after a huddle between Pershing, Milner, and Foch, an agreement covering June and July was reached. Under its provisions 500,000 men would be shipped, but only 310,000 of them would be detached infantry and machine-gunners. In other words, Pershing would get 190,000 troops of his own choosing. With this agreement reached, the three prime ministers composed a message to Wilson thanking him for the "remarkable promptness" of American aid and, with a suddenness that was itself remarkable, asking that America now plan to send over a total of 100 divisions.[70] One hundred divisions, all told, would total some 4,000,000 men, or twice the number until then contemplated. The prime ministers said they were basing their request on General Foch's estimates and were satisfied he had not exaggerated the needs of the case. Although Pershing subsequently ridiculed the notion that 100 divisions would be needed, at the time he confined his reservations on the point to a cryptic recommendation to Baker that "men be called out as fast as they can be handled."[71] Having finished its two pieces of business, the Supreme War Council adjourned, in Frazier's words, "with unexpected celerity."[72]

On June 5 Wiseman telephoned news of the Pershing-Milner-Foch agreement and the prime ministers' statement to House, on vacation at Magnolia. The latter, no doubt with Wiseman's encouragement, found the developments alarming and immediately concluded that a deal had been made between Pershing and the Allies. His conclusion was logical. The new shipping schedule still gave priority

---

Ambassador to the President. If General Pershing wishes to raise objection let it come from him to his own Government if he desires to do so."

[70] Minutes and resolutions of the meeting are printed in *U.S. Army in the World War*, Vol. 2, pp. 438-41. See also Pershing, *My Experiences*, Vol. 2, pp. 71-83.

[71] *Ibid.*, pp. 82-83, 105-106.

[72] Frazier to Lansing, June 3, 1918, HP 35:66C.

to infantry but it also gave Pershing a large number of other troops. The prime ministers' cry for a vastly increased American army could also serve Pershing if it jolted the Administration into a new crash program to rush men to Europe. The conferees at Versailles, House thought, had either panicked or, as was surely the actual case, had purposely exaggerated. House labeled the 100-division plea "stupid," particularly since Wiseman and Reading had assured Lloyd George that Wilson was willing to send an unlimited number of men and resented the constant and seemingly impulsive alarms for more men.[73] Wilson, however, took the 100-division request in good faith and began plans for raising that number. In August he learned indirectly that the British did not have enough shipping to accommodate 100 divisions, and he felt he had been duped. How characteristic it was, he complained to Baker; "Would that we were dealing with responsible persons."[74]

In the long run the stratagem was, as House said, "stupid," for it confirmed again Wilson's distrust of the British government. But in the short run the deal between Pershing and the Allies probably achieved what they intended. With a sense of extreme urgency the British and American shipping officials far outstripped their goals for June and July. Thereafter the numbers hauled continued to increase and at the same time British and French drafts for 1918 completed their training. As a result the man-

[73] House Diary, June 5, 1918. House's opinion that the request for 100 divisions indicated a deal between the prime ministers and Pershing is more convincing than the conclusion by Trask, *United States in the Supreme War Council*, p. 92, that the prime ministers' message "implied severe criticism of General Pershing."

Lloyd George later wrote: "Conceivably the 100-division figure was put forward in the hope that by asking for 100 American divisions we might get at least 50." *War Memoirs*, Vol. 5, p. 3,061. Note also the following sentence in Lloyd George to Reading, Aug. 26, 1918, Lloyd George Papers F/43/1/15: "As I told you . . . I am anxious to use the shipping lever for the purpose of bringing pressure to bear upon the French and the Americans to take over a part of our line and thus enable us to give a rest to our troops."

[74] Wilson to Baker, Aug. 9, 1918, Baker Papers, Box 8.

power shortage and the brigade controversy it spawned eased almost completely.[75]

So did the efforts of Wiseman and House to demote Pershing. Wiseman returned from Europe with the impression that Pershing, "an odd man," should devote all his time to the training and command of his troops. Pershing had too much to do, Wiseman told House, and in addition suffered from a "big head" that was bound "to grow until something happens to reduce it." Wiseman would reduce it by appointing a high commissioner, possibly House, to represent the United States in its dealings with the Allied statesmen. He proposed a consolidation of all American agencies (e.g., financial, shipping, and blockade representatives) in Europe, after the manner of the British consolidation under Reading in the United States.[76]

The President heard much of this directly from Wiseman[77] and subsequently from House. On June 3 House wrote: "What Sir William and others have told me concerning the lack of coordination of our interests in France and their constantly increasing magnitude leads me to suggest a plan looking towards a more orderly outcome." House went on to blame the German successes of the spring on the failure of Western generalship and specifically the failure of Western commanders to yield in fact to the over-all command of Foch. Pershing had acted as poorly as the others and by engaging in political negotiations had neglected the training of his staff. Even if Pershing confined himself to training and command it was doubtful, House said, that he had "the capacity to build up a staff adequate to the needs of the occasion." Therefore, House urged that Pershing be relieved of all duties not directly related to training and command. Specifically, House proposed that E. R. Stettinius, Assistant Secretary of War, take charge of

[75] Edward N. Hurley, *The Bridge to France*, Philadelphia, 1927, p. 123; Trask, *United States in the Supreme War Council*, p. 95.
[76] Wiseman to Reading, May 8, 1918, WWP 107; House Diary, May 25, 1918.
[77] Wiseman to Drummond, May 30, 1918 (CXP 627, 628, 629), WWP 129.

all behind-the-lines operations of the army and that Vance McCormick go to Paris as chairman of an American Board Overseas. McCormick would handle all negotiations with the Allied governments and would keep in direct touch with the President.[78]

Wilson referred House's proposal to Baker, with a note that the candor of the letter resulted from House's knowing "that he can say what he pleases to me without parliamentary circumlocution. . . ." Baker responded that House's remarks were essentially correct, but he objected to putting Stettinius or any other civilian in charge of Pershing's supply operation. Regarding Pershing, Baker promised to emphasize to him that his task was military and under Foch.[79] Apparently because of the weight of other problems (particularly studies required for implementing the 100-division plan and for determining the feasibility of dispatching troops to Siberia), Baker waited nearly a month before acting on the Wiseman-House plan of reorganization.[80] In early July he wrote Pershing that Gen. George W. Goethals would be appointed to head the supply department in Europe, "rather in a coordinate than subordinate relationship to you. . . ." In addition, Pershing was to surrender to Bliss responsibility for "military diplomacy," since the President had determined that all inter-Allied military questions must be handled by the Permanent Military Representatives.[81]

Pershing craftily beat Baker to the punch by creating a subordinate supply command and appointing one of his

[78] House to Wilson, June 3, 1918, HP 49:10. Reading thought House's proposal would be adopted. Reading to Balfour, June 11, 1918, FO 371/3492.

[79] Wilson to Baker, June 7, 1918, and Baker to Wilson, June 8, 1918, Baker Papers, Box 8.

[80] It is important to note that at exactly this time House and others were also suggesting some type of American commission to Russia and nominating the same people, notably Herbert Hoover and Vance McCormick, for the jobs in Russia and Europe. See, e.g., House to Wilson, June 4 and 13, 1918, HP 49:10. See pp. 182ff. below.

[81] Baker to Pershing, July 6, 1918, printed in Pershing, *My Experiences*, Vol. 2, pp. 181-87. See also *ibid.*, p. 180.

own officers to it. He did submit to Baker's instructions concerning military diplomacy, but not without remarking, with much truth, if diplomacy is equated with tact, that "very little of my time has been taken up with that sort of thing. . . ."[82] There is little doubt that Pershing found out the source of the attempt to curb him. A few days after replying to Baker he cabled House that he had never performed any diplomatic or political function aside from arranging for the associating of American troops with the Allies. "Anyway," he added tartly, "no one else could handle these details which . . . are largely of the past."

So they were. The course of actions set in motion by Wiseman to restrict Pershing's authority had not matured until the manpower crisis was virtually over. House informed Pershing on August 21 that he need not "have any anxiety whatever" over the matter.[83]

THE BRITISH search for manpower would have been exasperating enough had the people of the United Kingdom been really united. But the age-old dissidence of Catholic Ireland made the problem especially trying. The Asquith government was unsure that the Irish would submit to military conscription and exempted them from the provisions of the conscription act passed in June 1916. Later that same year, the government's brutal suppression of the Easter Rebellion, a small affair rendered sinister by German support, and the subsequent execution of the rebellion's leader, Sir Roger Casement, wiped out what-

[82] Pershing to Baker, July 28, 1918, in *ibid.*, pp. 187-91. See also *ibid.*, p. 179.

[83] Pershing to House, Aug. 7, 1918, HP 15:45. House had written Pershing on July 4 urging him to delegate some of his duties to others. On August 21 House cabled Pershing: "The President has been visiting me for several days at Magnolia and I do not believe you need have any anxiety whatever concerning matter mentioned in your [cable] 126. . . ." Both letter and cable are in HP 15:45.

Pershing at last enjoyed a minor revenge on Wiseman in November 1918, when he notified House that Wiseman was talking indiscreetly about the "secret" travel plans of the President. Pershing to House, Nov. 6, 1918, HP 15:45.

ever grudging sympathy Irishmen had previously shown Britain in the war. The number of Irish volunteers for the British army declined rapidly, and since indications were that conscription would only lead to full-fledged rebellion, Ireland as a source of manpower seemed hopeless after 1916.

In Parliament members from Protestant Northern Ireland demanded that the government extend conscription over Ireland, both for the men it would produce and as a symbol of British authority. Irish nationalists on the other hand demanded home rule, or independence in the case of the Sinn Feiners, as the only answer to the rebellion. At the beginning of the war Asquith had promised home rule once the war was over, and John Redmond, the Irish leader in Parliament, had pledged Ireland's support in the war in return. Now the truce was at an end.[84]

The Irish problem reached crisis proportions in the spring of 1918. It need not have, except that the manpower shortage forced Lloyd George's hand. When he introduced legislation in January 1918 to extend the draft to previously exempted categories, the Ulster members objected to the exclusion of Ireland. Nevertheless the bill passed. But when in the wake of the March offensive the government prepared to raise to age 50 the ceiling on men subject to the draft, the Ulster and Unionist members, as well as organized labor, demanded that Ireland also be conscripted. Labor informed Lloyd George that it would "bitterly resent" a further "comb-out" of English laborers "whilst we exempted the Irish peasantry which had done well out of the war and had given us nothing but trouble in return." Lloyd George decided it was necessary, in order

---

[84] The fundamentals of the Irish problem are presented entertainingly in A.J.P. Taylor, *English History, 1914-1945*, Oxford, 1965, esp. pp. 16-17, 21, 55-58. Charles Callan Tansill, *America and the Fight for Irish Freedom, 1866-1922*, New York, 1957, gives much greater detail, pervaded by an unrestrained anti-British bias. See David W. Savage, "The Irish Question in British Politics, 1914-1916," unpub. doctoral diss., Princeton University, 1963, for a balanced treatment of developments prior to 1917.

not to rile Ulster men, Unionists, and labor, to assert the British authority to draft Irishmen. To sweeten the pill for Ireland, he tacitly held out the possibility of home rule.[85]

Before deciding to press for the principle of Irish conscription, Lloyd George sounded out another party interested in Irish affairs—the United States government. The United States was the traditional refuge of oppressed Irishmen and the source of much of the financial and moral backing of the Irish independence movement. Irish-Americans formed a vocal and often influential faction in American politics, especially in the Democratic party. Americans generally sympathized with Ireland's aspirations; the executions resulting from the Easter Rebellion caused widespread anti-Irish feeling in the United States. Thereafter Irish-American hostility hampered the likelihood of American partiality toward Britain and the Allies. Some Irish-Americans aided German agents in the United States, and one of Wiseman's chief duties in 1916-17 was to uncover their subversion of British interests.[86]

The American declaration of war did not automatically transform Irish-Americans into Anglophiles. In April 1917 Wilson emphasized to the British that failure to arrange some form of self-government for Ireland made "absolutely cordial" cooperation difficult for his government. Ever deft, Lloyd George responded by suggesting that the President would do well to make his complaint to Balfour (who was en route to Washington). It was, after all, Lloyd George pointed out, Balfour's Unionist Party that was opposed to home rule.[87] Not surprisingly, the Prime Minister's shifty suggestion was not adopted.[88] Shortly thereafter he

[85] Lloyd George, *War Memoirs*, Vol. 5, pp. 2,664-68. See also Taylor, *English History*, pp. 103-104.

[86] Link, *Wilson*, Vol. 3, pp. 22-23, 161-62, Vol. 4, pp. 14, 65-66, 161.

[87] Wilson to Lansing (for Page), Apr. 10, 1917, *Foreign Relations, The Lansing Papers, 1914-1921*, 2 vols., Washington, D.C., 1940, Vol. 2, pp. 4-5; Page to Lansing, Apr. 18, 1917, SD 841d.00/106.

[88] Balfour to Foreign Office, May 2, 1917: "Neither President nor any Member of Government has said a word to me about Ireland. . . ." But four days later he reported that the Irish question "is apparently the only difficulty we have to face here and its settlement would

himself took the initiative by calling a convention of all Irish factions to work out a mutually acceptable formula for home rule. The convention chairman was, significantly, Sir Horace Plunkett, who had ranched in Wyoming and considered himself a confidant of Wilson and House. For the remainder of the war British efforts to conciliate the Irish were as much directed to American as to Irish sensibilities.[89]

During his visit to London in August 1917 Wiseman impressed on Plunkett House's concern over the home rule question and arranged for Plunkett to send Wilson and House the secret reports of the Irish Convention.[90] The convention soon bogged down as a result of the obstinacy of both northern and southern Irishmen. Although Lloyd George showed sporadic interest in the convention's labors, it seemed doubtful that he expected any result. His main hope was to buy time. When he was obliged to consider home rule legislation in April 1918 he found that the result of the convention was not the desired "substantial agreement" but a final report endorsed by less than half of the convention members.[91]

While the War Cabinet was considering both conscription and home rule, Balfour consulted House for a prediction as to the effect conscription in Ireland would have in America.[92] House passed Balfour's cable on to Wilson,

---

no doubt greatly facilitate vigorous and lasting co-operation of United States Government in the war." Both cables in FO 371/3070.

[89] Taylor, *English History*, pp. 83, 103. On Plunkett, see Seymour, *Intimate Papers*, Vol. 3, pp. 75-76; Link, *Wilson*, Vol. 4, pp. 108-109; and Margaret Digby, *Horace Plunkett, An Anglo-American Irishman*, Oxford, 1949, *passim*. L. S. Amery took credit for the idea of the Irish convention; Amery Diary, Dec. 31, 1917.

[90] Wiseman to House, Aug. 2, 1917, WWP 27; Plunkett Diary, Aug. 2, 1917, Plunkett Papers, Plunkett Foundation, London. See also Seymour, *Intimate Papers*, Vol. 3, p. 76.

[91] Tansill, *America and the Fight for Irish Freedom*, p. 243.

[92] Balfour to House, Apr. 2, 1918, HP 2:23. F. S. Oliver, a Unionist and no admirer of the United States, wrote thus of Balfour's inquiry to House: "I have just read such a document as I never thought to see an English Statesman put his name to—A.J.B.'s cable to House. He asks H. in effect to make up the minds of the War Cabinet as

who scribbled in reply that the measure "Would accentuate the whole Irish and Catholic intrigue which has gone hand in hand in some quarters in this country with the German intrigue." House incorporated these words verbatim in his response to Balfour.[93] Drummond, making preparations for a Cabinet discussion, then asked Wiseman to amplify House's reply and to state his own opinion.[94] Wiseman said that House had represented Wilson's view correctly but that he himself disagreed with both of them and did not believe that they felt very strongly about the matter. Wilson's concern, Wiseman said, naturally was to avoid any anti-war agitation in America by "Irish extremists." But the vast majority of Americans, even though they desired home rule for Ireland, had little sympathy for the Sinn Fein brand of Irish nationalism, according to Wiseman. Most Americans would, he thought, weigh the step of conscription on the basis of the reasons the British government gave for taking it. Since these reasons would be presented through the press, Wiseman urged, as he had several times previously, that Britain make a friend or at least less of an enemy of Hearst's International News Service by freeing it from restrictions imposed earlier in the war because of Hearst's pro-Germanism. Wiseman also thought an attempt might be made to persuade American Catholic leaders of the necessity for conscription. "In short," he concluded, "I consider that America's view would depend largely on how the case is presented through the Press, and I do not believe the possibility of bad effects here should influence your decision."[95]

---

to whether they should or should not conscript Ireland." Oliver to Austen Chamberlain, Apr. 3, 1918, Austen Chamberlain Papers, AC 15.

[93] House to Balfour, Apr. 3, 1918, HP 2:23. Wilson's note is in the margin of Balfour to House, Apr. 2, 1918, *ibid.*

[94] Drummond to Wiseman, Apr. 5, 1918, WWP 69.

[95] Wiseman to Drummond, Apr. 5, 1918, WWP 69. Wiseman consulted the opinion of Frank Cobb, editor of the New York *World* and one of Wilson's advisers, before writing his cable. Wiseman to Reading, Apr. 5, 1918, WWP 107.

With Wiseman's statement that Wilson did not feel strongly about the matter, the British government went ahead with the conscription bill, which became law on April 18.[96] Simultaneously the government lifted its punitive restrictions on the International News Service.[97] And in Washington Reading, left alone with the problem by Wiseman's departure to Europe, busied himself with explanations and courtesies to American Catholic leaders. Among other things he got Monsignor Francis Kelley of Chicago to agree to propagandize on behalf of the Allies and asked, in vain, for $10,000 per month to finance the Monsignor's work. He entertained Cardinal Gibbons of Baltimore at the embassy and later suggested, perhaps at Gibbons' request, to President Wilson that the United States accredit a confidential agent to the Vatican. Wilson replied with a definite no. Balfour also vetoed most of Reading's proposals (such as interceding at the Vatican in behalf of Monsignor Kelley's desire to become bishop of Detroit) for raising British stock in the Catholic hierarchy.[98]

Reading had taken the advice of Wiseman perhaps too seriously. He was ably assisted by Shane Leslie, an Anglo-Irish writer with pro-British sentiments, who was in close touch with Joseph P. Tumulty, President Wilson's secretary and a Catholic.[99] It may be that Reading interpreted Tumulty's insistence on home rule to be that of the President. On May 1 he cabled Wiseman that the Irish question in the United States was "as delicate as can be."[100] He persistently asked Lloyd George to push through a generous

[96] Lloyd George, *War Memoirs*, Vol. 5, p. 2,670.

[97] The restrictions were lifted by April 25. Wiseman to House, Apr. 25, 1918, WWP 64. See editorial entitled "Who Saved Hearst?" in the *New York Tribune*, May 1, 1918.

[98] Reading to Drummond, Apr. 10, 1918; Reading to Balfour, Apr. 10, 1918; Reading to Balfour, Apr. 11, 1918; Balfour to Reading, Apr. 15, 1918; Balfour to Reading, Apr. 20, 1918; Drummond to Reading, May 13, 1918; Reading to Drummond, May 23, 1918; all in Reading's Private Papers, FO 800/211.

[99] See Leslie to Tumulty, Apr. 23, 1918, Wilson Papers, File 6, Box 558, and Leslie, *Long Shadows*, London, 1966, Chap. 14.

[100] Reading to Wiseman (via Paris embassy), May 1, 1918, Reading's Private Papers, FO 800/209.

home rule measure, and confirmed Wiseman's prediction that Irish nationalists would besiege Wilson for his support.[101] Wiseman warned that an Irish delegation was coming to Washington in hope of securing Wilson's blessing. He vainly sought for some innocuous method by which Wilson could indicate sympathy to both the Irish and British; he need not have bothered, for Wilson maintained a stony silence against all appeals.[102]

The British government never issued an order-in-council to implement conscription in Ireland—the Chief Secretary for Ireland remarked it would be as prudent to try to recruit Germans as conscript Irishmen. Merely by its presence on the statute books, however, the conscription law prompted more and more southern Irishmen to support the Sinn Fein, which would eventually win Irish independence. By interning Sinn Fein leaders, by revealing evidence of German complicity in the Sinn Fein movement, and by asking the Vatican to curb the anti-British activity of Irish prelates, Britain managed to keep the lid on the Irish revolution in 1918. And so the government had an excuse for procrastinating in the matter of home rule.[103] Wiseman continued to keep an eye on Irish affairs—for instance he

[101] The numerous cables exchanged by Reading and Arthur C. Murray on home rule are in Reading's Private Papers, FO 800/209. At last Murray reported: "For the moment Home Rule bill has been buried, and its resurrection depends upon unforeseeable events." Murray to Reading, June 26, 1918, WWP 69.

[102] Wiseman to House, Apr. 25 and 26, 1918, and House to Wiseman, Apr. 26, 1918, WWP 64. Wilson explained in his interview with Wiseman on May 30, 1918 why the American government could not cooperate with the British in publishing materials to show the connection between Sinn Fein and Germany. "It would have been regarded here as too obviously helping the British Government in a political situation . . . ," Wilson said. Wiseman to Drummond, May 30, 1918 (CXP 627, 628, 629), WWP 129.

[103] The conclusion of the Irish Cardinal Logue seemed to be essentially correct, if harsh. He accused the British government of having "kept Home Rule dangling before our eyes for a purpose, and cast it aside when the purpose was served. Now that America is involved in the war beyond the possibility of retreat or slackening, it is no longer necessary to keep up pretensions." Logue to Plunkett, Aug. 9, 1918, WWP 69.

alerted the United States Justice Department to actions of Irish nationalists which, he thought, violated the American espionage act[104]—but the status of Ireland did not threaten Anglo-American cooperation again until the Paris Peace Conference.

[104] Wiseman to Reading, Sept. 19, 1918, and Wiseman to Murray, Sept. 21, 1918, WWP 69.

CHAPTER SEVEN

INTERVENTION IN RUSSIA

> Anyone who has studied his [Wilson's] Mexican policy will
> understand the remarkable parallel which the Russian situation
> presents, and realize that this is to him more than a passing
> political question, but a matter of principle. I am not saying
> that he is right, but I think we should realize that we are up
> against a new conception of foreign policy which no amount
> of argument will reconcile with, for instance, traditional British
> policy.
>
> Wiseman to Arthur C. Murray,
> July 4, 1918

WISEMAN returned to the United States at the end of May
1918 convinced that the most urgent problem in Anglo-
American relations was the dispute with Pershing over the
use of American troops. He soon learned, however, that
the most difficult issue for President Wilson was Allied insistence on intervention in Siberia. This was the first subject the President broached when Wiseman saw him on
May 29. Wilson linked the two problems, pointing out that
no American military expedition of any consequence could
be sent to Siberia without diminishing the flow of troops
to France. Nor would Wilson permit a purely Japanese intervention, for that, he said, would only succeed in turning the Russians toward Germany. Within six weeks, however, Wilson reversed himself, ordered 7,000 American
troops into Vladivostok, and invited the Japanese to send
a like number. He did this at precisely the time Secretary
Baker completed the process, initiated by Wiseman, of
curbing Pershing's independence in military diplomacy.[1]

Guiding the American government toward a policy of
intervention in Siberia was, however, an infinitely more
delicate operation than that of restraining Pershing. American and British attitudes toward and aims in Russia differed so radically and so passionately as to prohibit the

[1] See above, p. 155.

formulation of a joint policy. Wiseman therefore strove gradually to persuade each government that the other's position was somewhat similar to its own. Bit by bit he tried to convince the Americans that British interest in Russia was unselfish and humanitarian. He encouraged the British to think that the tentative and idealist plans of the Americans for Russia would lead to the ruthless, unsentimental brand of intervention desired by London. This process of incremental persuasion had only indirect relation to the condition of Russia itself. To Wiseman Russia was a problem not because of its chaos, its Bolshevism, or its domination by Germany. These attributes became problematical only when they produced responses from the British and American governments which were antagonistic to one another. In dealing with these responses Wiseman appreciated the greater capacity of the United States to enforce its will. Therefore, no matter how compelling the British prescription for the Russian malaise, if it conflicted with the American position it must defer to the latter. Wiseman was unwilling to risk the hard coin of American amity to cover a British gamble in Russia.

Wiseman's interest in a role for the United States in Russia dated from the summer of 1917. His propaganda expedition, as we have seen, won the approval of House and Wilson, but his suggestion at the same time that an American army go to Russia[2] produced no result. By January 1918 he was well aware that House and Wilson, while willing to lend encouragement and limited material aid to the Russians, were wholly opposed to military intervention. The Bolshevik seizure of power in November 1917 intensified rather than lessened the United States' determination to avoid involvement in Russian internal affairs. Undoubtedly mindful of the complications which resulted from her recent intervention in Mexico, the United States settled on a Russian policy of "Do Nothing." The phrase was Lansing's and represented his belief that no government based on na-

[2] Wiseman, "Some Notes on the Position in August 1917," HP 20:45.

tionality and private property could afford to traffic with the "dangerous idealists" of Bolshevism. "Do Nothing" was also the attitude of House and Wilson, though for different reasons. They feared contact with the Bolsheviks less than they feared that foreign involvement in Russia would strengthen reactionary forces and smother the sparks of democracy released by the original revolution of March 1917. In addition, interference in Russian affairs would violate the principle of self-determination and thus cost the United States the moral esteem gained from the pronouncements of Wilson. Lansing, House, and Wilson all expected the Russian situation to resolve itself. Lansing hopefully predicted the emergence of a dictator, and House and Wilson looked forward to the rise of representative government.[3]

Initial British policy toward Bolshevik Russia was more opportunist. Naturally distressed by the disappearance of Russia from the coalition fighting Germany, Balfour stated in February that his government would cooperate with the Bolsheviks as well as and simultaneously with any other Russian group that actively opposed Germany. To that end Britain supported the anti-German but also anti-Bolshevik movements of Kaledin and Semenov, urged the Japanese to march across Russia to engage the Germans, and at the same time sent Bruce Lockhart to Petrograd to encourage the Bolsheviks to renew the war against Germany. Although Balfour repeatedly disclaimed any desire to influence domestic politics in Russia, others in the British government clearly opposed Bolshevism almost as much as Germany.[4] Lockhart, for instance, undertook his mission with the understanding that "our two main objects in the

[3] Lansing, "Memorandum on the Russian Situation December 7, 1917," Lansing Private Diaries, Box 1, Vol. 2; Arno J. Mayer, *Political Origins of the New Diplomacy*, New Haven, 1959, pp. 340-41.

[4] Richard H. Ullman, *Intervention and the War*, Princeton, 1961, pp. 74-75, 123.

war are (1) the defeat of German militarism and (2) the suppression of Bolshevism."[5]

Generally the British were less concerned with the public opinion of the world than the Americans were, and increasingly military necessity, as they saw it, shaped their Russian policy. As 1918 progressed this military necessity required, in sequence, (1) the occupation of the Trans-Siberian railroad by Japan as the mandatory of the Allies; (2) the Allied occupation of Vladivostok and Murmansk; and (3) a general intervention in Siberia by Japanese, American, and Allied troops (or some combination thereof) for the purpose of resurrecting the Eastern Front against Germany.

British aspirations, however, outran British resources. The military intervention the War Cabinet so ardently desired had to be supplied either by Japan or the United States or the two in combination. Japan showed a willingness to oblige, but only in a limited way and only if the United States interposed no objection. The United States not only refused to intervene herself but refused as well to condone a Japanese expedition.[6] The key to the realization of any one of the phases of British policy lay therefore in persuading the United States that intervention was necessary and desirable.

Wiseman, as the Englishman with greatest sway over House, was ideally situated to secure American accession to the plan for Japanese intervention. For House, as the President's close adviser, staunchly and effectively opposed a Japanese entry into Siberia. He rejected the idea when it was first presented by the French at the Inter-Allied conference in December.[7] Similarly he begged Wilson to reject the British proposal, made at the end of January, for a Japa-

[5] Lockhart to Lord Milner, Jan. 24, 1918, Milner Papers, Private Correspondence.

[6] James William Morley, *The Japanese Thrust into Siberia, 1918*, New York, 1957, pp. 41, 49, 56, 125; George F. Kennan, *The Decision to Intervene*, Princeton, 1958, pp. 85-88.

[7] Seymour, *Intimate Papers*, Vol. 3, pp. 386-87.

nese occupation of the Trans-Siberian railroad. Just after receiving this proposal Wilson invited Wiseman to visit him. House assumed (incorrectly) that Wilson wished to discuss this new proposal with Wiseman. He assumed further that if Wilson was willing to discuss intervention, his opposition to it had weakened. House therefore wrote a strong letter to the President, warning that the appearance of a Japanese army in Russia would consolidate the Slavs of Europe in opposition to the Allies.[8]

In addition, House had a long talk (February 2) with Wiseman before the latter left New York for Washington. Unquestionably in this talk House elaborated on the wickedness of the intervention proposal. Significantly, he also spoke to Wiseman of the latter's future and suggested that when Reading completed his term Wiseman might become ambassador. Since House was to repeat this suggestion later, there is no reason to doubt that he meant it sincerely.[9] Nonetheless, the suggestion obviously implied that Wiseman's rise would depend on House's support. And to qualify for that support Wiseman must sympathize with House's views, including disapproval of Japanese intervention. As Wiseman went to his appointment with the President, therefore, his loyalty to British policy was complicated by his knowledge of House's views.

If Wiseman felt torn between the duty to press the British position and the compulsion to soften it in order to please House, he learned with relief that Wilson's summons arose from concern over the problem of troop amalgamation, not Japanese intervention. The latter topic occupied only a fraction of their conversation, but Wiseman was able to glean the impression that Wilson was not unmovably opposed to intervention. He reported to London:

[8] House to Wilson, Feb. 2, 1918, HP 49:10.
[9] House Diary, Feb. 2, 1918; House to Wiseman, Oct. 3, 1929, HP 46:1: ". . . I always thought you leaned more to the Am. side than to the British. This, I think, was the opinion of many of your colleagues, and notably that of the Prime Minister himself. When your appointment as ambassador to Wash. was under discussion, I believe it would have been made had it not been for this feeling."

"With reference to the proposed Japanese co-operation in Russia, I think President can be persuaded to agree if you persuade Bliss that the military end is practicable and likely to have substantial results and if the Japanese are approached confidentially and carefully sounded as to their attitude. The President is particularly anxious not to appear as obstructing any of your schemes."[10] Whatever the President's feelings, he could hardly refuse to take into account a British proposal at the same time he was asking them to understand his difficulties regarding amalgamation.

Wiseman had suggested consulting Bliss during his long conversation with House on February 2. With House's approval he drafted a cable to Bliss, which was dispatched practically verbatim over Lansing's signature on the same day.[11] Wiseman was not very optimistic that the cable would cause a change in American policy. "Unless," he informed Balfour, ". . . Bliss cables strongly in favor, I think the President will reject the proposal as far as he is concerned."[12] Bliss did not reply strongly in favor, and Wilson in effect did reject the proposal.[13] Still, Wiseman's action proved to be doubly shrewd. By wording the cable to Bliss to read that the Japanese intervention seemed "dangerous" politically he appeared to be agreeing with House. By involving the Permanent Military Representatives of the Supreme War Council in the controversy, Wiseman both prolonged the life of the issue and opened a new route of approach to the President.

The Wiseman-inspired cable, which for some reason took 12 days for delivery,[14] caused Bliss to convene a special meeting of the Permanent Military Representatives and resulted in their adoption of Joint Note 16 (February 19). This note recommended that the Japanese assume control

[10] Wiseman to Drummond and Balfour, Feb. 4, 1918, WWP 129.
[11] House to Wilson, Feb. 2, 1918, HP 49:10; Lansing to Bliss, Feb. 2, 1918; Bliss Papers, Box 67. Wiseman's draft of the cable is in HP 20:45.
[12] Wiseman to Drummond, Feb. 1, 1918, WWP 113.
[13] Trask, *United States in the Supreme War Council*, pp. 105-106.
[14] Bliss to Baker, Feb. 25, 1918, Bliss Papers, Box 74.

of the railroad from Vladivostok to Harbin. Although Bliss drafted and signed the note, he wrote Washington that the military advantage resulting from its implementation would be slight. Consequently Wilson withheld approval of the note.[15] The Supreme War Council, however, continued to study the Siberian situation and in the succeeding weeks again urged intervention.

Wiseman meantime explored another approach to the Russian problem. On February 12 House remarked that he and Wilson had concluded that the United States ought to recognize the Bolshevik government. This extraordinary idea, nowhere mentioned by House in his diary, was entertained by House, and presumably by Wilson, at a time when there seemed to be a possibility of inducing Austria to desert her German co-belligerent. It was in line with what Wiseman described as Wilson's hope of "talking" the Austrians into peace. According to Wiseman, Wilson and House foresaw two benefits from recognizing the Bolsheviks: (1) recognition would encourage the liberals in Germany and Austria; (2) recognition would rob the Germans, already in a de facto relationship with the Bolsheviks, of the opportunity to link in propaganda the Western powers with Russian reactionaries.

Predicting that he could "probably" get Wilson to adopt whatever policy the British preferred, Wiseman asked Balfour and Reading for guidance. Reading thought the Bolsheviks were not resisting the Germans sufficiently to merit recognition, and Balfour repeated that it was impossible to recognize the Bolshevik government, which did not control all of Russia, and still render aid to non-Bolshevik groups that were continuing to fight against Germany. On February 27 Wiseman reported that Wilson had abandoned the idea of recognition.[16] The President's de-

[15] Trask, *United States in the Supreme War Council,* pp. 104-106.
[16] Wiseman to Reading (Memorandum No. 3), Feb. 12, 1918; Reading to Wiseman, Feb. 13, 1918; WWP 107; Wiseman to Drummond, Feb. 19, 1918; Drummond to Wiseman, Feb. 22, 1918; Wiseman to Drummond, Feb. 27, 1918; WWP 109.

cision, assuming he did in fact consider recognition, probably resulted from the breakdown of negotiations with Austria and from the Bolshevik acceptance on February 24 of Germany's peace terms. The preferences of Wiseman and the British probably influenced him very little.

At the beginning of March there occurred, or rather almost occurred, a complete shift in American policy regarding Russia. Balfour warned Wilson that Allied military supplies in Vladivostok were about to fall into German hands and predicted that the Japanese, for their own security and ambitions, would invade Siberia. From Siberia John F. Stevens, the American sent in the summer of 1917 to help the Russians rehabilitate their railroads, reported that the Japanese seemed poised for an invasion. Attracted to Balfour's idea of putting an Allied bridle on an inevitable Japanese intervention, Lansing and Wilson composed a note saying that the United States would not object to the Allies asking Japan to serve as their mandatory. The note stated, however, that the American government would refrain from endorsing or participating in the project. Polk showed this note to the French, British, and Italian ambassadors, and Wiseman relayed it to the Foreign Office.[17] But before it could be sent to the Japanese, House objected, saying to the President that Japanese intervention might be "the greatest misfortune that has yet befallen the Allies." House excoriated the "fatuous determination" of France and Britain to push Japan into Russia. "The French," he wrote, "have come to hate the Russians and do not care what ill fate befalls them. . . . The English that are in power have such an intense hatred for Germany that they have lost their perspective."[18]

Wilson immediately withdrew the note and replaced it with one which opposed intervention altogether. House re-

[17] Balfour to Reading, Feb. 26, 1918; Balfour to Wiseman, Feb. 28, 1918; FO 115/2445; Wiseman to Drummond, Mar. 4, 1918, WWP 113; Betty Miller Unterberger, *America's Siberian Expedition, 1918-1920*, Durham, N.C., 1956, pp. 28-33; Kennan, *Russia Leaves the War*, Princeton, 1956, pp. 473-81.

[18] House to Wilson, Mar. 3, 1918, HP 49:10.

joiced, but found that Wiseman, on the only occasion on record, "wholly disagreed" with him. For Wiseman the substitution of notes meant that the British campaign for Japanese intervention was back to where it started.[19]

On March 7 Wiseman took stock. Wilson's recent actions had shown a certain flexibility in attitude toward Japanese intervention, but House remained passionately opposed. The problem was to maneuver the American government back into the position it had so fleetingly held. Essentially this meant converting House. Wiseman therefore decided the British must:

(1) arrange for the Japanese to state that intervention would be undertaken to aid the Russians and not for any Japanese gain

(2) silence those who argued that intervention was necessary to prevent a German threat to India

(3) emphasize that military stores in Russia might fall into German hands and be used against American soldiers

(4) justify intervention on liberal and humanitarian grounds

Wiseman in short hoped to establish in the minds of House and Wilson that intervention would be a crusade, not just a military operation.[20]

[19] House Diary, Mar. 5, 1918. One of Wiseman's objections concerned the wording of this second note. In the original draft (as printed in Seymour, *Intimate Papers*, Vol. 3, p. 419) Wilson speaks of the proposed "invasion" of Siberia. The note as sent (*Foreign Relations, 1918, Russia*, Vol. 2, p. 67) substituted the word "intervention," the word Wiseman preferred.

In commenting on House's opposition to Japanese intervention, Wiseman said: "I think House may exaggerate the effect Japanese action will have in the U.S. although there will be undoubtedly considerable opposition, particularly in the West, and it is this which President's note . . . is intended to allay." Wiseman to Drummond, Mar. 4, 1918, WWP 113.

[20] Wiseman, memorandum dated Mar. 7, 1918, and "Notes for a Cable from the Ambassador to the Foreign Office," Mar. 9, 1918, WWP 113. In the latter, Wiseman emphasized that the President feared Americans in the West would accuse him of permitting "a

Anticipating Wiseman, the British government on March 11 began pressing the Japanese to state publicly that their interest in Siberia was one of unselfish concern for the welfare of the Russian people.[21] But London was slow in realizing that the consideration of keeping the "road to India" safe was an argument which aroused resentment rather than sympathy in the United States. Indeed, reference to the security of India was such a ritual for some British officials that they introduced it into papers on almost any subject.[22] Reading on March 10 cautioned against the mention of India in messages directed toward the Americans, yet the practice continued well into April.[23] It finally ceased when Wiseman, in London, pointed out the danger of leading Americans to assume that "Japanese intervention is intended to secure the British position in India rather than as an effective factor in the present fighting in Europe." Balfour agreed with Wiseman and directed the Foreign Office to omit the mention of India from subsequent messages regarding intervention.[24]

As the first step in his strategy to maneuver the American government toward intervention, Wiseman prompted Wilson to make a dramatic gesture of sympathy toward the

---

yellow-race to destroy a white one" if he consented to Japanese intervention.

[21] Morley, *Japanese Thrust into Siberia*, p. 132.

[22] See Ullman, *Intervention and the War*, pp. 302-29, on the defense of India. Sir Henry Wilson, Chief of the Imperial General Staff, was obsessed by the threat of both Bolshevism and Germany to India. Lloyd George, *War Memoirs*, Vol. 6, p. 3,119; Paul Guinn, *British Strategy and Politics 1914 to 1918*, Oxford, 1965, p. 321. L. S. Amery, a close adviser to Sir Henry Wilson and Lord Milner, consistently stressed the security of India in his memoranda on the future of the British Empire. See, e.g., Amery to Wiseman, Dec. 7, 1917, enclosing the memorandum, "The Future of the German Colonies," WWP 59. See also Cecil to Lloyd George, June 7, 1918, Cecil Papers, 51076, British Museum.

[23] Reading to Balfour, Mar. 10, 1918, WWP 113, and Balfour to Reading, Apr. 19, 1918, Reading's Private Papers, FO 800/209.

[24] Wiseman, "Comments on Foreign Office Cable No. 2303 to Lord Reading, April 19th," including the marginal note by Balfour, Balfour Papers, 49741, British Museum.

Russian people. On March 10 he suggested to Colonel House that the President should send a friendly message to the Soviet congress due to assemble to consider the Brest-Litovsk treaty. House wrote the suggestion to Wilson as his own, and Wilson, apparently having similar advice from William Bullitt, complied with the suggestion.[25] The President's message deplored his present inability to aid the Russian people but assured them that the United States was determined to "secure for Russia once more complete sovereignty and independence in her own affairs and full restoration to her great role in the life of Europe and the modern world."[26]

Perhaps Wiseman thought such a message had a slight chance of stiffening the Bolsheviks against Germany's peace terms, but primarily he wanted to advance the idea of America's duty to come to the aid of Russia.[27] In a memorandum to House he outlined how the United States might both create the threat of pressure on Germany's Eastern Front and prevent the stifling of "Russia's new-born democracy." A commission composed of Red Cross, Y.M.C.A., propaganda, and military recruiting units should go to Vladivostok and Murmansk to help the Russians organize themselves against German militarism. But before the commission could embark on its work, its way would need to be cleared by a Japanese military force. The Japanese would also be able to protect the military stores in the two ports and, depending on their reception by the Rus-sian people, might open additional areas of Russia to the

[25] Wiseman claimed credit for suggesting the message in his cable to Drummond, Mar. 14, 1918, WWP 113. House's letter to the President, Mar. 10, 1918 is printed in Seymour, *Intimate Papers*, Vol. 3, p. 399. Kennan, *Russia Leaves the War*, pp. 509-10, credits Bullitt with the idea. In HP 34:107 there is a memorandum addressed to Frank Polk, apparently from Bullitt, urging that "Mr. [Thomas W.] Lamont's suggestion" of a message from the President be sent. There is no doubt that House's letter influenced Wilson, but there is no way of establishing conclusively that Wiseman was or was not the first to make the suggestion to House.

[26] Baker and Dodd, *War and Peace*, Vol. 1, p. 191.

[27] Wiseman to Drummond, Mar. 14, 1918, WWP 113.

missionary work of the American commission. It was very important to note, Wiseman wrote, that no one could accurately predict how the Russian people would react to this program until it was actually inaugurated. "The mass of the Russian people," he stated, "probably do not understand what is going on, nor do they know what they want themselves; thus the propaganda or information department of the Commissions would be of the greatest importance."[28]

Wiseman's plan of coating Japanese military intervention with American good works gained no immediate headway with House. Wiseman told London it was most unlikely that anything would come of his plan unless the Bolsheviks or some other body of Russian opinion reacted sympathetically to Wilson's March 11 message. Unfortunately, the Bolsheviks answered the President with an insult, and no other Russian group invited American aid either. But the sending of the message, Wiseman thought, had familiarized the American people with the unsatisfactory conditions in Russia and made them more amenable to action of some sort, even Japanese intervention, in the future. At the moment, however, the American public still showed little interest in the Russian situation.[29]

On March 18 the British government again asked the President to agree to Japanese intervention. Again House and Wilson reacted negatively, as they did yet again when Balfour the following week proposed a Japanese expedition accompanied by a civilian Allied mission.[30] Regarding the former proposal, House recorded that he "talked Sir William quite out of" it and that Wiseman in turn so shook Reading's views "that the Ambassador could not put up any arguments for his Government."[31] Whether or not

[28] Wiseman, memorandum dated Mar. 11, 1918, WWP 113 (also HP 34:109).

[29] Wiseman to Drummond, Mar. 14, 1918, WWP 113; Kennan, *Russia Leaves the War*, p. 513.

[30] Seymour, *Intimate Papers*, Vol. 3, p. 401; Drummond to Wiseman, Mar. 26, 1918, WWP 114.

[31] House Diary, Mar. 18, 1918. In returning to the State Department memoranda from the British Embassy urging approval of inter-

Wiseman and Reading changed their views, there was little point in their putting up an argument. The American government in late March was reassured that Japan would not move into Siberia without American approval[32] and was also almost totally absorbed by the military developments on the Western Front (following the great German offensive of March 21). When Wiseman interviewed Wilson on April 1, the President mentioned Russia only in order to condemn the imperialist terms Germany had imposed on her at Brest-Litovsk.[33]

IN THE COURSE of a conversation with Reading and Wiseman on March 27 House remarked that intervention in Siberia might be acceptable if some expression of Russian assent could be secured. Reading passed the remark on to Balfour,[34] and the next phase of the British campaign for intervention concentrated on this idea. Balfour instructed Bruce Lockhart[35] to persuade Trotsky, the Soviet foreign

---

vention, Wilson said of the memoranda, "They still do not answer the question I have put to Lord Reading and to all others who argue in favor of intervention by Japan, namely, What is it to effect and how will it be efficacious in effecting it? The condition of Siberia furnishes no answer." Wilson to Lansing, Mar. 22, 1918, SD 861.00/1433-1/2.

[32] Japan assured Wilson on March 19 that she would "refrain from taking any action on which due understanding had not been reached between the United States" unless Japanese national security was threatened. Morley, *Japanese Thrust into Siberia*, p. 141. Wiseman to Drummond, Mar. 21, 1918, WWP 114: "President has just received a very sympathetic and entirely satisfactory message from Japanese regarding intervention in Siberia."

[33] Wiseman, "Notes on Interview with the President—April 1st, 1918, at 5:30 p.m.," Balfour Papers, 49741, British Museum.

[34] Reading to Balfour, Mar. 27, 1918, Reading's Private Papers, FO 800/210. Reading to Balfour, Apr. 7, 1918, FO 115/2445, stated that the President was "more confirmed than ever in his opinion that America should not assent to or take part in intervention of Japanese unless there is at least something in nature of request from Russian Government for this assistance." See Wilson to Lansing, Apr. 4, 1918, SD 861.00/1439-1/2, for indication that Reading's report was accurate.

[35] Lockhart apparently began working for an invitation independent

minister, to invite Allied assistance. By April 19 Lockhart appeared to have succeeded, and the War Cabinet accordingly instructed Reading to secure American endorsement of a joint overture to Trotsky. Reading, believing "Best way to gain President's assent is by first convincing House," unveiled the new plan to the Colonel on April 24.[36] House approved. "It is what I had in mind in the beginning," he cabled Wiseman, now in London. House notified Wilson of the new proposal and predicted that he too would find it satisfactory.[37]

But House was wrong. When Reading read the War Cabinet's message to Wilson, Wilson warned that the Allies had better take care lest Trotsky lead them into a trap. The President said he was "daily expecting" the arrival of a person (Edgar Sisson) bringing documents to "prove conclusively" that Trotsky and Lenin were in the pay of the German government. Wilson also suspected that Trotsky's influence in the Soviet government had declined so that an invitation from him would be meaningless. More important, Wilson thought the War Cabinet's hopes of re-creating an Eastern Front were unrealistic. He said he doubted that the Japanese would agree to intervene "at all" and that the United States could spare no more than a regiment of troops.[38]

Wiseman, who arrived in London too late to influence the April 19 proposal, anticipated (in notes prepared for Balfour) the practical objections made by Wilson. He questioned the validity of virtually all the War Cabinet's assumptions regarding the reestablishment of an Eastern Front and criticized the proposal for its imprecision:

---

of and prior to Balfour's instructions. Ullman, *Intervention and the War*, pp. 136-42.

[36] Balfour to Reading, Apr. 19, 1918, Reading's Private Papers, FO 800/209; Reading to Balfour, Apr. 22, 1918, *ibid.*, FO 800/210.

[37] House to Wiseman, Apr. 25, 1918, WWP 64; House to Wilson, Apr. 24, 1918, HP 49:10.

[38] Reading to Balfour, Apr. 25, 1918, Reading's Private Papers, FO 800/210.

The President will probably observe that there are still no estimates available as to the force which the Japanese would be able to put into the field; the demands for money and material which they would be likely to make on America; the distance which the Japanese Staff estimate they could penetrate with the force at their disposal; and, on the other hand, no estimate of the supplies the Germans might otherwise obtain from the area which would be controlled by the Allied force. The President sees grave political objections to the proposal, but he is prepared to balance against them the military and economic advantages which might be gained. He would like a more definite estimate of these advantages.[39]

The arrival of Reading's report on Wilson's reaction to the proposal proved that Wiseman had read the President's mind correctly.

In the days following, Wiseman canvassed officials in London for more information on intervention. He learned that the chief proponents were the military, who were "strongly anti-Bolshevic and even anti-revolutionary."[40] He did not report this finding to House. In fact, he cabled House on the topic of intervention only once during the whole of his month's stay in Europe. In that one cable (May 1) he predicted that Trotsky would not invite the Allies to intervene because Trotsky knew that such a step would cause the Germans to turn the Soviet government out of Moscow. The Allies, Wiseman said, thus had three alternatives: do nothing; intervene against the wishes of the Bolsheviks; or establish a Russian government in exile to attempt "what Trotzky will not do." Wiseman made no rec-

[39] Wiseman, "Comments on Foreign Office Cable No. 2303 to Lord Reading, April 19th.," Balfour Papers, 49741, British Museum. Kennan, *Decision to Intervene*, p. 346, suggests that Wiseman helped formulate the April 19 cable, but Wiseman did not arrive in London until after the cable was dispatched.

[40] Wiseman to Reading, Apr. 26, 1918, Reading's Private Papers, FO 800/211.

ommendation. He merely stated that the British government urgently wished an intervention, built largely around a Japanese force, and that in his opinion the re-creation of an Eastern Front would have a "very depressing effect" on Austria. If he personally favored intervention he gave no evidence of enthusiasm for it.[41]

By the time Wiseman returned to the United States, Wilson's attitude toward Russia had undergone considerable change. He believed the Sisson documents, now in hand, which portrayed the Bolsheviks as German puppets. The arrival of the documents apparently intensified his interest in Russia and caused him to continue his search for Siberian *"nuclei* of self-governing" authorities which he could encourage. In addition, his reading of public opinion revealed considerable sympathy for Russia. He was surprised to find the well-dressed audience that he addressed in the Metropolitan Opera House on May 18th enthusiastically responsive to his rather casual pledge to "stand by" Russia. If these people had feeling for the Russians, surely more ordinary men did too. Wilson was coming close to admitting the need for the sort of intervention for relief that Wiseman proposed in March.[42]

When Wilson on May 29 invited Wiseman's frank views on the European situation, the first question the President asked concerned Japanese intervention. Wiseman explained that advocates of the project hoped both to aid the Russian people and to reestablish the Eastern Front. Wilson said that these were of course desirable goals, that he himself would be willing to intervene against the wishes

[41] Wiseman to House, May 1, 1918, WWP 64. In his cable to House of April 27, 1918, WWP 64, Wiseman did mention in passing that Trotsky seemed to be losing influence in the Bolshevik government.

[42] Kennan, *Russia Leaves the War*, p. 446; Kennan, *Decision to Intervene*, pp. 350-58. As another example of the "intelligence" which concluded there was complicity between Lenin and the Germans, see Wilson to Lansing, Jan. 28 [?], 1918, SD 861.00/1011, which encloses a second-hand report from Emanuel Voska. Wilson said, "I have heard very favorable things of Mr. Voska from Charles R. Crane."

of the Russian people if it were for their own eventual good, but that no military man had been able to convince him that there was any practical scheme for renewing the Eastern Front. The Japanese, Wilson continued, had stated they would go no farther west than Omsk, meaning that to give them a mandate would accomplish no more than to deliver to them maritime Siberia. Wilson then explained to Wiseman why he thought Japanese intervention was so undesirable:

> If we could have put a large British-American force into Vladivostock [sic], and advanced along the Siberian railroad, we might . . . have rallied the Russian people to assist in defense of their country. But if we relied mainly on Japanese military assistance we should rally the Russians against us, excepting for a small reactionary body who would join anybody to destroy the Bolsheviki. I remarked that in any case it was not possible to make the situation worse than it was now. He said that that was where he entirely disagreed. We could make it much worse by putting the Germans in a position where they could organize Russia in a national movement against Japan. If that was done he would not be surprised to see Russian soldiers fighting with the Germans on the Western Front. "Then," I said, "are we to do nothing at all." "No," he said, "we must watch the situation carefully and sympathetically, and be ready to move whenever the right time arrived."

Wilson's own preferred plan, as he told Wiseman, was to send a mission of American, French, and British civilians to Vladivostok and Murmansk to help organize a system of barter. Of course, he said in Wiseman's paraphrase, "it would take a long time before any results could be expected from such a movement. If in the meantime we were invited to intervene by any responsible and representative body, we ought to do so. An oral or secret arrangement with Trotsky would be no good since he would repudiate it. He [Wilson] realized that the U.S. Government held the key to the situation in that Japanese Government would not intervene without their sanction; but it would be odious for him to use such power except the best interests of the common cause demanded it."[43]

Here was a clear statement of Wilson's thinking at the time and a guide to the action he later took. He would have none of the Allied scheme for Japanese intervention because it was militarily impractical and would antagonize the Russian people. He wanted to organize relief for the Russian people, but he wanted time to perfect a system, such as barter, which would not allow commercial interests[44] to exploit the Russians. And he felt no urgency. The Japanese were checked and he would release them to act in Siberia only if the "common cause," that is, his concept of the aims of the war, demanded it.

As the month of June progressed, Wilson's time for planning a policy for Siberia began to run out. Demands to "do something" in Russia bombarded the White House. The press, State Department officials, American agents in the Far East, a special French delegation, Thomas Masaryk —all brought great pressure to bear upon the President.[45] On June 13 Gordon Auchincloss, after talking with Vance McCormick and other Democratic party officials, wrote a letter on the Siberian situation which Lansing signed and sent to the President. The letter began by asserting that agitation of the Russian question in the press required the

[43] Wiseman to Drummond, May 30, 1918 (CXP 627, 628, 629), WWP 129.

[44] Wilson's preference for a barter system on this date foreshadowed his scepticism regarding a commercial or economic mission to Siberia. On June 19 Wilson told Masaryk that "he had a plan for the coordination of the Red Cross which makes for the barter and exchange of commodities in Russia; and that he intended to place this under the charge of one man and that this man was not a business man." Auchincloss Diary, June 19, 1918. See Kennan, *Decision to Intervene*, pp. 359, 400.

[45] Unterberger, *America's Siberian Expedition*, pp. 60-66. On June 22 House had the cable censor at New York kill every cable concerning intervention. House wanted to diminish discussion of the matter in the press while Wilson had it under "active consideration." House Diary, June 22, 1918.

181

Administration to take immediate action. It proposed that Herbert Hoover lead an American relief commission to Siberia. This commission would, the letter said, "dispose of the proposal of armed intervention." Auchincloss's letter received the enthusiastic approval of Wiseman and House before it was sent, and in Auchincloss's mind it was his most important proposal yet. The novelty in his suggestion, however, was the nomination of Hoover, for the plan itself was similar to the one offered by Wiseman back in March and was a variation on numerous other plans then being studied in Washington.[46]

Wiseman knew the proposed Hoover commission would not satisfy London, but, as he cabled Drummond, "I do not believe it is possible to persuade the President to agree to armed intervention without some such preliminary movement." The advantage of the plan, from the British standpoint, was the President's assumed confidence in Hoover. According to Wiseman, Hoover was no "sentimentalist," was pro-British, and once in Siberia could probably convince Wilson of the need for armed intervention. If the plan received Wilson's approval, Wiseman thought "we should be on the right road. . . ."[47]

Wiseman might have added that House's endorsement of the Hoover plan meant that the Colonel was now definitely on the "right road." House's conversion to advocacy of some form of intervention was apparently a gradual process and no doubt related to the swing in public opinion that animated Auchincloss and McCormick. House was

[46] Auchincloss Diary, June 13, 1918. Auchincloss's diary contains a copy of the letter, which is also in *Foreign Relations, The Lansing Papers, 1914-1920*, Vol. 2, pp. 362-63. See also House to Wilson, June 4 and 13, 1918, HP 49:10. See Christopher Lasch, *The American Liberals and the Russian Revolution*, New York, 1962, pp. 97-126, for the rationale of American liberal support of intervention. The Foreign Office feared that American liberals opposed intervention because of the influence on them of "foreign socialist elements," especially Slav elements, among whom "social revolutionary ideas" appeared to supersede "nationalist aspirations." Balfour [or Cecil?] to Reading, June 18, 1918, FO 371/3492.

[47] Wiseman to Drummond, June 14, 1918, WWP 115.

also subjected to the arguments of visiting European interventionists, although, significantly, there is no direct evidence that Wiseman put any great pressure on him. Apparently Wiseman, repeating a tactic successful in other instances, allowed others to press forcibly the argument for
intervention and seemed himself detached and objective
in the matter. At any rate, by June 21 House was urging
the President to take immediate action in Russia. "It has
now become a question of days rather than months," he
wrote Wilson, after Reading read him a fresh appeal from
Balfour. In addition, he asked Wilson to receive Reading
for a presentation of the conclusions which House, Reading, and Wiseman reached during a day-long conference.[48]

The most striking thing Reading told Wilson during their
talk on June 24 was that House believed a relief commission would have to be accompanied by an American military force. Reading mentioned 15,000 American troops
and said that he and House thought that this number
would have to be supplemented by a gradually increasing
and eventually dominant number of Japanese troops. Wilson responded in a noncommittal way, but the Ambassador
sensed a definite change in the President's thinking: "I
think his views have changed to this extent, that he now
recognises that such a Commission would be useless unless of vast dimension and importance and protected by a
military force. It is the accompaniment by a military force
which to my mind is of such importance in this new proposal. It is obvious that once that military force has entered

---

[48] House to Wilson, June 21, 1918, HP 49:10. See House Diary,
June 11, 12, 14, 17, 26, 1918, for his consideration of the intervention question. Wiseman to Reading, June 12, 1918, WWP 107,
reported, "There is no doubt that House and the State Department
are modifying their views on this subject, and are now persuaded
that it is necessary for the United States to take some action." Urging
House not to agree to intervention, William C. Bullitt charged:
"Except for a few upperclass Russians and French who are consciously selfish in advocating this policy, the gentlemen investors who
are now working on the President believe that they are actuated by
the highest motives. But most of them are simply panic-stricken
because of recent events on the West Front." Bullitt to House, June
24, 1918, HP 3:45.

Siberia it must be supplemented as and when necessities arise, as they assuredly will."[49] Thus, while (in the view of one authority)[50] most men in the Administration thought the President was thinking of an entirely civilian commission, Wiseman, Reading, and House knew different. They knew he now leaned toward a military expedition and had come to question the feasibility of a relief scheme.

On June 30 Wiseman cabled London that American public opinion was "far more favorable to Japanese intervention than three months ago." He hinted that Wilson was on the verge of a decision regarding Siberia but cautioned that undue pressure on him would have the opposite effect from that desired. What would influence the President more than anything else, Wiseman said, was a strong endorsement of intervention by Foch.[51] If this was the case (and it was) why had not Wiseman urged such an endorsement earlier? He had, after all, during the controversy over troop amalgamation emphasized the importance of approaching Wilson through the Supreme War Council and Foch, and more recently the American government had agreed to divert a few battalions from France to Murmansk if Foch thought it necessary.[52] But Wiseman relized that in the case of Siberia, Wilson considered more to be at stake than military expediency. "I know he feels the responsibility of the situation, and is anxious but unconvinced," Wiseman wrote. "He hesitates—wondering where interven-

[49] Reading to Balfour, June 25, 1918, Reading's Private Papers, FO 800/210.

[50] Kennan, *Decision to Intervene*, p. 389.

[51] Wiseman to Drummond, June 30, 1918, WWP 115. Wiseman cabled only twice during June specifically on the intervention question, but he said he helped Reading compose all the latter's cables to the Foreign Office. Wiseman to Arthur C. Murray, June 4, 1918, WWP 85.

[52] Kennan, *Decision to Intervene*, p. 270. The request to send American troops to Murmansk was always considered in relation to the Western Front and never required the decision as to principle that Siberian intervention did. *Ibid.*, pp. 266-68. Trask, *United States in the Supreme War Council*, p. 19. Wiseman and House never expressed any worry over the Murmansk question.

tion would lead the United States. It would be, he thinks, a political adventure, the far-reaching effects of which it is impossible to foresee."[53]

At this point Wiseman drew an analogy between Wilson's Mexican and Russian policies.[54] In both cases Wilson's objectives were the same, the establishment of a representative government by the people themselves. But if intervention in adjacent Mexico had failed of its purpose, how much more likely this would be in distant and barely known Russia. Principle, not self-interest, had motivated Wilson in Mexico. But profane interests, notably American business investments, had obscured and vitiated the purity of his motives. Hence, as Wiseman appreciated, Wilson wanted to avoid any sort of exploitative commercial or political involvement in Siberia that would contaminate an official policy of selflessness. Wilson's foreign policy was truly different from Britain's traditional self-interested policy; it was with the realization that the two policies were virtually irreconcilable that Wiseman tried to present the American position to his superiors in the best light possible. He hoped to restrain British pressure on Wilson. If he succeeded he would prevent a dangerous split between the two governments. But he would also run the risk of misleading the British into thinking there was some similarity between their policy and Wilson's.

At Versailles on July 3 the British delegation secured the

[53] Wiseman to Drummond, June 30, 1918, WWP 115.

[54] Wiseman to Murray, June 4, 1918, WWP 85. This is the source of the quotation which opens the present chapter. Wilson's Mexican policy is best covered by Arthur S. Link, *Woodrow Wilson and the Progressive Era, 1910-1917*, New York, 1954, Chap. 5. See also Howard F. Cline, *The United States and Mexico*, New York, 1963, pp. 185-88.

It was probably not entirely for illustrative purposes that Wiseman drew the analogy. While he was in London the general staff attempted to get the Cabinet to consider means, even intervention, by which the United States could bring order to Mexico, the site of vitally important British-owned oil wells. See Balfour's marvellously sarcastic memorandum (May 13, 1918) on this matter in Blanche E. C. Dugdale, *Arthur James Balfour*, 2 vols., London, 1936, Vol. 2, pp. 244-45. See also p. 211 below.

endorsement of intervention from the Supreme War Council and Foch, as Reading and Wiseman had rather belatedly recommended.[55] The British had decided on this tactic, in fact, long before Reading's and Wiseman's recommendation. They had gone to the previous meeting of the Supreme War Council in June with the same intention, but had relented when Bliss told them the United States could not assent. Failure to press for a resolution at that time so infuriated Lord Robert Cecil, Under Secretary of State for Foreign Affairs, that he wrote his resignation to Lloyd George. Cecil's blistering letter charged that if the Prime Minister "attached the same importance to Allied intervention in Siberia that you do to the increase of American troops in France, I feel confident the whole treatment of the question would have been very different." Assured by Lloyd George that he did indeed attach importance to intervention,[56] Cecil decided to retract his resignation. But so great was his passion for quick action that he plotted with Lord Milner to remove Balfour, his own cousin and party leader, from the foreign secretaryship. Cecil was particularly disgusted with Balfour's failure to "take steps as to the Czechs."[57]

The Czechs referred to by Cecil added a new and ultimately decisive factor to the question of intervention. After the treaty of Brest-Litovsk some 50,000 Czech soldiers who had been fighting with the Russian army retained

[55] Trask, *United States in the Supreme War Council*, pp. 119-23. Reading to Balfour, June 25, 1918, Reading's Private Papers, FO 800/210, which Wiseman helped prepare, and Wiseman to Drummond, June 30, 1918, WWP 115, recommended endorsements by Foch and the Supreme War Council. Reading to Balfour, Lloyd George, and Milner, June 22, 1918, Reading's Private Papers, FO 800/210, recommended endorsement by the Supreme War Council. Gen. Tom Bridges, military adviser to Reading, had made the same recommendation. Bridges to Reading, June 18, 1918, Reading's Private Papers, FO 800/210. See also Kennan, *Decision to Intervene*, p. 391.
[56] Cecil to Lloyd George, June 7, 1918, and Lloyd George to Cecil, June 7, 1918, Cecil Papers, 51076, British Museum.
[57] Milner to Cecil, June 13, 1918, and Cecil to Milner, June 13, 1918, Cecil Papers, 51093, British Museum.

their discipline and organization and were thus the most important military force in Russia. Masaryk, their national leader, realized the diplomatic asset the army constituted in his campaign for national independence. In an agreement with the French he exchanged the use of his army for their promise of recognition to the future Czech state. The French then ordered the Czech army to leave its location at Kiev and debark from Vladivostok for the Western Front. The British, however, saw the possibility of using the Czech army as the nucleus for an Allied force in Siberia and in May convinced the French to permit the Czechs to divide into two groups, one to head toward Vladivostok and the other toward Murmansk.[58]

Although the Czechs never deployed themselves in a line from Murmansk to Vladivostok as the British desired, their movement across Siberia did succeed in precipitating the American decision to act in Russia. Progressing eastward, the Czechs clashed with Austro-Hungarian prisoners of war and with Bolsheviks, and their units became separated. Those in the vanguard who reached Vladivostok therefore took over the city and set about establishing contact with their comrades in the interior. Reports concerning the Czechs which reached America and Europe were ambiguous, but out of them one point emerged clearly: the army of a small national state struggling for independence was under attack, partially at least from agents and assumed puppets of Germany.[59] Here was an element in the Siberian situation that touched directly the "common cause" on whose behalf Wilson had told Wiseman he would intervene.

Coincidentally, news of the Czech rising reached Versailles in time to be incorporated in the July 3 resolution of the Supreme War Council.[60] But the rising became more important than the resolution. As Wiseman recorded, "The

[58] The Czech legion is described in detail in Kennan, *Decision to Intervene*, Chap. 6.

[59] *Ibid.*, Chap. 12.

[60] Trask, *United States in the Supreme War Council*, pp. 117-19.

Czech-Slovak [sic] position has . . . materially altered the situation, and will be . . . the determining factor."[61]

So it was. The fortuitous difficulties of the Czechs provided Wilson a nearly perfect way out of the dilemma posed by his impulse to grant the requests of Foch and the Supreme War Council and his belief that (aside from any consideration of principle) the United States simply did not have enough men and supplies to undertake a military role in Russia.[62] An intervention to rescue the Czechs, however, would permit the United States to focus on a very specific and limited objective. No more convinced now than previously of the soundness of Allied plans for intervention, Wilson would be able to appear to be going along with their recommendation but would in fact be following a much more restricted policy. Previously the idea of a relief commission seemed the best way to make a token gesture of cooperation with the Allies. But that plan, to be effective, would require extensive planning, vast amounts of commodities, and constant vigilance against a takeover by businessmen. In addition, a commission would have to be escorted by a protective military force. To rescue the Czechs required only the latter and would still represent an acceptance of the Allied position.

The basis of the President's decision, made on July 6, was

[61] Wiseman to Murray, July 4, 1918, WWP 85. The same day Wiseman wrote House: "The Czech-Slovak incidents seem to me likely to be the determining factors in the whole affair. I wonder incidentally how much Mazaryk has had to do with them?" Wiseman to House, July 4, 1918, WWP 64.

[62] It must be emphasized that Wilson was making his decision at the time when the Allies were demanding 100 American divisions. See above, p. 152. An indication of the impact of practical considerations on the President's thinking is given in Reading to Balfour, July 8, 1918, WWP 129. Reading said the President was obviously disturbed by the demands for supplies and equipment: "He explained that vast as it was the productivity capacity of the U.S. was limited and was being already very heavily taxed by the requirements for so large a force as 100 divisions and he assumed that it was not in contemplation to reduce this programme in order to carry out either the Siberian or Murmansk proposals."

recorded by Lansing: ". . . the present situation of the Czecho-Slovaks requires this Government and other Governments to make an effort to aid those at Vladivostok in forming a junction with their compatriots in western Siberia; and . . . this Government on sentimental grounds and because of the effect upon the friendly Slavs everywhere would be subject to criticism if it does not make this effort, and would doubtless be held responsible if they were defeated by lack of such effort. . . ."[63] Nothing here or in related evidence indicated that Wilson was concerned to forestall a unilateral intervention by the Japanese, who had assured him on June 26 that they would not take action without an understanding with the United States.[64] But if American troops entered Siberia the Japanese obviously would expect to do so too. Consequently, Wilson invited them to send 7,000 troops along with the 7,000 he would send.[65] These numbers of Japanese and Americans, combined with the 50,000 Czechs, would mean that the foreign force in Russia would be predominantly white and thus less likely, in Wilson's view, to antagonize the Russians on racial grounds.

After initiating negotiations with the Japanese for the implementation of Wilson's decision, Lansing outlined it to the Allied ambassadors.[66] Reading complained that the United States was acting without consulting the Allies and stated that he must report the unilateral aspect of the intervention plan to his government. Wilson warned him that such a report would "make trouble" and promised that an opportunity for consultation would arise once an answer was received from Japan. Partly consoled, Reading cautioned London against making a protest and remarked

[63] Lansing, "Memorandum of a Conference at the White House in Reference to the Siberian Situation July 6, 1918," Lansing Private Diaries, Box 1, Vol. 3.

[64] Morley, *Japanese Thrust into Siberia*, p. 229; Kennan, *Decision to Intervene*, p. 390.

[65] *Ibid.*, p. 397.   [66] *Ibid.*, pp. 406-408.

that Lansing had said "this expedition may well be the means eventually of creating a Russian front."[67]

Lloyd George greeted the American démarche with contempt. The plan was, he said, "preposterous" and insufficient to attain the objects the Allies had in mind.[68] Lord Milner, however, was better pleased. Before news of the American plan reached London he informed Wiseman that if Wilson would not agree to large-scale intervention the next best thing was a "small force to join up with and support the Czecho-Slovaks and to assist in restoring and maintaining order in Siberia." It was better, Milner said, to go slow to begin with than to suggest that no start at all was possible without a large military force.[69] In response, Wiseman cabled: "I agree . . . and it is along these lines that I have been working. I feel that the President is now committed to intervention on a small scale and that this will eventually lead to what we want. We must now work to end that he shall commit himself finally and irrevocably when I think we will find the whole matter will go through in entire accordance with our wishes. I was going to wire . . . these views when I received your message. I take a more cheerful view of the situation than Lord Reading."[70]

This cable owed much to Wiseman's desire to please the addressee. His "more cheerful view" most likely derived from Milner's own view, which meant that the War Cabinet, of which Milner was next to Lloyd George the most prominent member, was unlikely to express serious objection to Wilson's plan for intervention. Wiseman could hardly tell London that Wilson's plan probably represented

[67] Lansing Desk Diary, July 10, 1918. Reading to Lloyd George and Balfour, July 10, 1918, Reading's Private Papers, FO 800/209.

[68] Lloyd George to Reading, July 10, 1918, Reading's Private Papers, FO 800/211.

[69] Murray to Wiseman, July 9, 1918. Murray was forwarding remarks made by Milner on July 8. Reading's first report to London on the President's planned intervention was filed at 9:10 p.m. July 9. Reading to Balfour, July 9, 1918, WWP 115.

[70] Wiseman to Murray, July 10, 1918, WWP 116.

the maximum rather than the minimum extent to which the Americans would intervene. To do so would reveal the irreconcilable difference between Wilson's and the British position, and Wiseman was trying hard to camouflage that difference. Yet a hint of the minimal nature of Wilson's commitment revealed itself in a cable drafted largely by Wiseman and dispatched on July 12 over Reading's name to the Prime Minister. The President and the American people, Wiseman said, had been from the beginning much more sympathetic than Europeans to the Russian revolution and still feared that interventionists were eager to mold the form of Russian government. "The President," continued the cable, "is still opposed to intervention and somewhat apprehensive lest the step he is now willing to take should lead him into a much more extended policy."[71]

Wiseman's real opinion emerged again when he analyzed —for Reading, but not for London[72]—the July 17 aide-memoire distributed by the American government to explain its policy in Siberia. The aide-memoire defined American aims to be to "help the Czecho-Slovaks consolidate their forces," to guard military stores at Vladivostok, Murmansk, and Archangel, and "to render such aid as may be acceptable to the Russians in the organization of their own self-defense." The United States, the aide-memoire stated, would not take part in "organized intervention" and would feel free to withdraw its troops if the character of Allied involvement in Siberia developed beyond the "modest and experimental" plans of the United States.[73]

Wiseman thought, correctly, that this statement of American policy would annoy London because of its "finality." He confided to Reading: "It would be preferable if it did

[71] Wiseman to Murray, July 12, 1918, WWP 88. This cable was sent as a "personal and most secret" message from Reading to Lloyd George. But the manuscript draft of it (WWP 107) reveals that virtually all of it was drafted by Wiseman. The line here quoted is in Reading's hand but surely represented Wiseman's thought also.

[72] See footnote 74 below.

[73] Lansing to the Allied Ambassadors, July 17, 1918, *Foreign Relations, 1918, Russia*, Vol. 2, pp. 287-90.

not commit the U.S. so definitely against any other kind of action than that which it prescribed with regard to the Murmansk and Vladivostok 'modest and experimental' plans. If it allowed for a change of attitude in the case that these projects corroborate, in any considerable degree, the evidence already to hand to the effect that the Russian people desire Allied intervention on a large scale." "In truth," Wiseman concluded, "the President gives every excuse except the real one, which is that he believes the interventionists are reactionaries under another name."[74]

THE American and Japanese governments haggled over terms to govern the Siberian intervention until August 2. The Japanese never agreed to put a ceiling on the number of troops they might send, but did intimate that 12,000 would probably be sufficient. Then, without prior notice, the Japanese proceeded unilaterally with their intervention. There was nothing left for the American government to do but proceed with its as well. The first American troops landed at Vladivostok on August 16. They found that a British detachment had been there since August 3.[75]

Indeed, the British, though distressed by the independence of Wilson's course and the "misconceptions" of his policy, moved quickly to include themselves in the Siberian intervention.[76] Already an economic mission under Sir William Clark had set out for Siberia, and on July 10 the War

[74] Wiseman to Reading, July 19, 1918, enclosing undated critique of the July 17 aide-memoire, Reading's Private Papers, FO 800/210. From Washington, Arthur Willert informed his editor, Geoffrey Dawson of the London *Times*, that there should be no comment on the aide-memoire, "in the sense that the mouse may gradually develop into an elephant. Great emphasis will be laid here upon American determination not to countenance any taking sides with Russian Parties or Factions. Comment about the obvious difficulties of this policy will not be popular." Willert to Murray, July 23, 1918, FO 115/2448.
[75] Kennan, *Decision to Intervene*, pp. 412-15.
[76] The War Cabinet response to Wilson's July 17 aide-memoire is contained in Balfour to Reading, July 22, 1918 (No. 4543), WWP 116. In a personal cable to Reading on the same day (WWP 116), Balfour stated: "For obvious reasons it is not very easy to devise a satisfactory message to the President."

Cabinet appointed General Alfred Knox to lead a military mission there.[77] On July 25 Balfour informed the State Department that Britain wished to participate in any "inter-Allied organization" for the distribution of goods in Siberia.[78] On August 12 the British chargé told Lansing that because of the "critical" position of the Czech army the British government intended to ask the Japanese to send in more troops.[79] These acts angered Wilson, and on August 23 Wiseman reported that the President "is beginning to feel that the Allies are trying to rush, even trick, him into a policy which he has refused to accept. He is well aware that he is committed to the task of rescuing the Czechs, but thinks the Allies are trying to change the character of the expedition into a full-fledged intervention with the object of reconstituting the Eastern Front."[80]

The British, or at least Lord Reading, now back in London, were genuinely concerned that the Czechs were in danger. But as Wiseman cabled Reading, the Americans found British concern hard to credit when Masaryk in Washington seemed satisfied that the Czech army was relatively secure.[81] American distrust of British motives was so strong by mid-September that Masaryk went to the British embassy to ask that reassurances be given the President. Masaryk testified that he heard suspicions of the British frequently expressed in the State Department and even by the President himself.[82] Masaryk was not exaggerating.

[77] Ullman, *Intervention and the War*, p. 220. Reading did not learn of Clark's economic mission until the first week of July. He then insisted that he be allowed to tell the American government about the mission, because "The U.S.G. will assuredly get to know it if it is the fact." Reading to Balfour, July 6, 1918, FO 115/2448. See also the memorandum (G.T. 4812) "British Economic Relations with Russia," June 11, 1918; British Embassy to State Department, July 17, 1918; and Reading to Balfour, July 26, 1918; all in FO 115/2448.

[78] Balfour to Reading, July 25, 1918, WWP 117.

[79] Ullman, *Intervention and the War*, pp. 259-60.

[80] Wiseman to Reading (London), Aug. 23, 1918, WWP 108.

[81] Reading to Wiseman, Aug. 20, 1918, WWP 108; Wiseman to Reading, Aug. 23, 1918, WWP 108.

[82] Barclay (chargé in Washington) to Balfour, Sept. 13, 1918, and

Wilson wrote Lansing that the Allies were utterly disregarding American policy and instructed the Secretary to let the Allies know in a "pointed" way that he recognized no such combined military command as they were attempting to organize in Siberia.[83] On September 21 Lansing told Wiseman that the Allies misunderstood American policy. "He says," Wiseman reported, "the policy of the U.S. Government is perfectly clear, unaltered and in entire accord with the policy of the Japanese Government, viz., to rescue the Czechs and not to assist them to re-create an Eastern Front."[84]

On September 22 Wiseman reported further that Wilson felt "control of the Russian situation is slipping from his grasp."[85] Five days later Lansing reasserted America's Russian policy in a firmly worded memorandum to the Allied governments. In this last comprehensive statement of policy prior to the war's end, Lansing labeled the military operation at Murmansk a failure and called Allied hopes of erecting a front along the Volga "impossible." The United States therefore would send no more troops to Murmansk and would insist that the Czechs retire to the east of the Urals. In addition, the United States must postpone indefinitely its wish to "bring succor" to the Russian people.[86] Bal-

---

Hohler (commercial attaché, Washington) to Drummond, Sept. 13, 1918, Balfour Papers, 49748, British Museum.

[83] Wilson to Lansing, Sept. 8, 1918, quoted in Ullman, *Intervention and the War*, p. 264, and Wilson to Lansing, Sept. 17, 1918, *Foreign Relations, The Lansing Papers, 1914-1920*, Vol. 2, pp. 385-86.

[84] Wiseman to Reading and Drummond, Sept. 21, 1918, WWP 108.

[85] Wiseman to Reading, Sept. 22, 1918, Reading's Private Papers, FO 800/212.

[86] Lansing to Page, Sept. 26, 1918, *Foreign Relations, 1918, Russia*, Vol. 2, pp. 394-95. A copy of Lansing's memorandum, dated Sept. 27, is in WWP 118.

Wiseman reported on August 27 that Wilson seemed in no hurry to develop the idea of an economic commission. Wiseman to Reading, Aug. 27, 1918, WWP 117. Under prodding from the State Department, Wilson at last charged the War Trade Board with the responsibility of relieving the immediate economic necessities of the Russian people. See Auchincloss Diary, Sept. 9, 13, 1918, and Polk to Allied

four, in reply to the memorandum, stated that British military authorities did not agree with the American analysis, that Britain was "honourably bound" to stand by her friends in European Russia, and that his government would not ask the Czechs to withdraw to the east.[87]

The predictable clash between British "traditional" policy and Wilson's "new conception of foreign policy" had occurred. Neither House nor Wiseman could think of a way out of the impasse. Realizing the President's stubbornness they did not even try to modify his position. Wiseman concluded that, despite a briefing by Masaryk, he lacked the necessary information both on the situation of the Czech army and on Allied policy to make such an attempt. He and Reading decided that the search for a "common formula" must be deferred until Reading returned with the latest views of the War Cabinet.[88] Reading did not return until February 1919.

In October indications of an early German surrender focused the attention of statesmen and their advisers on the problems of concluding the war. On October 14 Wilson ordered House to proceed to Paris to represent the United States in armistice negotiations. House asked Wiseman to accompany him and arranged for Wiseman to lunch with Wilson on October 16. The purpose of Wiseman's visit was to secure the President's views on topics which would arise in armistice and peace discussions.[89] Here is what he learned regarding Russia:

Ambassadors, Oct. 10, 1918, *Foreign Relations, 1918, Russia*, Vol. 3, pp. 147-50.

[87] Balfour to Barclay, Oct. 2, 1918, *ibid.*, Vol. 2, p. 404.

[88] Wiseman to Reading, Oct. 2, 1918, and Reading to Wiseman, Oct. 5, 1918, WWP 108. Masaryk to Wiseman, Oct. 1, 1918, WWP 80: Masaryk asked to see Wiseman on this date; it is reasonable to assume that it was for the purpose of discussing the status of the Czech army and British policy. A copy of Masaryk's notes (Sept. 30) on Lansing's Sept. 27 memorandum is in WWP 118.

[89] Seymour, *Intimate Papers*, Vol. 4, pp. 82-83; House Diary, Oct. 22, 1918.

I asked the President why he would not send any political Commissioner, or join in any political conferences with the Allies regarding action to be taken in Russia. "My policy regarding Russia," he said, "is very similar to my Mexican policy. I believe in letting them work out their own salvation, even though they wallow in anarchy for a while. I visualize it like this: A lot of impossible folk, fighting among themselves. You cannot do business with them, so you shut them all up in a room and lock the door and tell them that when they have settled matters among themselves you will unlock the door and do business." I suggested that in this case you would probably lock in a lot of Germans with them who would bolt the convention. He thought it was impossible to eradicate German influence from Russia. Hundreds and thousands of Germans had gone to live in Russia; had taken Russian names, and were apparently Russians. How could you get rid of the influence of these men? The Bolsheviki, he agreed, were impossible. He had watched with disgust their treatment of Lockhart, who had tried hard to help them.

The question of Russia, he thought, should . . . be left to the Peace Conference. I protested that would be too late; that the stage was even now being set by the Germans, and we should find forces and conditions had been created in Russia which would be difficult, if not impossible, to alter at a Peace Conference. The President said there was a great deal in that view, and the whole question was causing him great anxiety. I gathered the impression that it is not impossible that he will modify his policy regarding Russia.[90]

As subsequent events proved, Wiseman was right about the danger of postponing action to the peace conference. But there was little in American policy of the past few months to justify his "impression" that Wilson would modify his

[90] Wiseman, "Notes of an Interview with the President at the White House Wednesday, October 16th, 1918," WWP 129.

attitude. Most likely, Wiseman was once again hoping to make London believe that the gap between American and British policies was bridgeable. At the peace conference the British would learn first-hand that this was not so, that Wilson was still fundamentally committed to a policy of "Do Nothing."

CHAPTER EIGHT

THE APPROACH OF PEACE

> . . . whether we like it or not, Wilson will be President for
> another three years . . .
>
> Wiseman to Drummond,
> January 25, 1918

> . . . the approach of peace emphasizes the problems of recon-
> struction and the inevitable competition for trade after the
> war. I think trade rivalry after the war and freedom of the seas
> are going to be the two dangerous rocks for Anglo-American
> relations.
>
> Wiseman to Drummond,
> January 25, 1918

THE MOTIVATING and unifying force behind Wiseman's
various enterprises of 1917-18 was his belief that, properly
managed, the Anglo-American war partnership would
flower into a permanent entente. He expected that the two
countries working together in war would gradually realize
how similar their traditions and ideals were, with the result that the peace settlement would be an Anglo-American structure. But there was no guarantee that such a desirable outcome would automatically occur. Wiseman repeatedly reminded the British that the American attitude
toward and objectives in the war differed from Britain's. And particularly he emphasized that Woodrow Wilson was the embodiment of American foreign policy, was
the irremovable war leader, and would be the powerfully
armed peace arbiter. To defer to Wilson and to gain his
trust during the war were undeniable prerequisites to securing his sympathy at the peace conference. Thus Wiseman
was willing to forgo certain efficiencies in the conduct of
the war, such as American political representation on the
Supreme War Council, rather than irritate Wilson. And thus
he prevailed on Balfour to send a copy of the notorious
Treaty of London to House. By such tactics and by the
continuous cultivation of House Wiseman surely improved

the prospects for Anglo-American unity at the peace conference. But in the closing months of the war Wiseman found that some of Wilson's anti-British principles and prejudices did not respond to conciliatory gestures. On the contrary, while Wilson grew fond and trusting of Wiseman he became increasingly suspicious of the British government.[1]

From the time of the American declaration of war Wiseman realized that for Wilson and particularly for House war-making was an unwelcome but necessary prelude to the more important task of writing the peace. Even as belligerents they considered themselves rather as umpires than as participants. Wilson's sense of special responsibility for the peace prompted him in September 1917 to establish a body of experts to prepare solutions for the political and territorial problems which would confront the peace conference. House took charge of this peace-planning project, named the Inquiry and quartered in New York, safe from the supervision of the State Department. Immediately Wiseman assumed that House would become the chief American delegate to the peace conference and began, on his own initiative, to expound British war aims to House.[2]

But neither Wiseman nor House had much time for postwar plans in the fall of 1917. They were soon caught up in schemes for coordinating American and Allied war efforts. House turned over the day-to-day direction of the Inquiry to his brother-in-law, Sidney Mezes, and embarked for the

[1] For Wiseman's views on Anglo-American cooperation see memorandum dated Mar. 7, 1917; "Memorandum on Anglo-American Relations August 1917," WWP 4; and "Some Notes on the Position in August 1917," HP 20:45.

Regarding the Treaty of London see Balfour to Wiseman, Jan. 31, 1918, WWP 4. See also Reading to Wiseman, Mar. 3, 1918, WWP 107, and Seymour, *Intimate Papers*, Vol. 3, pp. 50-51, 60-63. Seymour mistakenly dates Balfour's letter Jan. 30, 1918.

[2] Memoranda by Wiseman cited in previous footnote. Lawrence E. Gelfand, *The Inquiry: American Preparations for Peace, 1917-1919*, New Haven, 1963, pp. 26-31. Wiseman to Drummond, Oct. 4, 1917, WWP 42; Wiseman to House, Sept. 26, 1917, enclosing Wiseman's "Some Thoughts on War-Aims and Peace—September 1917," HP 20:46; Seymour, *Intimate Papers*, Vol. 4, pp. 5-7.

inter-Allied meetings of November and December. The Inquiry managed to produce some notes for Wilson's use in the preparation of his Fourteen Points speech of January 8, 1918, but not until later that month were the experts pursuing their studies in a systematic way.[3]

When Wiseman went to London in April 1918 he arranged to establish communications between the Inquiry and its nearest British counterpart, the Political Intelligence Department of the Foreign Office. This department had sent occasional information to the American embassy in London but apparently had not yet made contact with the Inquiry.[4] Wiseman explained to Balfour the nature of House's organization and the eagerness of Wilson and House to inform themselves regarding European public opinion, which, Wiseman perhaps added, Wilson intended to exploit. "We may be quite sure," Wiseman wrote, "that House will find means of keeping in touch with all shades of political opinion, particularly in England. The question is whether he shall do so through me, or through someone else, presumably an American." Wiseman argued that information from the Inquiry would obviously be useful to the British and that the chances of obtaining it would be greater if he could convey more information from the British side. "It must be quite clear to you," he wrote, "that when in New York I occupy practically the position of political Secretary to House. I think he shows me everything he gets, and together we discuss every question that arises."[5]

Besides wishing to establish a mutual exchange of data by the peace-planning bureaus, Wiseman evidently feared that Ambassador Reading was about to ask for his assignment to the embassy staff.[6] Reading, still the Lord Chief

---

[3] Gelfand, *The Inquiry*, pp. 35, 38, 136-53, 89.

[4] Arthur C. Murray to Wiseman, Apr. 5, 1918, and July 3, 1918, WWP 88.

[5] Wiseman to Drummond, Apr. 27, 1918, Balfour Papers, 49741, British Museum.

[6] Wiseman to Reading, July 26, 1918, WWP 108.

Justice of England, planned to return to London for a period in the summer, and Wiseman was the logical substitute for him. But Wiseman did not wish to be chained to embassy routine, which would have separated him from House at Magnolia and the Inquiry in New York. Balfour agreed that Wiseman should become the liaison between the Inquiry and the Political Intelligence Department and that he should continue his independence from the embassy. Said Balfour: "I do not see why W.[iseman] should narrow down his activities. No doubt any broadening of them will increase his labours—but I cannot see that it would be otherwise than beneficial. His position is already somewhat anomalous & therefore difficult. But it is this very characteristic which makes his services so valuable. I should let him do anything which he thinks worth doing."[7]

With this carte blanche from Balfour, Wiseman proceeded to place a representative in the Political Intelligence Department. He chose Arthur C. Murray, a member of Parliament on friendly terms with Lloyd George and Reading. In addition, Murray was recently returned from Washington where he served several months as an assistant military attaché to Reading and where he gained an acquaintance with numerous American officials.[8] From May 1918 to the war's end Murray regularly sent Wiseman British documents on various topics and through long letters and cables kept him abreast of events and gossip in the British government. As a result Wiseman was able to satisfy the curiosity of House and Wilson about political figures and movements in Europe. In September, evidently without intended hyperbole, Wiseman reported that "House and the President have come to regard me as perhaps their chief source of information. . . ."[9]

Wiseman aspired to be the chief source of British information to the State Department and the Inquiry as well.

---

[7] Minute by Balfour on the margin of Wiseman to Drummond, Apr. 27, 1918, Balfour Papers, 49741, British Museum.

[8] Murray to Wiseman, July 3, 1918, WWP 88; Murray, *At Close Quarters*, London, 1946, pp. 7-18.

[9] Wiseman to Murray, Sept. 14, 1918, WWP 86.

He requested Murray to halt the transmission of any Political Intelligence Department reports to the American embassy. Wiseman preferred that these reports come directly to him so that he could decide which, if any, should go to the Inquiry or to the State Department, whose security arrangements he distrusted. He hoped in return to secure American documents to send to the Politial Intelligence Department. The latter concluded that it could not abolish its communication with the American embassy without causing offense.[10] So information was exchanged through several channels; it is impossible today to determine exactly which information reached the Americans via Wiseman. Wiseman did forward to the Political Intelligence Department Inquiry data which otherwise would not have been sent, and presumably the numerous Political Intelligence Department documents which reached House and the Inquiry came from Wiseman.

With one exception Wiseman did not contribute substantively to the deliberations of the experts of the Inquiry. The exception involved the retention by the British Empire of colonies captured from Germany. Wiseman came to expound British claims to the colonies reluctantly. In the summer of 1917 Lord Northcliffe agitated for a propaganda campaign, including a speaking tour by Gen. Jan Smuts, to proselyte Americans on the necessity for British adoption of German colonies in Africa. In December 1917 L. S. Amery, political adviser to the British War Office, pressed upon Wiseman notes to be used in defending these British claims.[11] Wiseman objected to both overtures, believing it was unwise to raise a question that could lead to dissension. Finally an American initiative caused him to change his mind—slightly. George Louis Beer, the Inquiry expert on Africa and an ardent Anglophile, in June 1918 began seeking information directly from the Foreign Office and from

[10] Wiseman to Murray, July 19, 1918, WWP 85; Murray to Wiseman, Aug. 10, 1918, WWP 86.
[11] Northcliffe to War Cabinet and Smuts, Aug. 30, 1917, WWP 91; Amery to Wiseman, Dec. 7, 1917, WWP 59.

his friends on the staff of the journal *The Round Table*. Beer, whom Wiseman had not previously known, proved to be just the sort of discreet man in a position of influence with whom Wiseman believed such questions as the African colonies could profitably be discussed. Consequently Wiseman procured a large quantity of data for Beer and met with him occasionally to suggest ways for dealing with problems like Egyptian nationalism and the future of Mesopotamia.[12]

Colonial questions interested Wiseman only as a possible source of friction between Britain and the United States. He considered that they held that potential only if publicly agitated. In February 1918 Wiseman got from the President the impression that the United States would not demand the return of Germany's colonies. In June Wilson appeared sympathetic when Prime Minister Hughes of Australia outlined the arguments in favor of retention by the British Empire of German colonies in the Pacific.[13] In his long interview with Wiseman on October 16 Wilson indicated that his chief concern was to find a way to eliminate colonial competition and jealousies among the European powers. Commenting on the fifth of his Fourteen Points, Wilson told Wiseman:

> It was clear that the Colonies must not be given back to Germany; at least until we are satisfied that their form of government is very different from the present. For his part, he would be well content to see the German Colonies administered by Great Britain, whose Colonial government was in many respects a model for the world. He must warn the British, however, of the great jealousy of the other nations—including, he regretted to say, a

[12] Eustace Percy to Wiseman, June 18, 1918, and July 5, 1918, WWP 97; Wiseman to Percy, July 19, 1918, WWP 59; Beer to Wiseman, Sept. 8, 1918, WWP 9. See list dated July 1, 1918 of materials on Africa, and other areas of the world, received by D. H. Miller of the Inquiry from Wiseman, WWP 64.

[13] Wiseman to Drummond, Feb. 4, 1918, WWP 129; Reading to Balfour, June 2, 1918, Reading's Private Papers, FO 800/209.

large number of people in America. It would, he thought, create much bad feeling internationally if the German Colonies were handed over to us as a sovereign part of the British Empire. He wondered whether there was some way in which they could be administered in trust. "In trust," I asked, "for whom?" "Well, for the League of Nations, for instance," he said.[14]

Here, in a statement that reached the British well in advance of the peace conference, Wilson indicated that the "absolutely impartial adjustment of all colonial claims" demanded by his Point V[15] need not deny the British actual control over former German colonies. Wilson merely preferred that the power which administered the colonies do so as a trustee for the league and not as a sovereign possessor.

AMERICAN planning for the League of Nations, proposed by the last of the Fourteen Points, fell largely beyond the purview of the Inquiry.[16] Wilson considered the league to be the vital feature of a successful peace settlement and proved unwilling to delegate the planning of it. He did permit House to sketch a draft for a league covenant and to solicit the ideas of persons interested in a league. But he consistently refused to publish any detailed plans himself or to agree to such publication by the British or any private American groups. Thus Wilson reached the end of the war maintaining that the league should be the pillar of the peace settlement, yet with only the fragmentary draft by House as a blueprint.[17] In part, other duties prevented the President from composing a detailed league plan. But

[14] Wiseman, "Notes of an Interview with the President at the White House Wednesday, October 16th, 1918," WWP 129.
[15] The Fourteen Points speech is printed in Baker, *War and Peace*, Vol. 1, pp. 155-62.
[16] For the Inquiry's role in league planning, see Gelfand, *The Inquiry*, pp. 149-50.
[17] Seymour, *Intimate Papers*, Vol. 4, pp. 9-54; House's draft is printed on pp. 28-36.

Wiseman's notes and reports indicated that there was also method in Wilson's delay.

The British, unlike Wilson, were eager to complete league plans prior to the end of the war. Soon after Wilson's Fourteen Points speech the British government appointed a committee under the chairmanship of Sir Walter Phillimore, an expert on international law, to devise a constitution for the league. On February 9 the Foreign Office inquired of Wiseman whether the American government had a similar committee with which the Phillimore committee might consult. Wiseman answered in the negative and suggested that Lord Robert Cecil, the leading British exponent of a league, correspond directly with Colonel House. Cecil then wrote House, only to be told that American study of the question had not progressed sufficiently to warrant discussion between the two governments.[18] In fact, however, Wilson was trying to silence all but the most private deliberation.[19]

In his remarks to Wiseman on April 1, Wilson implied that he was necessarily considering more than one kind of

[18] Henry R. Winkler, *The League of Nations Movement in Great Britain, 1914-1919*, New Brunswick, N.J., 1952, pp. 233-36; Drummond to Wiseman, Feb. 9, 1918, HP 20:47, WWP 43; Wiseman to Drummond, Feb. 12, 1918, WWP 43; Seymour, *Intimate Papers*, Vol. 4, pp. 8-10.

[19] *Ibid.* Aside from reasons related to the conduct of the war, Wilson probably objected to deliberations over the league because of the initiative being taken by prominent Republicans. Lord Bryce urged Elihu Root, A. Lawrence Lowell, and William Howard Taft to constitute a committee of their own to communicate with the British if Wilson refused to appoint an official committee. House to Wilson, Mar. 8, 1918, HP 49:10. Wilson wrote Lowell: "I should consider it very embarrassing to have a private organization like the League to Enforce Peace take this matter up, since the immediate establishment of a league of nations is a question of government policy not only, but constitutes part of the intricate web of counsel now being woven between the associated governments. I am having this matter studied myself and hope very sincerely that if the League to Enforce Peace undertakes its study, it will not in addition undertake to establish international connections with committees of a different origin abroad." Wilson to Lowell, July 11, 1918, Wilson Papers, File 6, Box 600. See also Wilson to C. R. Macauley, May 16, 1918, *ibid.*

a league. At that moment the Allies were reeling under the impact of the German spring offensive, and Wilson felt obliged to contemplate the possibility of a negotiated peace with Germany. In case of an Allied defeat, Wilson said (in Wiseman's indirect quotation):

> He supposed we should have to make a compromise peace, but we could not deceive ourselves—it would be a German peace, and mean in effect a German victory. The Germans would no doubt be prepared to deal generously with France and Belgium, and other questions, providing she was allowed practically a free-hand in Russia. She would be, of course, subject to various restrictions and guarantees, which on paper would limit her success, but we would know that such guarantees would be quite worthless. The only bright spot would be that our economic resources would be very formidable. . . . It would mean, he said, that England and America would have to start building up again for another war, organizing ourselves as best we could.
>
> [A negotiated, compromise peace with the Germans] would be only a "scrap of paper," but they might be restrained from violating it by material rather than moral considerations.[20]

From this, Wiseman, who already knew the President's belief in the power of economic coercion,[21] concluded that unless Germany were decisively beaten Wilson's league of nations might be essentially an economic combination of the United States and Britain to restrain Germany. The league's composition and function must necessarily depend on the result of the war. There was no point in announcing that Germany could or could not be in the league until Germany's condition at the end of the war was known. This obvious necessity surely accounted for much of Wilson's re-

[20] Wiseman, "Notes on Interview with the President—April 1st, 1918, at 5:30 p.m.," Balfour Papers, 49741, British Museum.
[21] Wiseman, "Notes on Interview with the President January 23rd, 1918," WWP 43.

luctance to endorse a particular scheme prior to the war's end. It also affected Wiseman's proposals for a league, made in June 1918.

In May the Phillimore committee placed before the British government an interim report, which Cecil sent to Wiseman for House's inspection. Cecil was becoming impatient with the Americans and warned that unless the two nations soon reached some common position on the league, "we are merely deluding ourselves and others by advocating it."[22] After discussing the report with Wiseman, House sent Cecil a letter containing his own vague ideas, the chief one of which was the proposal that nations adopt the same standards of conduct which prevailed among "individuals of honor." Wiseman supplemented House's letter with the explanation that Wilson's "one-track mind" was too distracted by other problems to consider the league. But House, Wiseman said, was seeking advice from "various prominent people here who have interested themselves in the subject. . . ."[23] Cecil caustically replied that it was "inexpedient . . . to leave the discussions on so important a theme entirely in the hands of unguided amateurs." Cecil therefore intended to submit the Phillimore report to the Allies and to Parliament as a basis for debate.[24]

Wiseman was no less eager than Cecil to formulate definite plans for a league, but he objected to the Phillimore draft because it lacked provision for enforcing the league's will. It envisaged, as Wiseman put it, a judge but no policeman. The obvious way to overcome this difficulty was to provide the league with a police force. But Wiseman doubted that any of the great powers would permit such a force to operate within its jurisdiction. Besides, in his

[22] Cecil to Wiseman, May 17, 1918, WWP 76.
[23] House to Cecil, June 25, 1918, HP 4:38; Wiseman to Cecil, July 17, 1918, WWP 75; Wiseman to Cecil, July 18, 1918, WWP 98.
[24] Cecil to Wiseman, July 21, 1918, WWP 75. House's letter to Cecil of June 25 related so little to the Phillimore report that Cecil cabled: "Has Colonel House been given a copy of Phillimore's report and if so when? He has written me a letter . . . and I should be glad to know if I am to take it as a reply to this report." Cecil to Wiseman, July 15, 1918, WWP 75.

opinion there was a more effective method of preventing the outbreak or controlling the spread of war. Since the fundamental cause of such wars as the present one was the "economic factor," i.e., the competition for raw materials and markets, equal trade opportunities would eliminate the cause. And if they did not, an economic boycott could isolate and starve any war that did occur.[25]

In his emphasis on "teeth," in the form of economic suasion, for the league Wiseman paralleled the thought of the President. And when he attempted to apply these ideas he followed Wilson's line of thought, expressed in April, as to what must be done in case Germany was not totally defeated. Wiseman, doubting that Germany would be badly beaten, thought that a league must obviously utilize "the situation left by the war" and that it must be "as natural a growth as possible." The situation left by the war, he expected, would be characterized by balance of power tensions and by national obsession with economic security. Why not convert these unhappy factors into strengths for the league, he asked.

Cannot a means be discovered of giving the League an economic foundation and of simultaneously buttressing it upon the play of those human instincts which must for a long time perpetuate the spirit of the Balance of Power in the sense of distrust of the civilized world for the Teutonic nations? . . .

An economic foundation for the League . . . would give it the force not only of logic but of immediate and practical usefulness. If the allies are to make the most of their peace negotiations and of after-the-war conditions, it is essential that they should have a firm economic understanding. There must be an agreement before the peace negotiations for the control of raw materials as (1) a card

[25] Wiseman, "Memorandum. The League of Nations," June 22, 1918; and Wiseman, untitled and undated memorandum, c. June 30, 1918; both in WWP 98. These memoranda were written for House and copies were sent to Cecil. Wiseman to Cecil, July 18, 1918, WWP 98.

on the peace table; (2) a means toward equitable reconstruction; (3) a lever wherewith to secure . . . good behaviour on the part of Germany after the war. . . .

If the League had at its back the lever of even Anglo-American control of raw materials and could show Germany that, after reconstruction was over, she could be treated as well in trade matters as other countries so long as she behaved Germany's incentive to further wars would have been very much diminished.[26]

These lines were intended as much to suggest a preventive to an Anglo-American trade war as to put muscle in the league. Ironically, the closer the Anglo-American combination came to defeating Germany, the more likely appeared the chances of the combination's breaking apart over the question of postwar economic policy. Whereas the British would like to leave Germany out of the league and indeed use the league's economic might to restrain Germany, Wilson still hoped for a governmental reformation in Germany which would enable her to become a league member. The British government was not so sanguine about a reformation of Germany and considered the threat of economic punishment an effective war tactic. Wilson, on the other hand, thought such threats would both discourage liberals in Germany and commit the Allies to a harsh policy from which it would be difficult to recede. Yet, and to compound the irony, Wilson was not averse to using America's economic power to prevent Britain from using hers.[27]

The importance of the economic question emerged plainly in August. On July 31 Lloyd George addressed the (British) National Union of Manufacturers on the future of the British economy. The Prime Minister's remarks, printed on the front page of the *New York Times*, included the sentence, "The longer the war lasts the sterner must be

[26] Wiseman, memorandum, c. June 30, 1918, WWP 98.

[27] These points will be substantiated in the development of the present chapter. See also Winkler, *League of Nations Movement in Great Britain*, pp. 241-42.

the economic terms we impose on the foe." He went on to say that it was vitally important for the United States and Britain to reach "complete agreement" on economic policy and implied that the United States should endorse the so-called Paris resolutions. These resolutions, produced by the Paris Economic Conference of the Allies in June 1916, called for postwar tariff and transportation discrimination against Germany. They had caused consternation in Washington at the time of their conception and were still repugnant to Wilson. Their spirit characterized the remarks of Bonar Law, also delivered on July 31, regarding "imperial preference" in the British Empire. Law stressed that the British must arrange to control sources of raw materials so as "to prevent old enemies from organizing a corner in them." To perfect the offensiveness to Wilson of Law's and his own remarks, Lloyd George proposed that the league of nations consist of the British Empire and Germany's other enemies, following the economic policy he outlined.[28]

Wiseman cabled on August 7 that the Prime Minister's speech had caused "much comment" in the United States and hinted that Wilson might declare his dissent from it.[29] Two weeks passed with no direct comment on the mat-

[28] The *New York Times*, Aug. 2, 1918. On the Paris Economic Conference, see Laurence W. Martin, *Peace Without Victory: Woodrow Wilson and the British Liberals*, New Haven, 1958, pp. 33, 69-71, 112.

Lord Eustace Percy, formerly attached to the Washington embassy, warned the British of American opposition to the Paris resolutions. He was quoted in a memorandum circulated to the Cabinet in May 1918 as saying: "The original intense hostility evoked in the United States in 1916 by the publication of the Paris Resolutions has in no sense abated since then." Balfour, memorandum, May 1918, Private Secretary Archives, 1917-1924, A. J. Balfour, FO 800/199. Arthur Willert to Wiseman, June 23, 1918, WWP 3, called "the so-called Paris Economic Conference . . . the most unpopular thing done by the allies while the U S was neutral." See also memorandum "Economic Policy," July 12, 1918, by Percy and A. E. Zimmern, WWP 96.

[29] Wiseman to Reading, Aug. 7, 1918, WWP 108. Wiseman said: "The State Department . . . while admitting that the speech follows much the same line as some of the President's pronouncements, claims that no definite Inter-Allied Economic Policy has been as yet settled, and evidently feels that the hearty support that public

ter from the President. He went to Magnolia on August 15 for a few days' vacation with House.[30] Wiseman, not accidentally, was also at Magnolia. On August 17 he received a cable from Balfour for House which again raised the question of economic policy. Balfour intended the cable as a courtesy and an indication of the British willingness to confide in Wilson. But the subject of the cable, a contemplated interference in Mexico to "secure honesty and order in the public administration" (i.e., to protect British oil investments), could hardly have been better calculated to anger Wilson.[31] Here shortly after Wilson's announced determination to avoid interference in the domestic affairs of Siberia and only days after his criticism of Lloyd George's talk of commercial ambition, the British revealed they might support a revolution in Mexico in order to improve their commercial position there. Undoubtedly Wilson's strong reaction to this cable accounted for Wiseman's reiterated emphasis thereafter on the necessity for an understanding on commercial matters between Britain and America.

The immediate result of Balfour's Mexican cable was the dispatch by Wiseman of two cables outlining the President's attitudes. The first dealt with Mexico:

> The President most earnestly hopes that HMG will not contemplate supporting [Roblez] Dominguez [the Mexican rebel] with money or otherwise, either directly or indirectly. You will recollect that the President has adopted a carefully considered and, for his part, unalterable policy regarding Mexico and the Latin-American states generally. The guiding principle of this policy is non-interference with the internal affairs . . . and non-

opinion here seems inclined to give to the Prime Minister's proposals may force Administration to declare their policy before they are ready."

[30] House Diary, Aug. 15, 19, 20, 1918.

[31] Balfour to House, Aug. 17, 1918, HP 2:23, including marginal note by House saying that the President was "much disturbed." Wiseman to Balfour, Aug. 20, 1918, WWP 82.

recognition of revolutionary leaders. . . . While it is practically true that the United States are not entirely satisfied with the attitude of Carranza [president of Mexico], or with the situation in Mexico, they believe the position is improving, and . . . hope that economic assistance will help Mexico to recover her stability. Any allied support of a counter-revolutionary movement would, in the President's opinion, be fatal to such a policy. . . . The President will insist that the Mexican Government shall deal with the Oil supply of the country in accordance with the recognized principles of international law and the rights of foreign nations.[32]

The second cable, which probably would not have been sent had not Wilson been provoked by the proposal concerning Mexico, dealt directly with Lloyd George's July 31 speech and the Paris resolutions. Wilson, Wiseman said,

had understood that the Allied Governments decided they would not officially endorse the punitive trade policy advocated by the Paris Conference. He was disturbed, therefore, on reading the reports of Mr. Lloyd George's speech . . . which seemed to be recommending the crushing of Germany's trade after the war. . . .

He is convinced . . . that it is a great mistake to threaten Germany now with any kind of punitive postwar measures against her trade. In his view this threat is one of the strongest levers with which the German

[32] Wiseman to Balfour, Aug. 20, 1918, WWP 82. An unsigned, undated [but c. May 1917] memorandum in the papers titled Balfour's Mission (Foreign Office Library) contains the following: "Situation is bad & growing worse. Only possible solution appears to be a new Mexican candidate, short of intervention. Such a candidate is in sight, but unless endorsed by USG he would have no success. . . . Any movement to be made in Mexico must start from the oil fields otherwise they would be destroyed. Pelaez [?] who is in charge of the fields is friendly and is interested personally in their preservation." And Reading to Balfour, May 12, 1918, FO 115/2446 stated laconically: "There is no doubt State Dept. is well aware of the happenings in Mexico." See also Reading to Wiseman, Aug. 23, 1918, HP 16:30.

militarists suppress the growth of any Liberal movement in Germany. They point out, he thinks, to their people that the Allies, especially Great Britain, are manifestly jealous of Germany's commercial position, and that if the Allies are not forced to accept a German peace they will crush Germany's trade. . . . It is true that the Allies will come to the Peace Conference practically controlling the supply of the world's raw material, but there will be no need to advertise that fact or to threaten anyone. Everyone—especially the Germans—will be quite aware of the facts.

Wiseman concluded with a warning, from Colonel House, that if the Allies again advocated a punitive trade policy against Germany the President would be obliged to dissociate the United States from that policy. Wiseman also pointed out that Wilson intended to seek from Congress authority for presidential control over American exports of raw materials for a period of years after the close of the war. Wilson would thus have, in Wiseman's words, "a formidable weapon for the United States to bring to the Peace Conference."[33]

There was no question that Wilson expected the "formidable weapon" might be needed against the British Empire as well as against Germany. When he learned at the end of August that Australian Prime Minister Hughes intended to come to the United States on a speaking tour he exploded in anger. Hughes, a delegate to the Paris Economic Conference, was one of the staunchest advocates of commercial punishment for Germany, and Wilson assumed that the Prime Minister planned to spread his wicked doctrine in the United States. To stop Hughes, Wilson ordered Lansing to instruct the London embassy to refuse Hughes an American visa. When Lansing objected to so extreme a step, Wilson agreed that a better procedure

[33] Wiseman to Reading, Aug. 20, 1918, WWP 108. But see also Willert to Wiseman, June 23, 1918, WWP 3, which predicted opposition from Southern Democrats to any measure which would inhibit "the freest trading possible in raw cotton."

would be for Wiseman to ask the British government to persuade Hughes not to come.[34] Wilson noted that "Sir William Wiseman is fine in his helpfulness and I hope with his kind help the incident will be avoided altogether."[35]

Wiseman was able to stop Hughes. But Wilson's suspicion of British commercial greed continued unabated. He complained to his aides of British profiteering in the sale of supplies to the American army and accused the British of trying to gain "every economic advantage that is within their reach." His Cabinet members freely alleged that Britain was charging extortionate rates for the transport of American soldiers and talked of using American power to make the British "listen to reasonable arrangements after the war."[36] This criticism was so evident among American officials in Europe that Lord Reading (in London) asked Wiseman if a deliberate policy of non-cooperation had been instituted by the American government.[37]

[34] Wiseman to Reading, Aug. 31, 1918, WWP 108. Reading was in Paris and did not answer Wiseman until September 6, when he noted it would be difficult for the British government to appear to wish to control Hughes. On September 12 Reading cabled that Lloyd George "quite understands the situation and will deal with it." Wiseman to Reading, Sept. 5, 1918; Reading to Wiseman, Sept. 6, 1918; Reading to Wiseman, Sept. 12, 1918; all in WWP 108. See also Auchincloss Diary, Aug. 30, 1918.

[35] Quoted by Auchincloss from a note from Wilson to Lansing. Auchincloss to Wiseman, Sept. 3, 1918, London WWP.

[36] Baker, *Wilson Life & Letters*, Vol. 8, pp. 364-65; E. David Cronon, ed., *The Cabinet Diaries of Josephus Daniels, 1913-1921*, Lincoln, Neb., 1963, pp. 332, 338.

McAdoo vehemently opposed any step that would benefit British commerce. Typical was his letter to Wilson of November 16, 1918, in which he said: "As you know, we have been extending liberal credits to the British Government, and as a result of the relief America has afforded in this way, Great Britain is now in a position to buy these [American] ships. It would requite us in an extraordinary way if Great Britain should take advantage of the strength we have imparted to her to strike this blow at America's essential ocean transportation system." McAdoo Papers, Box 525.

[37] Reading to Wiseman, Aug. 28, 1918, WWP 108. One day earlier House recorded that Assistant Secretary of State Phillips thought "the President and Lansing are so prejudiced against the British Government that there is danger of serious complications." House Diary, Aug. 27, 1918.

Wiseman replied, in a message he cleared with House, that friction had inevitably resulted from the working out of difficult war problems. "The real danger-point," he continued, ". . . is in trade questions. . . . Both nations and their representatives find it difficult to give way to each other's views and policies without apparently sacrificing their interests and principles."[38] In a subsequent cable, not cleared with House, Wiseman said: ". . . I must admit that our most practical difficulty is the attitude of the President himself. During his week's holiday at Magnolia, I saw a great deal of him, and, while I do not alter my own affectionate admiration for him, I realize that he is a most difficult person to deal with as head of the government. His attitude lately has tended to become more arbitrary and aloof, and there are times when he seems to treat foreign governments hardly seriously. Col. House realises this, and any influence he has will be used to the uttermost to remedy it. Of course the rest of the Administration and officials generally take their "time" by the President and tend to treat foreign representatives in a somewhat patronizing and impatient manner."[39]

At Magnolia Wiseman found Wilson's arbitrariness notably prominent in regard to the league of nations. There Wilson tentatively approved House's draft of a league covenant, based in part on the Phillimore report.[40] But he condemned the report as indefinite and again refused to appoint an American committee to consult with the Phillimore committee. "How then," Wiseman asked him, "are we ever to exchange views and urge a common basis, because no one nation can make a league all by itself." Wilson replied that he planned to consult with Lloyd George at the peace conference. To arrange a league before then, the President said, would be to construct a sort of Holy Alliance against Germany. The American people wanted no such alliance, he continued, but rather a family of na-

[38] Wiseman to Reading (CXP 731), Sept. 5, 1918, WWP 108.
[39] Wiseman to Reading (CXP 732), Sept. 5, 1918, WWP 108.
[40] Seymour, *Intimate Papers*, Vol. 4, pp. 24, 49.

tions, including Germany. Wiseman cabled these views to London and advised against the publication of the Phillimore report. The President, he said, "has given us this clear warning, and it may easily embarrass our whole relations with him if we cannot meet his views."[41]

By early September, then, American and British policies, particularly regarding the league and postwar commerce, were diverging rather than meeting. Alarmed, House attempted to play on Wilson's suspicion of the "hostile" composition of Allied governments to get him to define publicly what he meant by a league. "Do you not think," House asked the President, "the time has come for you to consider whether it would not be wise to try to commit the Allies to some of the things for which we are fighting?" House pointed out that as the Allies began to feel that the war was won Wilson's influence on them would diminish. Wilson agreed but declined House's suggestion to consult with the Allies on the terms to be included in the league's constitution. Instead Wilson chose to make a speech outlining generally his ideas and inviting the Allies to accede to them.[42]

On September 27 Wilson delivered the speech in New York. In it he demanded that the league be an integral part of the peace settlement, that there be no "special, selfish economic combination within the league," and that the power of economic boycott be reserved solely to the league. He said he spoke not because he doubted that the Allied leaders agreed with him but because of the necessity to clear the air of "mists and groundless doubtings and mischievous perversions of counsel."[43]

At some point during his visit to New York Wilson

[41] Wiseman to Reading, Aug. 16, 1918, WWP 75. The version of this cable printed in Seymour, *Intimate Papers*, Vol. 4, pp. 52-54, with no ellipsis marks or any indication of alteration, varies radically from the original. Neither of the two sentences here quoted appears in the Seymour version.

[42] House to Wilson, Sept. 3, 1918, HP 49:11A; Seymour, *Intimate Papers*, Vol. 4, pp. 66-67.

[43] Baker and Dodd, *War and Peace*, Vol. 1, pp. 253-61.

learned that at least one important source of counsel in the British government was not mischievously perverted. Wilson read a letter from Lord Robert Cecil to Wiseman in which Cecil described the league in distinctly Wilsonian tones. Cecil said that the architects of the league should aim for a Hebraic-Christian "reign of Peace." They must act swiftly at the war's end to mobilize the public revulsion of war against the "heresies" of militarism, which existed in Britain as well as in Germany, and against the obstructions offered by "European bureaucracies." Cecil also suggested the continuation of inter-Allied economic organizations for the purpose of healing Europe and fitting Germany for membership in "International Society." His sense of urgency, his wish "to create and focus public opinion," Cecil concluded, had accounted for his eagerness to publish a league plan.[44]

Wilson was pleased with Cecil's letter. Cecil in turn enthusiastically approved Wilson's speech, calling it "the finest description of our war aims yet uttered. . . ." Thus by October the two men who would be most responsible for the league covenant at the peace conference had come, through the agency of Wiseman, to admire the similarity of one another's ideas.[45]

Whether Wiseman carried to London a copy of the House-Wilson draft for a league covenant is not clear. He did, however, know the contents of the draft[46] and had in addition Wilson's latest thoughts, expressed on October 16. Wilson told Wiseman on that date that the league of nations must be the "very centre" of the peace settlement, the "pillars upon which the house will stand." He also specified that Germany should be present when the league was constituted, that there must be "equal trade opportunities for all nations everywhere," and that there could be "no

[44] Wiseman to Drummond, Sept. 17, 1918, WWP 75, asked permission to show Cecil's letter, dated Aug. 19, 1918 (WWP 98) to Wilson. House to Cecil, Oct. 2, 1918, WWP 75.

[45] *Ibid.*; Cecil to House, Sept. 28, 1918; Seymour, *Intimate Papers,* Vol. 4, p. 72.

[46] House Diary, July 15, 1918.

economic boycott except as a penalty imposed by the League of Nations."[47]

Thus Wiseman's hope of constructing the league as a "natural growth," as an Anglo-American economic combination utilizing the "human instincts" of anti-Germanism, was shattered. But an open break between the United States and Britain had been avoided, and the prospect of cooperation between Wilson and Cecil cordially established.

ONCE Wilson's determination to push forward his Fourteen Points became unmistakably clear, Wiseman realized that Point II, the demand for "Absolute freedom of navigation upon the seas, alike in peace and war," would cause grave difficulties. Freedom of the seas, a term frequently espoused by Germany, was anathema to Britain, dependent on mastery of the seas for her position in the world. On the other hand, Wilson attributed America's involvement in the war and indeed the basic cause of hostilities in 1914 to the unsatisfactory state of maritime conditions. He insisted as early as 1916 that freedom of the seas was the *sine qua non* of a peace settlement.[48] Not surprisingly, Wiseman during most of the war was very reluctant to initiate discussions on the matter.

Freedom of the seas and other naval questions came to the fore when Sir Eric Geddes, First Lord of the Admiralty, paid a visit to the United States in October 1918. Geddes was alarmed that while Britain was forced to concentrate on building warships the United States was building a merchant marine which threatened to surpass Britain's. He therefore came to Washington to seek compensation, in the form of destroyers, for British tonnage lost in the service of the United States and to persuade the Administration to adjust its ship-building program so that the British and American ratios of merchant ship to war ship construction

[47] Wiseman, "Notes of an Interview with the President at the White House, Wednesday, October 16th, 1918," WWP 129.

[48] Martin, *Peace without Victory*, pp. 109, 125.

would be the same. Lord Reading deplored the opening of such questions with the Americans and tried vainly to prevent Geddes' visit.[49] Arthur Murray alerted Wiseman to the visit with the comment, "There is no saying what harm he might do. The bull in the china shop would be nothing to it."[50]

Geddes received no satisfaction regarding ship-building.[51] And he did irritate Wilson by some remarks to the press implicitly criticizing the President's readiness to negotiate with Germany. But he came away from an interview with Wilson (arranged with some difficulty by House, at Wiseman's urging) impressed that freedom of the seas might not be intolerable. When Geddes on October 12 asked Wilson the meaning of the term, Wilson replied that no one nation could be allowed to close the seas to another but that should a nation like Germany become an "outlaw" the united naval force of the world should discipline the outlaw.[52] Geddes reported to Lloyd George that the President was most cordial and that "his views are obviously unformed but his intention appears to be to deal with that [freedom of the seas] if possible in generalities. . . ."[53]

[49] Balfour, "Minute of a meeting in F.O.," Aug. 16, 1918, Balfour Papers, 49748, British Museum; Balfour to Drummond, Aug. 28, 1918, *ibid.*; and Reading to Geddes, Sept. 5, 1918, Reading's Private Papers, FO 800/212, make clear the purpose of Geddes' visit. Balfour to Sir Joseph Maclay, Aug. 21, 1918, Balfour Papers, 49748, British Museum, said that Balfour and Reading agreed it was unwise even to raise the question of equal ratios with the Americans.

[50] Murray to Wiseman, Sept. 16, 1918, WWP 87.

[51] Polk Confidential Diary, Oct. 11, 1918, said that Secretary of the Navy Daniels interpreted Geddes' trip as an effort to get destroyers. Apparently Geddes only got noncommital responses. He described his visit as "only . . . partially successful." Geddes to Lloyd George, Oct. 13, 1918, WWP 53.

[52] House Diary, Oct. 13, 1918; Geddes to Wiseman, Oct. 24, 1918, London WWP.

[53] Geddes to Lloyd George, Oct. 13, 1918, WWP 53. Geddes' whole sentence read: "In talking of his 14 conditions conversation with me naturally turned on freedom of seas upon which his views are obviously unformed but his intention appears to be to deal with that if possible in generalities and acceptance of principle that no one power in League of Nations shall exercise its Naval strength to crush

Wiseman, too, gathered from his interview with Wilson on October 16 that the President, though insistent on the principle of freedom of the seas, was not altogether clear as to how the principle would be implemented. Wilson conceded that the British navy theretofore had acted as a naval police for the world and had never abused its power. He reminded Wiseman, however, that "Many nations, great and small, chafed under the feeling that their sea-borne trade and maritime development proceeded only with the permission and under the shadow of the British Navy. He had always felt that the deepest-rooted cause of the present war was this feeling in Germany—an unjust fear and jealousy of the British Navy, but a feeling none the less real. I gathered that the President was searching for a remedy which he might suggest, but that he had found none; in his mind there is an idea that the great power of the British Navy might in some way be used in connection with the League of Nations and thereby cease to be a cause of jealousy and irritation."

Wilson also indicated his awareness that technological advances had rendered existing international law obsolete. That was why, he told Wiseman, he had not "in his neutrality days . . . insisted more strongly on the strict observance of international law in his dealings with the British Government." New laws taking into account the submarine, the greater range of modern guns, and new concepts of blockade must be devised, and Wilson hoped for a conference soon after the peace treaty to deal with these matters.[54]

With Wilson's personal explanation of the freedom of the seas and the other items of the Fourteen Points, Wiseman was well equipped to interpret the President's peace program in the armistice negotiations soon to open. He sailed

a belligerent Power without consent of the League leaving until the occasion arises any decision as to nationality of Naval police force."
[54] Wiseman, "Notes of an Interview with the President at the White House, Wednesday, October 16th, 1918," WWP 129.

for England on October 17 better acquainted than any other Englishman with the new order which Woodrow Wilson planned for England and the whole world.

IN September 1918 the Allied armies, powerfully augmented by the American Expeditionary Force, clearly seized the initiative from the enemy. As Germany's weaker allies began to falter, the British directed Wiseman to ask Wilson to declare war on the weakest of them, Bulgaria. This would be enough, the British thought, to cause Bulgaria to quit the war. Wilson refused, however, maintaining that it would be bad form to attack the Bulgarians when they were in full flight.[55]

Wilson displayed no such tenderness toward the Austrian enemy. On September 14 the Austrian government appealed to all belligerents to send representatives to a neutral state for "confidential, non-binding conversations over the fundamental principles of a peace treaty." Wilson replied on September 17 that the United States, having repeatedly stated its terms, could "entertain no proposal for a conference upon a matter concerning which it has made its position and purpose so plain."[56] This "brusque" reply, Wiseman reported to Reading, was very popular with the American public, whose desire was "to march to Berlin and dictate terms." But House, Wiseman said, considered that Wilson's answer, by alienating the "semi-pacifist, socialist, and advanced labor group," constituted probably the biggest political mistake of the President's career. Wiseman went on to suggest, "In my opinion there is a valuable opportunity for the Prime Minister to show greater statesmanship than the President if he seized on the suggestion of secret negotiations and insisted that before entering into confidential negotiations, the enemy governments must openly state what terms they are prepared to accept in order that the democracies, who are fighting, may judge

[55] Balfour to Wiseman, Sept. 17, 1918, enclosed by House to Wilson, Sept. 18, 1918, HP 49:11A; House Diary, Sept. 24, 1918.
[56] Harry R. Rudin, *Armistice 1918*, New Haven, 1944, pp. 32, 41.

221

whether they are acceptable. He could reject the proposals just as definitely as the President but at the same time satisfy labour opinion."[57]

Wiseman probably did not expect any serious peace talks to result from such a step by Lloyd George. Nor, needless to say, did he send this suggestion at the instance of Colonel House. Apparently he wished to improve the British government's stock with left-of-center groups, and the reaction of the *Manchester Guardian* to Wilson's stern answer indicated that Wiseman's reading of liberal opinion was sound.[58] At any rate, Reading took Wiseman's suggestion. Ill in bed in London, Reading telegraphed Lloyd George, who was ill in Manchester, that he had a "special and secret . . . extremely important" proposal to make before Lloyd George answered the Austrian note. And presumably Reading did communicate Wiseman's idea to the Prime Minister; at least on September 21 Lloyd George in conversation with friends described Wilson's reply as "very brusque" and said he himself might make a "more reasoned answer."[59] But by the time he did make his reply Bulgaria had requested an armistice and the expediency of wooing liberal opinion on the basis of the Austrian note disappeared.[60]

On October 5 Germany dispatched to Wilson an appeal (received October 7) to arrange an armistice on the basis of the Fourteen Points. In the following days Wilson skillfully maneuvered the Germans into accepting all the preliminary conditions he set for armistice talks. He chose not to consult with the Allies until the Germans satisfied him that they seriously wanted a cessation of the war. Then he submitted his correspondence with the German government to the Allied Council, consisting of the Allied Prime

[57] Wiseman to Reading, Sept. 17, 1918, Reading's Private Papers, FO 800/212.
[58] *Manchester Guardian*, Sept. 18, 1918. See also Murray to Wiseman, Sept. 18, 1918, HP 20:47.
[59] Reading to Lloyd George, Sept. 19, 1918, Reading's Private Papers, FO 800/212; Lord Riddell, *War Diary*, p. 356.
[60] Rudin, *Armistice*, pp. 41, 45.

Ministers and Colonel House, to determine the military terms of the armistice. This council, acting on the advice of General Foch and Allied naval authorities, actually wrote and contracted the armistice agreement. Nonetheless, the Allied Prime Ministers resented the initiative and independence of the President. Wilson appeared to them to be acting as an arbiter between Germany and the Allies. Worse, he had woven the Fourteen Points inextricably into the armistice negotiations. While the Allied Council was free to shape military terms, it could not disavow the political Fourteen Points without wrecking the possibility of an armistice. Neither Wilson nor the Germans would negotiate on any other basis.[61]

Wiseman reached London from New York to find Lloyd George "very bumptious and . . . much disposed to throw off the leadership of the President and to play a lone game." The Prime Minister bristled at Wilson's secretive independence. He ridiculed the league of nations as impractical and resented the rumored plan of Wilson to visit Europe. Wilson, whose nation had fought so briefly, had no right in Lloyd George's opinion to come to Europe as a conquering hero.[62] But most of all, Lloyd George disliked Wilson's freedom of the seas. The interpretation of this Point (Point II) which Wiseman brought from his recent interview with Wilson failed to appease Lloyd George. He determined, out of regard for Britain's traditional means of defense, and perhaps also out of pique, not to accept the Point. And never during the negotiations among the Allies, from October 29 through November 3, did he depart from that determination.

Wiseman came to Paris from London on October 28, in advance of the British delegation, with the news that the British Cabinet would not agree to freedom of the seas. House then instructed Wiseman to tell his superiors that the United States would no more "willingly submit to Great

[61] *Ibid.*, pp. 89-176, covers the negotiations in exhaustive detail. See also Seymour, *Intimate Papers*, Vol. 4, pp. 73-147, esp. p. 92.
[62] Auchincloss Diary, Oct. 29, 1918; Willert, *Road to Safety*, pp. 160-61.

Britain's complete domination of the seas . . . than to Germany's domination of the land." The United States, House continued, possessed more money, men, and natural resources than the British and would, if challenged, maintain an army and navy greater than theirs. As further tactical preparation for the approaching showdown with Lloyd George, House asked Reading to be present in Paris and directed Wiseman to send for Lord Northcliffe as well. House hoped to use Reading and Northcliffe, the latter now estranged from Lloyd George, as clubs over the British government as he had in the conference of the preceding November. Wiseman revealed to House yet another probable confederate from the British side. Sir Eric Geddes, Wiseman said, was so sympathetic to Wilson's policies that Lloyd George had accused him of falling under the President's influence.[63]

Having received House's strong threat, Lloyd George opened the negotiation with one of his own. He planned to dissociate Britain from the Fourteen Points altogether. But when House countered with the suggestion of a separate peace between the United States and Germany, Lloyd George withdrew objection to all the points except the second, the freedom of the seas.[64] Concerning it he entered the following reservation, which became part of the final armistice: "They [the Allies] must point out . . . that clause 2 relating to what is usually described as the freedom of the seas, is open to various interpretations, some of which they could not accept. They must, therefore, reserve

[63] House Diary, Oct. 28, 1918. Wiseman may have misjudged Geddes' opinion. See Geddes' memorandum (for the War Cabinet) "United States Naval Policy," Nov. 7, 1918, Lloyd George Papers F/163/4/7.

House reported to Wilson the following from Frank Cobb: "General opinion of all American correspondents in Paris is that the one definite policy of the Allies at this time is to take the control of the peace negotiations out of the [hands] of President Wilson. . . ." House to Wilson, Oct. 29, 1918, *Foreign Relations, 1918*, Sup. 1, Vol. 1, p. 413. Brackets in original.

[64] Rudin, *Armistice*, pp. 269-70; House to Wilson, Oct. 30, 1918, *Foreign Relations, 1918*, Sup. 1, Vol. 1, pp. 421-23.

to themselves complete freedom on this subject when they enter the peace conference."[65]

Informed of Lloyd George's attitude, Wilson stated on October 30 that he could not participate in peace talks which did not consider freedom of the seas, "because we are pledged to fight not only to do away with Prussian militarism but with militarism everywhere." The President the next day threatened to lay the difference between the United States and Britain before Congress.[66] House omitted this threat from his paraphrased reading of the President's cable to the council.[67] But House sent word through Wiseman that in the absence of "reasonable concessions" by the British "all hope of Anglo-Saxon unity would be at an end."[68] Moreover, Wiseman made a copy of Wilson's threat regarding Congress and no doubt showed it to Lloyd George. Still the Prime Minister refused to budge.[69]

On November 2 House, completely baffled by Lloyd George's obstinacy, made a new "suggestion" for Wiseman to give to the Prime Minister. A letter accompanied the suggestion. Both letter and suggestion are lost to the his-

[65] House to Lansing for Wilson, Oct. 30, 1918, Seymour, *Intimate Papers*, Vol. 4, pp. 170-72. The text of the official letter to the German government contains the same wording. Baker and Dodd, *War and Peace*, Vol. 1, pp. 291-92.

[66] Wilson to House, Oct. 30, 1918, Baker, *Wilson Life & Letters*, Vol. 8, p. 533; Wilson to House, Oct. 31, 1918, *ibid.*, pp. 537-39. This latter cable, as printed in *Foreign Relations, 1918*, Sup. 1, Vol. 1, pp. 427-28, omits the threat regarding Congress.

[67] The paraphrase is printed in Seymour, *Intimate Papers*, Vol. 4, pp. 182-83.

[68] House Diary, Nov. 1, 1918. House spent his "entire time outside of the scheduled conferences" working on the freedom of the seas problem. House to Wilson, cables no. 38 and no. 41, Nov. 3, 1918, *Foreign Relations, 1918*, Sup. 1, Vol. 1, pp. 448, 455.

[69] Wiseman's penciled copy of Wilson's threat is in WWP 94. Amery Diary, Oct. 29, 1918: "L.G. was very amusing on the way in which he and Clemenceau had pushed poor House about over Wilson's 14 points. He, L.G., had made it quite clear that we would sooner carry on the war single-handed than agree to the 'freedom of the seas.'" But on Nov. 3, 1918, Amery wrote in his diary of the "unpleasant" possibility of Wilson's laying the freedom of the seas question before Congress.

torian,[70] but the events of November 3 suggest their contents. When the council met that day, Lloyd George reiterated the impossibility of altering his reservation to Point II. House asked if the reservation constituted a challenge to Wilson's position. No, replied Lloyd George, "All we say is that we reserve the freedom to discuss the point when we go to the Peace Conference. I don't despair of coming to an agreement." House then asked Lloyd George to put his willingness to discuss freedom of the seas in writing. The result was the following letter, the main provision of which was drafted apparently by Wiseman and Frank Cobb, from Lloyd George to House (November 2):

> I write to confirm the statement I made in the course of our talk this afternoon at your house when I told you that "we were quite willing to discuss the Freedom of the Seas in the light of the new conditions which have arisen in the course of the present war." In our judgment this important subject can only be dealt with satisfactorily through the freest debate and the most liberal exchange of views.
>
> I send you this letter after having had an opportunity of talking the matter over with the Foreign Secretary who quite agrees.[71]

[70] The "suggestion" and letter are mentioned but not identified in House Diary, Nov. 2, 1918. There is no letter from House to Lloyd George dated November 2 in HP.

[71] Seymour, *Intimate Papers*, Vol. 4, pp. 183-85. There is in WWP 53 an undated note in Wiseman's hand which reads: "We are quite willing to discuss the Freedom of the Seas in the light of the new conditions which have arisen by reason of the war." Compare this to Lloyd George's letter here quoted and to Wilson's remarks to Wiseman on October 16, cited above, p. 220. See John L. Snell, "Wilson on Germany and the Fourteen Points," *Journal of Modern History*, Vol. 26, Dec. 1954, pp. 364-69.
Distinction must be made between this letter and the reservation itself. The letter was kept secret, the reservation published. Wiseman may also have helped word the reservation. Wiseman told Mr. Arthur Walworth "that he and Cobb of the *World* drafted a paper on 'freedom of the seas' that the *World* criticized editorially when it was made public—not realizing that its own editor had helped to draft it." Notes by Mr. Walworth on his interviews with Wiseman, Apr. 26, 1952, May 1, 1954, and Apr. 22, 1957. The New York *World*, Nov. 14, 1918, contains an editorial criticizing the reservation.

This compromise was not out of line with the attitude expressed by Wilson to Wiseman on October 16. On House's advice, Wilson approved the compromise, which House said "must not be published unless it becomes necessary."[72] Thus the official armistice statement revealed only Britain's reservation to Point II and not the commitment to discuss the Point. Thus, too, House's "suggestion" of November 2 became apparent. House had offered to let the reservation stand if Lloyd George would secretly agree to discuss freedom of the seas at the peace conference. Lloyd George thereby saved himself from the wrath of the British electorate, to whom he would be soon appealing, and House salvaged at least a basis for eventual freedom of the seas. And, incidentally, in the first compact signed under the aegis of the Fourteen Points, the signers violated the spirit of open diplomacy, espoused by Point I.[73]

Wiseman assured House that by securing Allied agreement to the bulk of the Fourteen Points the United States had won one of the "greatest diplomatic triumphs in history." How large a part Wiseman played in the triumph, or compromise, was not recorded. But that Wiseman worked tirelessly to mediate the differences between Lloyd George and House, while maintaining House's complete confidence (which Reading did not), was amply clear. At the close of the negotiations House cabled Wilson that "Wiseman has been splendidly helpful."[74]

[72] Baker, *Wilson Life & Letters*, Vol. 8, pp. 547, 550; House to Wilson, cable no. 41, Nov. 3, 1918, *Foreign Relations, 1918*, Sup. 1, Vol. 1, pp. 455-57.
[73] Significantly, Wilson in transmitting to Germany the Allies' qualified acceptance of the Fourteen Points failed to endorse the reservation on the freedom of the seas. He *did* agree to the Allied provision calling for compensation for damage done to civilian populations and property. Baker and Dodd, *War and Peace*, Vol. 1, pp. 291-92.
[74] House Diary, Nov. 4, 1918; House to Wilson, Nov. 5, 1918, HP 49:11B.
There is in WWP 53 a compilation of statements by Wilson and others regarding freedom of the seas. Wiseman probably used this in his mediation between House and Lloyd George.

NOVEMBER 11, 1918, the day of the proclamation of the armistice, found Wiseman not among celebrating London crowds but in bed with a newly contracted case of influenza. Within a few days, however, he was well enough to report to House (in Paris) that among British officials "those who admire the President, and want to see his authority maintained, are unanimous in advising against his taking part in the Peace Conference." If the President could agree on broad principles with the Allies, Wiseman said, then his presence would facilitate the settlement of those questions. "But after hearing what they all have to say, I am bound to tell you my own opinion is that the President would be taking a great gamble . . . he would be . . . likely to lose prestige and authority and be drawn into a very difficult diplomatic situation, which he would have to deal with under the worst possible conditions for himself."[75] In other words Wiseman was saying, discreetly, that leaders in London, or some of them, could not themselves agree with Wilson on broad principles and were ready to fight him openly at the conference. Frank Cobb, the President's newspaper friend, gained the same impression from observations in London and Paris and consequently reversed his earlier opinion that the coming of Wilson was necessary as well as desirable. Other observers noted the hostile attitude, personal as much as principled, which a number of British leaders felt toward Wilson in the weeks between the Armistice and the opening of the Paris Peace Conference. Added to their dislike of Wilson and/or his principles was the belief that Republican victories in the Congressional elections of November 6 had weakened the President's position as American spokesman.[76]

[75] House to Wiseman, Nov. 10, 1918, HP 44:25; Wiseman to House, Nov. 14, 1918, HP 20:47.

[76] Seymour, *Intimate Papers*, Vol. 4, pp. 210-13; Willert, *Road to Safety*, p. 161; Amery Diary, Oct. 25, Nov. 4, Nov. 8, and Dec. 24, 1918; Callwell, *Sir Henry Wilson*, Vol. 2, pp. 156-59; Riddell, *Lord Riddell's War Diary*, p. 380.
Cecil cabled from Paris in early October that "Lloyd George and Clemenceau vie with one another in scoffing at the President, and

Fortunately, Balfour was not disposed to foil the President. Had he been, an overture he received from Sen. Henry Cabot Lodge may well have been irresistible. On November 21 Colville Barclay, the British chargé d'affaires in Washington, cabled Balfour a message from a prominent "friend of a Republican." The "friend" urgently warned that in a general peace congress there might be a tendency in "certain quarters" to accede to the "maudlin appeals" of Germany. In a subsequent dispatch by diplomatic pouch, Barclay identified the "friend" and amplified the message. Lodge was the friend. He visited the British Embassy, and the French, to urge the Allies not to feel compelled by Wilson to negotiate with Germany. Wilson was, said Lodge, "an idealist, his great ambition was to be THE peace-maker, or the Arbiter of peace, and if it came to protracted discussions with the Germans he might well be inclined to be led too far by idealistic motives." Emphasizing the new power of the Republican party as a result of the recent election, Lodge stated that the party would uphold the President in his war policy but would "have a good deal to say as regards the reconstruction policy after the peace, and in this they would not give him a free hand." Lodge "sincerely hoped that Foreign Statesmen realized the influence which the Republican party would exercise in reconstruction problems."[77]

To make sure that his point got across to at least one foreign statesman, Senator Lodge took the unusual step of writing directly to Balfour. In more than four pages he stressed that the Administration had been defeated at the polls, that the Republicans had demanded the unconditional surrender of Germany, that his party wanted physi-

Sonnino is almost openly apprehensive of allowing him to interfere in European politics. In my view, the only satisfactory remedy would be for the President himself to come over here. . . . I have urged this view on my Colleagues, and they, without rejecting it, are not enthusiastic." Cecil to Balfour, Oct. 7, 1918, Balfour Papers, 49738, British Museum.

[77] Barclay to Balfour (cable), Nov. 21, 1918, and same to same (dispatch), Nov. 21, 1918, Balfour Papers, 49748, British Museum.

cal guarantees against future German aggression, and that the proposed league of nations seemed to him "hopelessly impracticable in many respects." A league ("if such a thing can be made") which attempted control over immigration laws, tariffs, the Monroe Doctrine, or the army and navy would meet "great and probably effective opposition." Thus, "it would be most unfortunate to have an agreement for a League attached to the peace treaty, for it might lead to great and most undesirable delays and probably amendments to the treaty of peace, which would be greatly to be deplored."[78]

None too subtly Senator Lodge was inviting the British to combine with the Republican party against Wilson's peace program. He arranged for other prominent men to write Balfour also, all with the intention of making the British "understand a certain person and what his characteristics are. . . ." Simultaneously Theodore Roosevelt was explaining to the British that the Republican party, not Wilson, was the true friend of the British Empire.[79]

Why did the British leadership, freshly reelected on a platform which if anything promised harsher treatment for the enemy than that espoused by Lodge or Roosevelt, not

[78] Lodge to Balfour, Nov. 25, 1918, Balfour Papers, 49742, British Museum. According to a notation on this letter, Balfour answered Lodge on Jan. 9, 1919. But I did not find the answer in either the Lodge or Balfour Papers.

[79] See Dr. W. S. Bigelow to Lodge, Nov. 26, 1918 (in which Bigelow offers to write Balfour about Wilson's "vanity and single-minded egotism, his treachery and cowardice, and his utter unreliability"); Lodge to Lord Charnwood, Nov. 28, 1918; Lodge to Bigelow, Nov. 29, 1918; Bigelow to Lodge, Dec. 3, 1918 (saying he has sent comments on Wilson to Balfour, via Balfour's cousin); and E. H. Darville to Lodge, Dec. 10, 1918; all in Lodge Papers.

See also Roosevelt to Rudyard Kipling, Nov. 23 and Nov. 30, 1918, in Elting E. Morison and Associates, eds., *The Letters of Theodore Roosevelt*, Cambridge, Mass., 1954, Vol. 8, pp. 1,403-1,408; Kipling to Lord Milner, Dec. 24, 1918 (enclosing Roosevelt's Nov. 23 letter), Milner Papers, Private Correspondence folder; and J. Murray Clark to Balfour, Jan. 9, 1919 (enclosing a Dec. 15 letter from Roosevelt, saying, among other things, "I have stood strongly and publicly for the right and duty of the British Empire to retain the colonies taken from Germany."), Balfour Papers, 49748, British Museum.

grasp the extended hand of Wilson's domestic opposition? First, and most obviously, there was no direct way in which the British government could bypass Wilson and enter into diplomatic relations with the Republican party or its legislative leaders. The most that could have been hoped for was a tacit approach parallel to Lodge's. Second, the overture was vague, not initially identified as Lodge's, and came at the time when British politicians' attention was focused on their general election (14 Dec. 1918). Third, when Lodge's attitude became unmistakable, the British position was clearly diverging from it. On December 21 Lodge, in a Senate speech which he specifically called to Balfour's notice,[80] warned that a peace treaty containing provision for a league of nations might not secure the upper house's approval. On the day before, Wiseman wrote (from Paris), "I think the outstanding feature here is the growing support—I might almost say: demand—for a League of Nations."[81] Fourth, and most important, Wiseman could report support for a league also because of the appearance of Wilson in Europe. Not only was the President the European public's hero, he dispelled many of the nationalist fears of Allied statesmen also. Lloyd George informed the Imperial Cabinet that when he met Wilson on December 26, Wilson had opened the talks "at once with the question of the League of Nations, and had given the impression that that was the only thing he really cared much about. There was nothing in what he said which would in the least make it difficult for us to come to some arrangement with him."[82]

That being the case, to cooperate with Lodge rather than Wilson was out of the question. Such a tack would have offended both those like Balfour who had a high sense of diplomatic legal procedures, and those like Cecil who ardently desired a league of nations. Cecil, in combatting

[80] Barclay to Balfour, Dec. 22, 1918, FO 115/2427.
[81] Wiseman to Frederick Cunliffe-Owen, Dec. 20, 1918, WWP 102.
[82] "Draft Minutes of a Meeting held at 10 Downing Street, S.W., on Monday, December 30, 1918, at 3-30 p.m.," WWP 102.

those at the Cabinet meeting who counseled an alliance with Clemenceau against Wilson at the peace conference, voiced the sentiment which actually guided the British at Paris. The greatest guarantee of a settled peace, he said, "was a good understanding with the United States, and that good understanding could not be secured unless we were prepared to adhere to the League of Nations." L. S. Amery, an imperialist and a realist, contemptuous of the league and other aspects of Wilson's idealism, implied agreement a few days later when he wrote: "To place Anglo-American relations on a permanent footing of mutual understanding and co-operation is the most important external object that the British Empire can aim at as the outcome of the war."[83]

Indeed there was no realistic alternative to accommodation with President Wilson. And Wiseman, who throughout the war stressed the ulterior goal of an Anglo-American entente, contributed, at least in a minor way, to the appreciation of this reality. Before leaving New York he asked J. P. Morgan, Britain's great private creditor, to comment on House's suitability as an armistice and peace negotiator. Morgan wrote, after the Congressional election, the following:

I have always taken every opportunity that presented itself to express my own personal satisfaction and confidence that he is just the man for this job, and that, in my own belief, the President could not have chosen anyone who could more adequately carry out the intentions of the whole country. . . . I know that the Colonel is very clear in his own mind on the rights of the Allies, and that he understands that a just peace does not mean justice to Germany, which involves injustice to the Allies. Should there be the necessity for injustice anywhere, I think we would all rather have Germany stand it than any of the Allies.

I hope you will see my partners in London and in

[83] *Ibid.* Amery, memorandum, in Amery to Balfour, Dec. 21, 1918, FO 800/209.

Paris, and I know that they will be perfectly delighted to do anything they can to help anywhere.[84]

Apparently Wiseman solicited Morgan's statement because he anticipated the sort of economic argument Lodge could make to Balfour in case of a Republican victory. In a memorandum written some days before the Armistice, Wiseman, like Lodge, referred to the reconstruction and other economic problems that would confront postwar Europe. These problems would be, in his succinct description, "difficult." Therefore, "We must remember that after peace is signed we shall by no means be finished with America. We shall not even have finished with President Wilson." Like it or not, Wiseman was saying, the Wilson Administration would control the American government for another two years. True it might be frustrated by the opposition party. But Wilson was a man of unusual force, in a unique governmental position, who on occasion did not hesitate to run counter to momentary public opinion. No foreign government could build its policy on cooperation with the Republicans that was not also cooperation with the President. "If we should have any difference of opinion with the Administration [Wiseman said], we might receive the enthusiastic support of powerful Republican interests, but we should, of course, find their very support our greatest handicap because the majority of Americans will always rally to the President in case of a dispute with a foreign country, and the ultra-British party have little political influence in America."[85]

Wiseman wrote these last words before he learned the depth of hostility to Wilson in London. They were part of a long, lucid defense of the Fourteen Points as a "complete and consistent whole" which need not be fatal to Britain. And Wiseman was confident that if House were the chief American negotiator accord between the two English-

[84] Morgan to Wiseman, Nov. 8, 1918, New WWP.
[85] Wiseman, "The Attitude of the United States and of President Wilson Towards The Peace Conference," no date (c. Oct. 20, 1918), WWP 102.

speaking nations could characterize the peace conference. For a time in November and early December, however, he feared that Wilson's determination to come to Paris would ruin the projected accord.[86] But when the President actually arrived Wiseman found him in a less dominating mood than expected. In a December 15th report to Balfour Wiseman wrote:

> I do not think [Wilson] has any specially cut-and-dried proposals to make regarding any of the important questions at issue, but will rather reaffirm his general principles and expect the Allies to make their definite proposals.
>
> On the question of the League of Nations, he is, however, very strongly of opinion that the formation of a League—at any rate a definite agreement as to its form among the great Powers—should be the first work of the Peace Conference. He considers that almost all the difficult questions—Colonies, Freedom of the Seas, the Balkan difficulty, Russia, and Reduction of Armaments—and, in fact, all the important problems that will arise, can only be satisfactorily settled on the basis of a League of Nations. He has a very open mind as to the form of the League, its scope and the machinery by which it should be operated. He is even willing to agree to the French proposal that the Germans should be excluded from the League for a time.
>
> The question of Indemnities may raise some difficulty, as the American view is that the Allies are bound by their Armistice formula. But the President is not disturbed by the [British] Election speeches, and quite understands the strong demand in Allied countries that Germany be made to pay the cost of the war.[87]

Wiseman's picture of Wilson as conciliatory was accu-

[86] Wiseman to House, Nov. 14, 1918, HP 20:47; Wiseman to Drummond, Dec. 15, 1918, WWP 125.

[87] Wiseman, "Memorandum," Paris, Dec. 15, 1918, Balfour Papers, 49741, British Museum.

rate, as Lloyd George's report of his December 26 conversation with the President indicated. Like Clemenceau, the British leaders dropped their opposition to Wilson's participation in the peace conference, and once the conference was underway they found themselves more often than not on the same side of an issue as Wilson was.[88] At Paris Wiseman was assigned to assist Lord Reading, still the absentee ambassador to the United States, and after Reading's return to Washington in February he became Balfour's special adviser on Anglo-American affairs. But his previous importance as intermediary and interpreter was over.[89] The American and British principals, as well as their staffs and expert committees, were in direct and frequent communication, with little need of peripatetic services such as Wiseman performed so well during 1917-18. Although his friendship with House did not wane, he came to feel that even his usefulness to the Colonel was redundant.[90] Over the past two years he had helped ensure that direct Anglo-American political consultation, so long denied by Wilson but at last permitted at the peace conference, was, when it came, generally harmonious. In the process he had worked himself out of a job.

[88] Seymour, *Intimate Papers*, Vol. 4, pp. 252, 256; Lord Derby to Balfour, Dec. 16, 1918, Balfour Papers, 49744, British Museum. Amery Diary, Dec. 30, 1918: "Imperial War Cabinet in the afternoon to hear L.G.'s report of President Wilson, who on the whole seems to have been not quite so tiresome as was anticipated, except perhaps on the question of Indemnity." Tillman, *Anglo-American Relations at the Paris Peace Conference*, pp. 401ff.

[89] Drummond to Wiseman, Dec. 5, 1918, and Balfour to Wiseman, Feb. 24, 1918, London WWP.

[90] Wiseman to House, July 11, 1919, WWP 65.

CHAPTER NINE

ENVOY

PERHAPS the chief remuneration from the study of Sir William Wiseman as diplomat is a typology of the difficulties which clogged the axis of Anglo-American collaboration in the First World War. Wiseman was uniquely situated to distinguish those points that most disturbed both Washington and London. Having decided that House was the best approach to Wilson, the British government routed its most urgent petitions to him through Wiseman. Similarly, House and Wilson directed their confidential messages to London through Wiseman. But though he was the link between the hierarchies of the two governments, Wiseman was independent of the embassy and consequently freed from a daily concern with routine matters. He thus enjoyed a certain detachment and perspective, and he used his freedom to locate trouble, present or potential, and to set in motion corrective measures.

The large problems Wiseman defined were those which form the chapter topics of this study: the nature of British representation in the United States, the financial crisis of 1917, the inclusion of the United States in the Supreme War Council and other inter-Allied organizations, the disposition of American troops, the intervention in Russia, and the plans for peace. These problems developed in dynamic succession. The financial crisis dramatically revealed faulty diplomatic contact. Resolution of the crisis involved the consolidation of all British agencies in America under a new ambassador enjoying influence with Lloyd George. Organizational overhaul also led to attempts to rationalize and institutionalize the coordination of American and British war efforts. Shortage of manpower emerged as the most troublesome of the difficulties of coordination. This shortage, in turn, complicated consideration of the most serious divergence between the two countries in war strategy—the

236

dissimilar attitudes toward Russia. Bitterness resulting from the disagreement over Russia reinforced Wilson's distrust of the British and strengthened his determination to pursue independent postwar plans. As peace approached, differences over the future economic treatment of Germany, the freedom of the seas, and the League of Nations added new tensions to Anglo-American relations.

Wiseman, as we have seen, significantly influenced developments in all these issues. His initiative brought close contact with Colonel House, helped ease the financial crisis, led to the streamlining of British representation in the United States, and brought over Lord Reading as ambassador. His advice resulted in House's trip to Europe in late 1917 and helped determine the extent of American participation in the international war bodies. His recommendations fashioned the British approach to Wilson for troop amalgamation, and his report from Europe to Wilson and House prompted the steps taken to circumscribe General Pershing's responsibilities. His restrained emphasis on the necessity for some sort of American action in Russia undoubtedly affected the change in attitude by House in this matter, and advice from him and Reading moderated British pressures on Wilson for intervention. Regarding future economic policy toward Germany and the British intention to publish their plans for a league of nations, Wiseman's firsthand warnings to London of the President's objections prevented an open clash between the two governments. Finally, Wiseman's interpretation of the freedom of the seas and the other thirteen of Wilson's Points, based on the President's own explanations, clarified the American peace program to Lloyd George and made acceptance of it as the basis of the armistice less difficult.

None of the foregoing is to denigrate the role of Lord Reading. But Reading was in America a total of only seven months, and virtually all of his recommendations to London were formulated with the advice of Wiseman. Reading himself acknowledged his dependence on Wiseman and despaired of ever forming as confidential a relationship with House and Wilson as Wiseman's. Although care must be taken not to exaggerate Wiseman's closeness to the aloof President, there are sufficient indications that relations between the two were candid and friendly. This was demonstrated by the substance of their several interviews at the White House and most strikingly by their frequent association during the week both were at Magnolia in August 1918. It is difficult to think of another foreign representative Wilson would have allowed to share his holiday, particularly one in which he was discussing with House his plans for a new world order.

Because of his access to the President, directly or through House, Wiseman was able to elaborate the generalities of Wilson's policies into specific applications the British government could understand. This was notably true regarding Wilson's concept of the Supreme War Council, his policy in Russia, and his peace program. Wiseman's observations also clarify these Wilsonian policies for today's student. Generally, they reveal that Wilson was more flexible and more affected by practical realities than has often been supposed. In military matters the President showed every willingness to meet the feasible demands of the Allies. He never authorized general troop amalgamation, partly because of his commander's opposition to it, but also because the Allies never clearly presented the dispute to him as one between Foch and Pershing whom he was willing to overrule. Regarding Russia, Wilson correctly concluded that Allied plans for a new Eastern Front were unrealistic, particularly in view of simultaneous demands for vastly increased numbers of American troops for the Western Front, and outweighed by the political disadvantages of military intervention. And concerning a league of nations, the President's thought was not static. After the March 1918 German offensive he believed that Germany must be completely defeated before his ideal league could be established. But, he indicated to Wiseman, if Germany were not beaten, the league would have to be an Anglo-American alliance designed for a future engagement with German autocracy.

There were also practical aspects and immediate determinants to Wilson's independence in diplomacy, as the experienced Balfour readily appreciated. After House was rebuffed by the Allies in his November 1917 plea for a joint declaration of liberal war aims, Wilson concluded that American war aims must be kept free of Allied selfishness. He did show a willingness, under pressure from House, to consult with the British through Wiseman prior to the announcement of his Fourteen Points. But Wiseman was unable to return to the United States in time for the consultation; in the meantime Lloyd George declared his war aims, without previously consulting Wilson. Though the two speeches were similar, Wiseman's divulgence of the origins and purpose of Lloyd George's speech caused Wilson to doubt the genuineness of it. Thereafter joint belligerency with Britain actually hindered rather than encouraged a merging of Anglo-American war aims. Britain's complicity in the consciously inflated Allied request for 100 American divisions, overt deviation from Wilson's purpose in the Siberian intervention, resuscitation of the Paris economic resolutions, and readiness to sponsor a counterrevolution in Mexico combined to heighten Wilson's suspicions. The British government, he concluded, could not be trusted, either as to the reliability of its word or the nobility of its intentions. Only after he had extracted British endorsement of the bulk of the Fourteen Points in the Armistice terms did he agree to negotiate particulars. Then, perhaps chastened by the election returns of November, Wilson manifested a willingness to entertain Britain's claims, so long as the basic principle of a league of nations was accepted.

Wilson's distrust of the British government never seemed to encompass Wiseman. Their association continued beyond the Paris Peace Conference, where Wiseman rendered the Wilsons personal courtesies, such as smuggling Mrs.

Wilson into the plenary session which heard the first reading of the League of Nations charter.[1] There are indications that Wilson desired Wiseman to become the ambassador at Washington. But Lloyd George and the new foreign secretary, Curzon, whether reluctant to appoint a 34-year-old man to such a high post or because of personal dislike of Wiseman, declined to consider him for anything but the secretaryship of the embassy.[2] Casting about for a business opportunity, Wiseman returned to America before the peace conference ended. Twice he talked with the President and afterwards sent the Foreign Office illuminating reports on the status of Wilson's struggle with the Senate over the Treaty of Versailles.[3] Following Wilson's physical collapse in September 1919 Wiseman called at the White House, apparently in the hope of establishing contact between the President and the British embassy, still empty of an ambassador. Mrs. Wilson, forgetful of her earlier pledge to "always bless and thank" Wiseman, turned him away and years later censured this initiative of "this plausible little man."[4] Hence, Wiseman's bond with Wilson was severed and his diplomatic career ended. It had lasted scarcely more than two and a half years, but it had been a remarkable experience.

[1] Edith Bolling Wilson to Wiseman, Feb. 15, 1919, London WWP: "I cannot go away without this word to tell you how I shall always bless and thank you for getting me permission to go to the Conference yesterday. I saw you in the distance & hope you got the 'thought wave' of appreciation I sent you. It was splendid, wasn't it? and I fairly glowed at being there. The President joins me in warm regard—and all sorts of good wishes."

[2] Edith Benham Helm, diary, May 2, 1919, Helm Papers, Library of Congress, Box 1. Also see note 9, p. 168, above. Arthur Murray wrote Wiseman in 1958: "In the First World War, Lloyd George . . . loathed you." Murray (Elibank) to Wiseman, Apr. 14, 1958, New WWP. Lord Curzon to Balfour, June 9, 1919, Balfour Papers 49731, British Museum.

[3] These are printed in E. L. Woodward and Rohan Butler, *Documents on British Foreign Policy, 1919-1939*, 32 vols., London, 1946-1965, First Series, Vol. 5, pp. 980-85.

[4] Edith Bolling Wilson to Wiseman, Feb. 15, 1919, London WWP; Edith Bolling Wilson, *My Memoir*, New York, 1939, p. 286.

APPENDIX: WISEMAN ON WILSON
(FROM THE WISEMAN PAPERS)

NOTES ON INTERVIEW WITH THE PRESIDENT

FRIDAY, JULY 13TH [1917]

(1). The President asked me to come to his study, and there we talked for more than an hour.

He began by asking me to explain to Mr. Balfour the misunderstanding regarding Morgenthau. Morgenthau was sent to the East for relief work, and instructed that, if opportunity arose to get in touch discreetly with some of the Turkish leaders, he might do so, and sound them on the subject of peace. He appears to have discussed his secret mission with a number of friends here before he left, and on arrival at Gibraltar to have discussed it again with British Naval officers, who discouraged the idea of his attempting it. He then proceeded to Paris, where he further discussed the proposition. He appears to have given the impression that he was authorised by the Preaident to express certain views as to the settlement of Turkey in peace terms. The President wished me to assure Mr. Balfour that Morgenthau was not authorised to express his views to anyone, or to approach any Turkish leaders officially. The President expressed to Morgenthau privately the same views regarding the disposition of Turkey that he explained to Mr. Balfour: He had no idea that they would be repeated, and certainly did not authorise Morgenthau to communicate them to anyone.

(2). The President then produced a memorandum from Col. House regarding the proposed modification of the U.S. ship-building programme. The President said that he was not familiar with this proposition, and was therefore discussing it somewhat in the dark. In his own words—he was "thinking aloud to me." His observations were approximately as follows:—

That in his opinion the war had proved that capital ships were not of much value; that future naval warfare depended on a large number of destroyers and submarines. That with this in view he did not consider the question of

U.S. delaying the building of capital ships as very important from a strategic point of view. He explained, however, that when Congress voted money for the Naval programme a specific estimate had to be made of the exact number of the different classes of ships upon which the money was to be spent. It would therefore be unlawful for him to change that programme and alter the number of ships to be built. The only way in which this could be done would be by laying the whole facts before Congress, which would probably be undesirable.

When asked for a suggested solution, he stated that he had always been opposed to allowing merchantmen to cross the Atlantic without convoys; that he was strongly in favor of forcing merchantmen to cross in fleets adequately protected by light naval craft. That he believed some such arrangement was now being put in force: that when the merchantmen reached some point near the British coast, lanes should be formed, strongly guarded by destroyers, through which the merchantmen could pass, and, again, when they were quite close to shore, they should radiate to the various ports. He suggested that if some such scheme could be devised as an American scheme, it would undoubtedly require a larger number of destroyers than the U.S. at present have, but that he could go to Congress with this scheme and ask for an appropriation specifically for this purpose. That, as far as shipbuilding accommodation was concerned, there would be no difficulty in delaying the building of capital ships and to make room for the laying down of destroyers, if necessary. He went on to say that Admiral Sims, who is always considered an original man, had done nothing since his arrival in London but report the views of the British Admiralty. That more than a week ago he had cabled Sims pointing out the submarine menace was as serious as ever, and that the only views reported to him had been those of the British Admiralty, and that he wanted Sims to cable him fully saying what steps he (Sims) would take if he had charge of the whole naval arrangements. Up to the present Sims has not replied, and the President assumes that he is studying the matter.

(3). With reference to finance, the President expressed his opinion that the recent crisis looked as though it was capable of solution. He urged strongly that more information, both as to actual financial needs and general policy of the Allies, must be given to the U.S.G. He pointed out that there was much confusion and some competition in the demands of the various Allies. Specifically, as far as the British are concerned, he pointed out that there was no one who could speak with sufficient financial authority to discuss the whole situation, both financial and political, with the Secretary of the Treasury. All these things should be remedied as soon as possible. That he was thoroughly in favor of a scheme proposed by the Secretary of the Treasury for a Council in Paris. This council, composed of representatives of the Allies, should determine what was needed in the way of supplies and money from America. It should also determine the urgency of each requisition, and give proper priority. I suggested that such a council should be composed of the Naval and Military commanders, or their representatives, and that the U.S. should be represented on it. The President did not seem to have any objection, but thought it would be unnecessary for the U.S. to be represented on it until they had their own portion of the front to look after and a large force in Europe.

(4). The President said he was disturbed by a dispatch which he had from Paris stating that the morale of the French troops and the French nation generally was low; and that even the arrival of the American contingent had not materially improved it.

(5). With regard to Mr. Balfour's suggestion covering the Naval shipbuilding difficulty by some species of defensive alliance:— The President stated that in his opinion the Allies had entered during the stress of war into various undertakings among each other which they would find it

245

very difficult, if not impossible, to carry out when the war was over; and he was not in favor of adding to that difficulty. Moreover, he pointed out that while the U.S. was now ready to take her place as a world-power, the strong feeling throughout the country was to play a "lone hand," and not to commit herself to any alliance with any foreign power. With regard to JAPAN, the President said that in his opinion a successful attack on the Pacific Coast was absurd owing to the long distance from the Japanese base and the difficulty they would have in obtaining any suitable base on the Pacific Coast. The possibility of their attacking the Phillipines [sic] or some outlying possession was, he thought, quite another matter, and presented a possibility which could not be overlooked.

Finally, he assured me that it was his intention to co-operate with Great Britain frankly and whole-heartedly in the common object of bringing the war to a successful conclusion as quickly as possible.

MEMORANDUM ON ANGLO-AMERICAN RELATIONS, AUGUST 1917

Our present relations with AMERICA present two problems:—

1. How to assist and encourage the United States to bring the full might of their power to bear upon the struggle as quickly and as effectively as possible.

2. How to promote a full agreement between the two countries both upon War-aims and terms of Peace.

PRESENT SITUATION:

The situation at present is not satisfactory, for, while the peoples of the United States and Great Britain probably have the same objects in view, there is by no means complete understanding between the two Governments as to the methods that must be employed to gain them.

There is danger of friction in the fact that the high officials of the two Governments are not personally known to each other, and in the normal difficulties of keeping the American authorities fully and constantly informed regarding the changing situation in Europe.

THE GOVERNMENT OF THE U.S.:

The essential fact to be grasped is that for the purpose of the War the Government of the United States means the personal decisions of PRESIDENT WILSON. The President of the United States is executively almost an autocrat for the period of his term in office, and such a crisis as War considerably increases his power. He can appoint and dismiss his Cabinet at will; and the Cabinet officers are not responsible to Congress but to the President alone.

Nor does the President entirely depend upon a majority in the Senate or in the House of Representatives. It has happened—as in the last year of Taft's administration—that there was a considerable majority against the President in Congress. Nor need pressure from his party be expected to have much influence since Mr. Wilson cannot in any event be elected for a third term.

PARTY-FEELING IN THE UNITED STATES:

But party feeling is very strong today. The President is normally a good party man, and it appears that AMERICA will run the War on party-lines. For many years after the Civil War the Republican party, with short interludes, remained in power. Towards the end of the Roosevelt administration, and during Taft's administration, the Republicans were drifting out of touch with the mass of the people; but the party-machine was strong and the traditions of the Civil War still made a majority of the people unwilling to place the power of the United States in the hands of the South, i.e. the Democratic Party.

President Wilson (particularly since his re-election) may be said to represent a stable majority definitely turned against the more reactionary Republican party, and his personal hold on the Middle West and West (less articulate but possibly more important of opinion than New York and the Eastern States) is very great. The Democrats, moreover, having been out of office so long, are determined not to share authority with their opponents, so that the chances for a Coalition Government seem remote. It is fairly certain that the President will not agree to a Coalition Government unless public opinion, aroused by some important disaster, should force him to do so. Any suggestion of this sort, however unofficial, any press campaign in its favor, however sympathetically conducted, would be a blunder of the first magnitude; for Great Britain, in particular, must avoid any semblance of interference in American domestic politics.

Of the two parties in the United States, the Republicans roughly represent the wealthier and better-educated classes. The Democrats are composed of the gentry of the South, and to some extent represent the rising wealth of the Middle West, but, beyond this, their intellectual outlook is that of the advanced Radical school of thought throughout the United States.

The present Administration is pro-Ally and even pro-English. Two of the members of the Cabinet are said to have been British-born subjects, and all of them have admiration and sympathy for England. It must be remembered, however, that they are bitterly antagonistic to what they imagine to be "Tory England"; and in nine questions out of ten they would be in complete agreement with our advanced Radical party.

PRESIDENT WILSON:

The President himself is of Scotch Presbyterian descent; Radical by conviction and training, but opposed to Socialism and the undue political power of Labour Unions. He has the greatest confidence in the future of the Anglo-

Saxon race, and believes that the security of the World can best be maintained by an understanding between the democracies of Great Britain and the United States. He has the most bitter and unyielding antagonism to the Kaiser, his form of Government, and anything which might appear to be militarism. He has been long getting into war, but he will not be found to be in a hurry for peace.

U.S. VIEW OF THE WAR:

The people of the United States sincerely believe that they are fighting solely for the cause of human liberty. They see themselves as the only disinterested parties in the war. They believe, too, that they, in participating, will be the deciding factor. Technically, the United States have made war against Germany to protect the rights of Americans, and they are not bound by any of the Inter-Ally treaties. They reserve for themselves the right to make peace with Germany at any time.

The sentiment of the country would be strongly against joining the Allies by any formal treaty. Sub-consciously they feel themselves to be arbitrators rather than allies.

On the other hand, the people are sincere in their determination to crush Prussian autocracy, and in their longing to arrive at some settlement which will make future wars impossible.

It is important to realise that the American people do not consider themselves in any danger from the Central Powers. It is true that many of their statesmen foresee the danger of a German triumph, but the majority of the people are still very remote from the war. They believe they are fighting for the cause of Democracy and not to save themselves.

There still remains a mistrust of Great Britain, inherited from the days of the War of Independence, and kept alive by the ridiculous History books still used in the National schools. On the other hand, there is the historical sympathy for France, and trouble could far more easily be created between the British and the Americans than with any of our allies. German propaganda naturally follows this line, and has been almost entirely directed against England.

WAR AIMS:

Public opinion will soon force the President to make some more definite statement regarding the concrete aims of the war, and the Allied Governments must be prepared for this. And any pronouncement they can make which will help the President to satisfy the American people that their efforts and sacrifices will reap the disinterested reward they hope for will be gratifying to him, and in the ultimate result serve to commit America yet more whole-heartedly to the task in hand. The more remote a nation is from the dangers of the war the more necessary it becomes to have some symbol or definite goal to keep constantly before it. The Americans are accustomed to follow a "Slogan" or simple formula. The President realised this when he gave them the watchword that America was fighting "To make the World safe for Democracy."; but the time has come when something more concrete and detailed is needed.

PRACTICAL DIFFICULTIES:

Our diplomatic task is to get enormous quantities of supplies from the United States while we have no means of bringing pressure to bear upon them to this end. We have to obtain vast loans, tonnage, supplies and munitions, food, oil, and other raw materials. And the quantities which we demand, while not remarkable in relation to the output of other belligerents, are far beyond the figures understood by the American public today.

The Administration are ready to assist us to the limit of the resources of their country; but it is necessary for them to educate Congress and the nation to appreciate the actual meaning of these gigantic figures. It is not sufficient for us to assure them that without these supplies the war will be lost. For the public ear we must translate dollars and tonnage into the efforts and achievements of the Fleets and the

Armies. We must impress upon them the fighting value of their money.

CONFUSION AS TO ALLIED REQUIREMENTS:

The demands for money, shipping, and raw materials come from the Allies separately and without reference to one another. Each urges that their own particular need is paramount, and no-one in America can tell where the next demand will come from and for how much it will be.

The Administration are too far from the war, and have not sufficient information to judge the merits of these demands. The Allies will have to use patience, skill, and ingenuity in assisting the American authorities to arrive at a solution of this one grave difficulty, which is, in a phrase, "The co-ordination of Allied requirements."

At present confusion reigns not only in the Administration Departments, but in the public mind. There is, on the one hand, a feeling that some of the money and material is not needed for strictly war-purposes, and, on the other hand, some genuine alarm is felt that even the resources of the United States will not be able to bear the strain.

German agents at work in the United States have seized upon this situation and are using it to the full. Their activities are aimed at confusing the issues and delaying the time when the full weight and power of America can be brought into the war. They are encouraging the idea that it would be better to conserve American resources for the protection of America, rather than dissipate them in a European quarrel.

SUGGESTED REMEDIES:

The main remedy for the present state of affairs is to see that the Administration better understand the real state of affairs in Europe, and realise the exact and practical significance of the information which is sent to them from the Allied Governments.

There is a feeling among the British authorities that the President ought to send expert missions to Europe for the purpose of ascertaining the facts and advising him as to the best steps to be taken. Possibly this would be the most practical method, but it is not one which is likely to be adopted. America, and especially the Democratic Party, lacks public men who can leave their personal affairs to look after themselves while they travel abroad, even though the call be one of public duty. It can be taken then as certain that the only way to settle any important negotiations with the States is by sending highly-placed and highly-competent envoys to Washington.

FINANCIAL COMMISSIONER:

There is, for instance, a very urgent need for an official of the highest standing to proceed to Washington and discuss with Mr. McAdoo financial problems. He should be a man who can not only grasp the strictly financial problems, but who will also understand the political situation in America and can discuss, with the Secretary of the Treasury the political problems involved in the raising of immense loans in the States. The mistake in the past has been to send purely financial experts who have had little knowledge of, or patience with, the serious political difficulties which face the Administration in Washington.

Then with regard to the four most important supplies, namely: Munitions, Shipping, Oil, and Food, there should be an official of high reputation in special charge of each; co-operating with, and their work co-ordinated by, the Chairman of the British War Mission. The existing British organisations in the States are admirably suited for the necessary routine work, but *in* certain cases lack the necessary weight in dealing with the high American officials.

CANADA:

In all questions of supplies, financial and otherwise, there must be close co-operation between the British Mission in the United States and the Canadian Government. An imperial representative of position and tact should be appointed to Ottawa to act as liaison between the Canadian Government and the British Mission.

NAVAL AND MILITARY INFORMATION:

It is absolutely necessary that the Administration should not only be kept fully informed as to the developments of the Military situation, but that care should be taken to see that they understand the information which they receive, and appreciate its significance. For this purpose, it is necessary to have in Washington naval and military officers who have had practical experience in the present war. They should not be considered as naval and military missions for the purpose of instructing the American army or navy, but as "Information Officers" whose duty it would be to receive all the information supplied to the War Cabinet and explain it to the responsible Naval and Military chiefs in Washington, and to the President himself if necessary, and to obtain from London further information that might be desired on any particular point.

POLITICAL INFORMATION:

America is for the first time keenly interested in European problems. Americans consider that Washington has become the diplomatic centre of the world. The American people, however, have no great knowledge of European problems, or any fixed ideas as to their settlement. Certain interested groups in America are actively engaged in furthering their own particular cause, but America as a whole has only the vaguest notions of the problems which would face a Peace Conference. America would never for a moment admit that she is prepared to follow the lead of England: but it is nevertheless true that unconsciously she is holding on to British traditions and would more readily accept the British than any other point-of-view, always provided no suggestion escaped that England was guiding or leading the foreign policy of the United States. It is no exaggeration to say that the foreign policy of America for many years to come is now in process of formation, and very much depends on the full sympathetic and confidential exchange of views between the leaders of the British and American people.

NOTES ON INTERVIEW WITH THE PRESIDENT,
JANUARY 23RD, 1918

On learning from Col. House that I was in Washington, the President telephoned Auchincloss at the State Department and left a message for me to call at 3.15 at the White House. I had about an hour's conversation (an unusual compliment considering how much he was occupied by the debate in the Senate), of which the following is a summary:—

After saying how glad he was to see me back, the President enquired most cordially regarding Mr. Balfour. He said that he often thought of him, and should never forget his visit.

I could not help noticing that he looked tired, and that his voice was decidedly weak. He admitted that the strain was very great, and remarked that, although he had only been in the war ten months, the strain of the period of neutrality was almost as great.

The Coal and Railway situation in America was causing him additional anxiety at the moment.

He remarked that he thought the States had done fairly well considering the difficulties of organizing such a vast country; that the people were totally unused to national organisation. The failures, he said, were apt to be magnified, and much of the good work could not be commented on for military reasons.

The President says that he is fully aware of the importance of the TONNAGE situation, and every effort is being made to increase and speed-up Shipbuilding; also to secure further existing tonnage (neutral and interned in neutral ports) for war purposes.

The immediate problem, he thinks, is to make the best use of the shipping now available. He does not consider the present arrangement satisfactory. The use of tonnage depends on Allied policy and military strategy. Here he referred to conflicting views among the Allies, and remarked that this made the problem of deciding priority even more difficult.

The Allies are making demands for more materials, tonnage, and money than can be supplied by the United States. The question is whether these demands are to be cut down all-round in simple mathematical proportion to meet the supplies, or, if not, how to determine which to grant and which to refuse.

I pointed out that before the States came into the war we had to make these decisions. Now the onus had fallen on him, and he must accept the position. Also that it was quite impossible to satisfy all the Allies. He must decide what was best for the cause as a whole. He said he realised this was true, and, though unwilling, he would not shrink from the responsibility of making the necessary decision. At the same time he pointed out that it was harder for him than for us because he is so far away from the Front. To my suggestion that he should delegate full authority to someone on the spot, he made no reply.

He does not consider the present arrangements for deciding priority are satisfactory, but hopes that General Bliss may be able to help the situation. I told him the purpose of READING's coming was to tell him on behalf of H.M.G. what we thought ought to be done for the common cause, and place at his disposal—in so far as one man was able—our experience in deciding these matters. He remarked that this arrangement ought to be very helpful to him. He repeated the difficulty was to decide on the questions of essentials and non-essentials and to determine the best priority.

ITALY:

The President said the Italian Ambassador called on him directly after his speech to thank him for his reference to Italian aspirations. He now hears from Rome that OR-LANDO has gone to Paris and London to protest against his and Lloyd George's speeches, and demand that the Allies live up to the full terms of their secret treaties. He would like to know what Lloyd George proposes to do about it. His judgment is not to commit himself any further. He is evidently not much in sympathy with Italian war aims, or particularly pleased with the part they have taken in the war.

FRANCE:

Referring to his last speech, he said the part about which he was most doubtful as to its reception in the Senate was the reference to ALSACE-LORRAINE. Much to his surprise it was most enthusiastically received by the Senate. It was hard to say—he observed—whether this feeling was really deep-rooted in America, or merely a romantic historic attachment. Alsace-Lorraine was, in his opinion, a wrong which had poisoned the air of Europe since 1871.

Regarding Lloyd George's speech, he was anxious to know the genesis of the speech—which he said was often as interesting as a speech itself. I told him of the discussions in London at the time of the House Mission; also of the pressure by the Labour party, which obviously interested him. He was delighted to find George's speech coincided so closely with his own views, which he earnestly believed were also the views of the American people. It was important that British and American world-policies should run on similar lines. He was glad to believe that was so at present.

Regarding George's speech—the liberal note, the policy of self-determination, and the absence of annexationist ideas would, he said, be duly appreciated in America.

He was anxious to know if British Labour was "fully satisfied" with the Prime Minister's speech. (I had no information beyond newspaper reports). The labour situation in the United States was causing some anxiety, and must be carefully handled. The American working men do not care about complicated national questions in Europe, and would be ready to take his judgment on what were fair terms of peace. Their purpose must be maintained by keeping firmly and constantly to the front certain very simple truths about the war.

ECONOMIC PEACE TERMS:

It might be true that Germany held the military advantage, but England and America held all the economic advantages. Referring to the scarcity which there will be of raw materials after the war, he said economic concessions would be cards as valuable as occupied territory. "I shall go," he said, "to the Peace Conference with these cards in my pocket, and there they will stay until the German military party give way." He had no doubt that the Senate would quickly ratify any Peace terms he submitted.

WAR AIMS:

The demand that had lately been made for a re-statement of war-aims was largely due, he believed, to the outrageous conduct of the Bolshevics [sic] in publishing the secret treaties, and the consequent fear of the people that they were being exploited for some imperial or capitalist purpose. Recent speeches he hoped and believed had put that right.

"I do hope," he said, "most earnestly that no-one in England thinks "that we are in this war for any material advantage. There is, I know, a party at the Capitol who would like to see us get material advantages out of the war, but if we did we should lose our moral authority and be false to our principles. I have been opposed to that party all my life, and rather enjoy watching their efforts now that I am in the saddle."

In general, he does not approve of speakers coming to this country for propaganda, or Americans going to England. An artificial Entente would be dangerous. Anglo-American relations must rest on surer foundations.

Apropos of HOUSE's Mission to Europe, the President remarked that House has a wonderful gift for getting a detached view-point and fixing on the really important issues. His last words were:— "Give my love to House, and tell him we have had a 'bully' talk."

CABLEGRAM CXP 521, 3 FEBRUARY 1918
FOLLOWING FOR BALFOUR FROM WISEMAN IN WASHINGTON:
No. 48.

A. I lunched today with the President and Secretary of War. The President asked me to send you a cable explaining his views regarding the disposal of American troops in France.

B. The following are the substance of his arguments.

C. In the first place the President is confident that you will believe that he is actuated solely by what he considers the best policy for the common good.

D. The President says American troops will be put into the line by battalions with the French or British if it should become absolutely necessary but he wishes to place before you frankly the very grave objections he sees to this course.

E. Apart from the serious danger of friction owing to different methods, it is necessary that an American army should be created under American leaders and American Flag in order that the people of America shall solidly and cheerfully support the war.

F. The placing of American troops in small bodies under foreign leaders would be taken as a proof that the recent criticism of the War Department was justified and that the American military machine had broken down.

G. The American people would not, he fears, understand

the military reasons, and the necessary secrecy would prevent a very full explanation being given.

H. Their resentment would be increased if an agreement was made between the American and British Governments for the disposal of American troops in this way before they left home. It would not have so bad an effect if Pershing as American Commander in Chief, decided after the men arrived in France that it was necessary to place some of them at the disposal of the British in this way.

J. The President therefore hopes you will provide transportation for the six American divisions at present under discussion without making a bargain that they are to be used to reinforce the British Line and that you will agree they are to be used by Pershing as he thinks best.

K. At the same time the President repeats most earnestly that he will risk any adverse public criticism in order to win the war and he has told Pershing that he may put American troops by battalions in the British line, or use them in any way which in his, Pershing's, judgment may be taken by the necessities of the military situation.

L. I would suggest that you send me something in reply to this that I may convey to the President.

CABLEGRAM CXP 522 AND 523, 4 FEBRUARY 1918
FOLLOWING FOR DRUMMOND AND BALFOUR FROM W.W.:
No. 49. MOST SECRET.

Further notes on my interview with the President and Secretary of War, which lasted about three hours and covered various subjects. BAKER only stayed during discussions on military matters.

They discussed recent attack on War Department: BAKER'S confidence is somewhat shaken, but the President is quite unmoved.

(A). President was entirely frank and showed a willingness to discuss any subject and listen to views opposed to his own. I am more than ever confident that he is most willing to cooperate with us, and is single-minded in his desire to win the war.

(B). I believe he will agree to have some American troops used with British in France. For political reasons, which in my opinion are sound, he feels that public opinion here must be carefully considered in carrying out such a scheme. It must not be said here that, instead of an American Army, the Americans are only depot battalions for British troops used thus to avoid trouble the British Government may have with their Labour Party on man-power. If it is done it must be shown as an effort on America's part additional to raising her national Army—as an emergency and temporary measure adopted by the American Commander-in-Chief in France. May I suggest a cable from you to the President appreciating difficulties with national sentiment here, and asking if we transport the six divisions mentioned we can rely on their being used in any way our Staff shows PERSHING to be necessary. I could get HOUSE to cable BLISS on the subject if you like.

(C). During the discussion I pointed out very plainly that it would be worse than useless to have an American Army in France too late—that is, if the line was broken. And equally useless to have an American Army if there was not sufficient shipping to carry supplies and food for civilian populations. Also that I did not think the American higher commands and staff would be sufficiently experienced this year to handle a large force, that is, half-a-million to a million men, even if the men and supplies were there. An inexperienced American Staff with however fine an army would be object of special attack by Germans and probably lead to disaster, terrible for the Allies but even worse for United States. The American failure to provide the estimated tonnage must now mean a readjustment of Allied plans on an important scale, and further emergency measures and sacrifices by America. I added READING would be here in a few days with definite proposals to lay before them, and begged that they should listen to him most carefully and act promptly on his suggestions in order to avoid the unthinkable failure of the Allied cause owing to lack of proper American cooperation.

(D). To all this the President and Secretary listened without taking offence and agreed there was much truth in it; also expressed themselves anxious for READING's advice and assistance.

(E). With reference to the proposed JAPANESE cooperation in Russia, I think President can be persuaded to agree if you persuade BLISS that the military end is practicable and likely to have substantial results and if the Japanese are approached confidentially and carefully sounded as to their attitude. The President is particularly anxious not to appear as obstructing any of your schemes.

(F). The Secretary of War wants to go to Europe on tour of inspection in order to learn needs of situation at first-hand, and will do so if and when he feels the Senate enquiry into War Department has been satisfactorily answered.

(G). GENERAL LEONARD WOOD was sent abroad by Administration in the sincere desire to use even their most bitter political enemies if they could serve the country, but they regret to hear that he has been freely criticising the Administration and casting doubt on their ability to make any satisfactory showing. Unfortunately he has found sympathisers among highly-placed French and British persons whom he has quoted indiscreetly. BAKER points out that Wood has not the necessary information to speak with authority.

(H). The President told me he was thinking of again addresssing CONGRESS on WAR AIMS in answer to HERTLING and CZERNIN. He wants to take the heart out of the German offensive by showing that German Government are sacrificing their soldiers for conquest, and that the Germans are not fighting a defensive war. He would say all questions at issue must be settled on basis of common sanction of all belligerents and not between any two. He remarked that as far as he was concerned he

261

would not allow IRELAND to be dragged into a Peace Conference. He is anxious to reaffirm most strongly the doctrine "No annexations and no punitive indemnities," with (he says) the accent on "punitive." He proposes to point out the difference between Austrian and German aims, and say he would listen to any proposal from Austria but it would have to be made in public. He will not hold secret conversations. This would not be intended as offer of separate peace between America and Austria, but as the United States leading the way to a separate peace between Austria and the Allies.

(I). He asked my views: I urged that before addressing Congress he should exchange views with you informally and generally. He replied that he was always glad to exchange views with you and get your criticisms.

(J). His insistence on "No annexations" made me think of Colonial questions, which, however, we did not discuss, but I pointed out the danger of Germany purposely misinterpreting "No annexations" and accepting it as an offer to return to the status quo. Also there might be some danger in publicly offering separate peace to Austria owing to ITALIANS who might consider such a peace would be made at their expense. He took the first point, but is not very sympathetic to ITALIAN aims.

(K). Shortly after I left White House a cable was received giving text of SUPREME WAR COUNCIL message from Paris. I learned today that President was not altogether pleased or quite in agreement with the tone of message. He may make it clear in future that United States is represented on Supreme War Council only as far as military matters are concerned.

(L). From what he said I gather he wishes to make a practice of sending for me for similar conversations. I propose, with your consent, to inform him that this will be undesirable so long as LORD READING is in the country.

CABLEGRAM, 4 FEBRUARY 1918
FOLLOWING FOR DRUMMOND FROM WISEMAN.

Yesterday President explained to me his views on proposed scheme for Japanese co-operation in Russia.

His judgment is against the proposal because

(a) He feels sure from conversations he had with Ishii that the Japanese will not agree to the proposition at any rate not in the way or on the scale which would make for success.

(b) He doubts if any military advantage which is likely to be achieved would justify the risk of our actions creating a serious anti-Allied and even pro-German sentiment in Russia.

On my suggestion President agreed to refer the proposition to General Bliss for his advice on the military part of the proposed undertaking and President will keep an open mind until he hears from Bliss.

He wants you to know that he is anxious to conform to any scheme for improving conditions in Russia which in his judgment the U.S. can join with any reasonable hope of success.

NOTES FOR A CABLE FROM THE AMBASSADOR TO THE
FOREIGN OFFICE. MARCH 9, 1918

The question of Japanese intervention in Siberia has largely occupied my attention during the past week in New York, and I have had long conferences with House on the subject, and also had the opportunity of ascertaining the views of other prominent Americans.

It may therefore be of advantage to review the position and to inform you as fully as possible as to the mind of the President and Colonel House.

It was first suggested to Col. House at the Paris Conference in November that the Allies should send a force over the Trans-Siberian railroad to assist the Roumanian Army and Cossacks of the Don. House thinks that the scheme was put forward and particularly favored by General Foch and the French; that the British military authorities doubted its practicability; and that the Japanese representatives stated it was most unlikely that their Government would be able to employ any considerable force in such an enterprise. At that time the danger of misrepresentation as to the motives of the scheme do not seem to have been specially considered. On his return House reported to the President that the matter had been fully discussed and rejected as impracticable from a military point of view.

When the matter was re-opened, I discussed it very frankly with the President, and have reported his views, which may be summarized as a general opposition to the scheme on the ground that the loss of the Allies' moral position would not be compensated by the very doubtful military advantage to be gained. His attitude was strengthened later by a report from General Bliss (whom he consulted at our suggestion), which we understand was to the effect that no military advantage would be likely to accrue from the scheme.

The President's position throughout has been that he is most anxious to cooperate in every way with the Allies, but he evidently fears that the proposed action will antagonize a large section of the public here and lessen American enthusiasm for the war generally. He thinks the Allies do not realise the resentment likely to be created in the Western part of America; though I must say that I have the impression that he is not sure American sentiment would be antagonistic to the scheme, but fears that it might be. The opposition would take the line that we are using a yellow-race to destroy a white one, and that, instead of helping Russian democracy, we should be dealing it another blow by invading Russian territory in opposition to the wishes of the Bolshevic authorities.

I consider, however, that it may yet be possible to secure the President's approval of the scheme, although he will never be enthusiastic about it. If this is to be done, definite assurances should be obtained from Japan, and the Allies should in some way guarantee the territorial integrity of Russia. It might be desirable to suggest that the United States themselves should become the guarantors of this integrity, as it could be pointed out that America would then be acting as a friend or trustee of Russia Democracy. Great stress should be laid on the importance of preventing Siberia from becoming a source of food-supply for Germany both immediately from existing stores, and next year when German activity would make the Siberian soil produce vast supplies. I do not think the President yet realises the danger that the war material furnished to Russia by the United States may yet be used against American troops by the Germans.

This cable is sent, of course, in ignorance of the Japanese attitude towards the matter but in the justifiable assumption that Japan awaits the arrival of BARON ISHII in Washington before discovering her stand. A satisfactory declaration from the new Ambassador would furnish a favorable opportunity for re-opening the whole question before the President, not only permitting us to bring pressure on him by further arguments, but it might also give him an opportunity of receding from his present standpoint.

After the above message was written I learned that BARON ISHII has not yet sailed from Japan. This modifies my last suggestion, but a declaration by the Japanese Government would still be a favorable opportunity for asking the President to reconsider his view.

Today's press despatches from London emphasize danger of German attack on INDIA. It would be most unfortunate if the idea prevailed here that we are encouraging Japanese occupation of Siberia in order to protect our own interests in India.

[DRAFT FOR A CABLEGRAM, C. 27 MARCH 1918—NOT SENT]
FOLLOWING FOR MR. BALFOUR. VERY SECRET.

It may be useful to explain to you the attitude of the President towards the present crisis.

The President never believed that the Germans would attempt the much advertized offensive.

He thought the morale of their troops was low and the influence of the military party waning.

The success of their present attack has been a great shock to him and necessitates a readjustment of opinions and hopes to which he has stubbornly clung in spite of much advice to the contrary.

The first effect here of the recent news has been to let loose a storm of criticism against the Administration which has been brewing for some time.

The events of the past week seem to justify the Republican charges that the American army would not be ready in time to take its proper share in the war.

Possibly the War Department is open to criticism but it [is] only natural that the President's mind should be alert to meet these charges and refute them—feeling, as he honestly does, that everything possible has been done in the face of enormous difficulties.

It will be hard for you to realise that anyone should be concerned with the credit of an Administration at a time like this, but we are very far from the great struggle in France.

The President, at any rate, regards his critics here as little better than traitors to America and the Allied cause.

The immediate consideration is, I take it, not what the U.S. might have done but what they can do now.

The authority of the President is so supreme that we must have his cordial personal co-operation if we are to secure the last ounce of American effort.

Expediency demands that we should help the President in order that he will help us. Our public statements, then, should be directed to strengthening the authority and prestige of the President and the unification of the war effort of America.

At the same time we are entitled to observe that the criticisms of the Administration in the American Press are most useful stimulants and providing they do not undermine the President's authority, must be regarded as definitely assisting the Allied cause.

Moreover, so long as our public attitude is entirely sympathetic we need not hesitate in diplomatic communications and interviews to point out to the President the exact truth even though it may carry with it criticisms of the Administration's shortcomings. But we should confine ourselves to insisting firmly on definite points to which we want him to agree rather than fevered appeals for greater efficiency.

It is also important that when we intend to insist on something to which we think the President may have objections, we should always make joint representations with the French.

It should not always be the duty of the British to lay unpleasant truths before the President.

It is my firm conviction that the President is determined to stand by the Allies whatever may occur with all the resources of the United States and to meet any demands which he considers practically possible.

Col. House is staying in Washington, at the President's request, during the crisis and is in the closest touch with Lord R[eading].

NOTES ON INTERVIEW WITH THE PRESIDENT—
APRIL 1ST, 1918, AT 5:30 P.M.

Remarking that he was glad the news from France is better, the President said he hoped Lord Reading had not misunderstood his remark the other day when he said that he hoped our Generals were not as rattled as our politicians. He had detected, he thought, a note of alarm which was almost panic in the telegram which he was shown, and all he meant to say was that such alarm was very contagious, and it would indeed be a very serious thing if the people generally, and the troops in particular, were to catch any spirit of panic. It was, he thought, a good time to keep very calm. His answer to Lord Reading, he observed, had been, of course, a foregone conclusion. He was prepared to do anything he possibly could to help. The number of American troops sent to France had, he said, been limited by the port facilities in France and the railroad facilities from the ports to the front. There had been, he said, enough men ready and enough ships to send over a considerably larger number. He hoped by sending them through England he would be able to get over at least 100,000 a month, and he hoped considerably more. He could not quite see the reason for such long training when American troops reached England and France. Surely half-trained troops could still take part in this sort of warfare.

The military situation was not, he said, at all clear to him. Names of French villages did not convey much without knowing the topographical significance of the lines held, particularly the numbers of troops engaged and in reserve. The important question, it seemed to him, was how many men we had available in reserve, and how many the Germans had. He wondered whether we had known the approximate numbers the Germans could bring against us at the time of Col. House's mission. If so, he said we ought to have pointed out that there was grave danger the Western line could not be held unless a larger number of American troops were available. This, of course, would have meant cutting down some other kind of supplies, because there was not enough shipping to go round: It was, he said, the old problem of priority, and the Allies must make up their minds as to the priority which they want the Americans to give to troops, munitions, etc. The German attack, he supposed, would go on in successions of waves. As a rule with these attacks the waves ebbed as well as flowed, but he feared we had not the necessary reserves for a serious counter-attack; at least, if so, he had had no indication of it.

The difficulty, he said, about this alternating fortune of war was that, when the Allies are victorious, they do not want to make peace as they expect to be still more victorious; and when things go the other way, and the Germans are victorious, we are then too proud to make a peace after a defeat. Let us consider, he said, a possible conclusion of this oscillation of the fortunes of war. If the Germans are unable to recover from some defeat, all will be well, and we shall be able to insist upon exactly the kind of peace we want. But we must consider the possibility that some time, when the wave of fortune has gone against us, the Allies will be too exhausted to recover. Obviously, he said, it will not be America which will be exhausted because she has only just started. But France, he felt, must be very weary, and in some senses almost exhausted. Great Britain, too, must be feeling a very heavy strain, as is evidenced by the Prime Minister's cable, showing that they proposed calling up men from 18 to 50. If then the Allies became exhausted, what should we do? He supposed we should have to make a compromise-peace, but we could not deceive ourselves—it would be a German peace, and mean in effect a German victory. The Germans would no doubt be prepared to deal generously with France and Belgium, and other questions, providing she was allowed practically a free-hand in Russia. She would be, of course, subject to various restrictions and guarantees, which on paper would limit her success, but we would know that such guarantees would be quite worthless. The only bright spot would be that our economic resources would be very formidable. Whatever we put in our treaties, he said: 'I could not persuade American merchants and traders to do business with Germany in such circumstances." It would mean, he said, that England and America would have to start building up again for another war, organizing ourselves and preparing as best we could. It would be, he said, an appalling prospect, and one which he would not believe for a moment possible.

He intends, he told me, to make a speech on Saturday to start the new Liberty Loan. He proposes to review the present situation, and say that we obviously must judge the Germans by what they are doing in Russia—not by what they are saying in Berlin; that he is disappointed to find the German Chancellor's speech on peace has no real meaning or sincerity. He will also say that he is ready to talk peace at any time, but it must be a peace based on justice, and nothing else. It would be wrong, he said, entirely to shut the door on peace discussions. I asked him what he considered our symbol of victory was; what our irreducible minimum. He said England and America have no symbol of victory. France had in Alsace-Lorraine; Belgium in the restoration of her country; Italy in her Irredenta; and so on; but the two most powerful countries on the Allied side had no such symbol. This, he thought, was a good thing because it made us better umpires, more disinterested in our discussion of peace terms. The leaders of these countries must judge the moment when the peace that could be made would be a just and lasting peace. When that moment arrived, he believed the people would accept the decision of their leaders.

It looked now as though we should be obliged to sign peace with the Military Party in Germany. That was not what we would have desired, but we should have to safeguard the terms as best we could. The treaty itself with such people would be only a 'scrap of paper', but they might be restrained from violating it by material rather than moral considerations.

He hoped Great Britain would not demand spoils from the war. That would injure our case, which was now so good. It was a great pity, he thought, that our public men could not make some definite pronouncement on this subject.

He also hoped that as a result of the present offensive we

and the French would not make any boasting or threatening statement. That would show weakness; a calm and generous statement would show strength.

He wanted to know, and be kept closely informed, of the political situation in England and France. It was his duty to ascertain the real feeling of the people of the Allied nations. For example, did British Labour really support the Government? How, for example, did Mr. Henderson stand? He foresees grave danger after the war from forces of anarchy which had been let loose. The submerged classes, lacking discipline and restraint, will tend to excesses.

He could not help being aware (he said) of the position of America. She was now supplying a large part of the material support of the war, and she was also the potential military factor. It meant, he said, that the decision as to whether the war should continue would rest in his hands. It was, he said, a terrible responsibility, and a question which he certainly would not regard from solely an American point of view: he must consider it also from the point of view of the Allies and indeed the whole world.

With regard to Mr. House, he said that he proposed to wait until the result of the German offensive is definitely ascertained. This he realised might be several months. After that he thought it likely that a new political situation might arise, and he might ask Mr. House to go to Europe again. He was the only person, he said, who knew the policy of the Administration so well that he could take decisions at a distance without having to refer everything by cable.

CABLEGRAM CXP 627, 628, AND 629, 30 MAY 1918
FOLLOWING FOR SIR ERIC DRUMMOND FROM W.W.:
No. 97

The President sent for me yesterday, and I had an hour's conversation with him. He asked me to tell him very frankly my views on the situation in Europe.

Starting with the question of JAPANESE intervention, he asked what was the genesis of the movement. I told him the idea was two-fold: First of all, to re-create a RUSSIAN front, and, secondly, to help the RUSSIAN people. I said that it was generally agreed among military experts that if an Eastern Front could be re-created it would have a decisive effect and might end the war in a few months in our favor. On the other hand, so long as the Germans could withdraw all their troops from Russia, there was a grave danger that we might be overwhelmed by superior numbers on the Western front. He said that he entirely agreed with everything I said, but no military man with whom he had talked had been able to convince him that there was any practical scheme which would re-create a Russian front. He remarked that he would go as far as intervening against the wishes of the Russian people—knowing that it was eventually for their good—providing he thought the scheme had any practical chance of success. The schemes put forward, however, were in his opinion impracticable, and would have the opposite effect to that desired. The Japanese themselves said they could not get any further than OMSK and were very doubtful if they could get as far as that. They were, he thought, anxious enough to have an invitation from us so that they might occupy the maritime provinces, but had no intention of engaging on a vast military enterprise sufficient to reach even the Ural Mountains.

If we could have put a large British-American force into Vladivostock, and advanced along the Siberian railroad, we might, he thought, have rallied the Russian people to assist in defence of their country. But if we relied mainly on Japanese military assistance we should rally the Russians against us, excepting for a small reactionary body who would join anybody to destroy the Bolsheviki. I remarked that in any case it was not possible to make the situation worse than it was now. He said that that was where he entirely disagreed. We could make it much worse by putting the Germans in a position where they could organize Russia in a national movement against Japan. If that was done he would not be surprised to see Russian soldiers fighting with the Germans on the Western Front, "Then," I said, "are we to do nothing at all." "No," he said, "we must watch the situation carefully and sympathetically, and be ready to move whenever the right time arrived."

His own idea was to send a Civil commission of British, French and American, to Russia to help organize the railroads and food supplies, and, since currency is worthless, organize a system of barter. He would send such missions to Vladivostock and Murmansk. Of course, it would take a long time before any results could be expected from such a movement. If in the meantime we were invited to intervene by any responsible and representative body, we ought to do so. An oral or secret arrangement with TROTSKY would be no good since he would repudiate it. He realized that U.S. Government held the key to the situation in that Japanese Government would not intervene without their sanction; but it would be odious for him to use such power except the best interests of the common cause demanded it.

(Part 2). CXP 628.

Regarding American infantry: He asked me to tell him what had happened. He thought the discussion somewhat academic as BAKER assured him that they were sending all the infantry and machine-gunners who were ready to go as quickly as possible. If PERSHING really stood in the way, he would be ordered to stand out of the way, but he thought that he was only asserting a principle which he was not putting into practice. For his part he stood on no ceremony regarding the use of American troops—they were to be used in any way that was necessary regardless if need be of national sentiment. It would, of course, distress him to have to override his Commander-in-Chief because he felt he ought to be loyal to him, and he did not like

273

overriding a man so far from home and possibly only understanding part of his case. He could not see the advantage at present of a civilian representative. PERSHING had full authority, and the part America was playing in Europe was purely that of rendering military assistance. He hoped the question of the new agreement regarding American infantry would not be raised at the next Supreme War Council because (he repeated) they could not in any event send more than they were sending, and it was no good discussing questions of principle with PERSHING when in practice you could not get anything better than you were getting now. "In any event," he said, "why limit your arrangement to June, July, and August. It is possible you may need American infantry for several months after that. Why not leave the time indefinite until the emergency has passed?"

I took the opportunity of impressing upon the President once more the problem of the American higher command and staff. "It was quite impossible," I said, "that PERSHING could train his General Staff behind the line, and the greatest disaster might befall the American army if they went into battle with inexperienced leaders and staff." He agreed entirely, and hoped some means could be found which would remedy this without discouraging the keenness or hurt the pride of the American commanders.

(Part 3). CXP 629.

Austria: He referred to the AUSTRIAN peace overtures, and said it was a thousand pities that CLEMENCEAU had acted as he did. He had no great sympathy for the Emperor Karl, but thought he had been sincerely looking for a means of breaking away from Germany, and now CLEMENCEAU'S action had fixed them to Germany and rivetted them there permanently; and all this, he said, merely to score a personal triumph. Now we had no chance of making a separate peace with Austria, and must look to

the other way—the way which he disliked most intensely—
of setting the AUSTRIAN people against their own Government by plots and intrigues. We were not good at that
work, and generally made a failure of it, but he saw no
other way. He intended to support the Czechs, Poles, and
Jugo-Slavs.

Ireland: He hoped the Government would not force
Conscription without Home Rule. I tried to explain that
these were two entirely different problems. He said that
he could well understand that himself—the mass of the
people in America would not understand it. It would not
have been wise for U.S. Government to make the Sein Fein
revelations as we had asked them to do. It would have
been regarded here as too obviously helping the British
Government in a political situation: the people would have
resented it. He was afraid the way the revelations had appeared in the press here had not caused a particularly
good impression. He deeply regretted the situation and
had no sympathy whatever for Irishmen either here or at
home who sought German aid.

I asked him his opinion as to the war generally. He said
he hoped and believed the Allies would be able to hold
back the German onslaught during the summer. That
the Americans must speed-up in every way the creation of
a great American army, so that in time we could beat the
Germans and force them to accept a peace we thought
right. He was, he said, telling everyone he came in contact
with that we could hope for no satisfactory compromise
with the present rulers of Germany.

Finally, I urged again that the American representation
in Europe was unsatisfactory; that PERSHING had far
more to do than should fall to the lot of a Commander-
in-Chief; and urged him to send more fully empowered
representatives to assist the military. He merely remarked
that he realised the difficulties of the situation, and was
even now considering what could be done to remedy it.

CABLE CXP 644, 14 JUNE 1918
FOLLOWING FOR SIR ERIC DRUMMOND FROM W.:
[No. 98] MOST SECRET. INTERVENTION IN RUSSIA

As reported in my cable No. 627 of May 30th, I discussed with the President the question of intervention in Russia and found that, while he realised the importance and urgency of action, he did not approve the plans we proposed. Since then House has been endeavouring to evolve a policy which would be acceptable to the President and has exchanged views with members of the Administration and others.

I have not troubled you with the various suggestions which have been put forward, but now a concrete proposal is being prepared and is likely to be accepted. Please treat this information as very secret for the present.

The President is still firmly opposed to intervention by the Japanese alone. He is also opposed to Allied-cum-Japanese intervention on the ground that this amounts to practically the same thing because the Japanese would supply the greater part of any military force. He is, in fact, totally opposed to armed intervention without invitation either from the de facto Russian Government or some body really representing Russian opinion. His objection is simply that such action on the part of the Allies would play into the German hands, and, quite apart from the moral issue involved, would do our cause more harm than good from a military point of view. He despairs of receiving any invitation from the Bolshevic Government. As reported in my cable No. 627 of May 30th, his mind has been working on the lines of a Civil commission, and this is what is now proposed:

It was at first suggested that the Commission should be under John R. Mott of Y.M.C.A. fame. While Mott has many admirable qualities he was clearly not the man for the task. The proposal now under consideration is that Hoover should proceed at once to Vladivostock at the head of an important Allied Relief Commission. In the first instance, the object of this commission will be to bring all the relief the Allies can spare in the way of food and other supplies, and, more particularly, to help the Russian people to organize their resources to better advantage. Mr. Hoover would take with him a large staff, and he has, as you know, a world-wide reputation for organization of food supply. A military force would accompany Hoover sufficient to protect his mission, and further troops would be held in readiness and sent later if Hoover so advised. When all is ready the Bolshevic Government will be asked to invite this Relief Commission, and I think they will find it very difficult to refuse if the suggestion is properly worded. In any event the commission would go. The Japanese Government would be requested to assist as well as the other allies. Having thus started the movement, the President would, I think, be very largely guided by Hoover's advice, and if he told the U.S.G. armed intervention (even mainly Japanese) would be acceptable to the Russian people, the President would probably support the proposal.

The objection which will no doubt occur at once to your mind is the delay between the sending of the Civil Commission and serious armed intervention. My reply is that at any rate we should be on the right road, and I do not believe it is possible to persuade the President to agree to armed intervention without some such preliminary movement. The advantages of the proposal seem to lie in the personality of Hoover, who knows Siberia, having spent some time there as a mining engineer. He is by no means a sentimentalist, but an ambitious and energetic man, and his recent achievements have gained him the confidence of the President and the country. He is, moreover, friendly disposed towards the British. We would, I think, be able to persuade U.S.G. to pursue their military preparations, and, if possible, to send with Hoover the nucleus of an armed force, such as a staff, to prepare the way for further troops.

277

This scheme has not yet received the approval of the President, but is now being considered. The information, therefore, is very secret.

CABLEGRAM CXP 701, 16 AUGUST 1918
FOLLOWING FOR LORD READING FROM W.:
Personal & Very Secret

Yesterday I showed the President a paraphrase of your No. 724 of 14th. Col. House was present during most of the interview. The President remarked that he was glad of the opportunity of further discussion because when he last saw you he had not read the PHILLIMORE report, and moreover he had been obliged to discuss with you a variety of subjects in a short interview. He asked me to cable you and say that he has no intention of making any public statement regarding the constitution of a LEAGUE OF NATIONS. In the first place, such a statement on his part would be a target for criticism here. One section of the Senate, led by Lodge, would say that he had gone too far in committing the United States to a Utopian scheme, and, on the other hand, the League enthusiasts would criticize him for not going far enough. Great harm might be done the scheme by arousing such controversy at this time. In the second place, he has not yet determined in his own mind the best method of constituting the League. He has ideas on the subject but not worked out in detail. I asked what his ideas were. He replied—"Two main principles; there must be a League of Nations, and this must be virile, a reality, not a paper league." I asked what he thought of the PHILLIMORE report. "It has no teeth," he replied. "I read it to the last page hoping to find something definite, but I could not." I asked whether he would appoint a Committee similar to Phillimore's to report on the subject, so that H.M.G. could ascertain the American view. He said he would not be in favour of appointing such a committee.

"How then," I asked, "are we ever to exchange views and urge a common basis, because no one nation can make a league all by itself?" He agreed it would be necessary to find common ground, and said he would like nothing better than to discuss the whole matter perfectly frankly with MR. LLOYD GEORGE, who he felt would substantially share his views. As this is impossible at present he would be glad to discuss the question with anyone H.M.G. care to send to him. In further conversation the President said he thought the LEAGUE OF NATIONS ought to be constituted at the Peace Conference and not before. If we formed the league while we were still fighting, it would inevitably be regarded as a sort of Holy Alliance aimed at Germany. This would not be the purpose of the American people. Germany should be invited to join the family of nations, providing she will behave according to the rules of the Society. The President sees grave danger in public discussions of the scheme now. Each nation, he fears, would become committed to its own plan and find fundamental objections in the methods proposed by others. It would, he thinks, even endanger the solidarity of those nations fighting Germany. He feels very strongly on this point and asked me to urge you from him to use your influence against the publication of the Phillimore report. He feels sure its publication would create much controversy here and that he would not be able to avoid expressing his opinion, when he would have to say definitely that he did not endorse the report. This would look like an important divergence of view between the two Governments and might have very ill effects. He asked me this morning if I had cabled you, and said he felt much relieved as you would appreciate his position, and be able to prevent the report being published.

I have tried faithfully to repeat the conversation which took place at intervals throughout a whole afternoon. In addition I will give you a few general impressions.

I think the President looks to economic pressure to supply the main force which might be used to support the

League. He feels there must be force, but recognises the practical difficulties. He has come up here to discuss the whole war situation with Col. House, but particularly the League of Nations. The President referred to the anti-British feeling still existing here as an additional reason for avoiding any appearance of friction between the two Governments. I reminded him that this might also create an anti-American sentiment in England, which happily did not now exist. He agreed that it was a possibility which too many Americans overlooked.

Regarding GERMAN peace offers, the President said U.S. representatives abroad had been instructed to listen and report anything that was said, without holding out any hope that such unofficial offers would be considered by U.S.G. The right policy, he said, would be for the German Government to state their terms through properly accredited representatives, so that they might be then considered officially by all the associated belligerents.

In conclusion, I would venture to urge you to impress Col. House's views regarding Phillimore report on H.M.G. He is willing, even anxious, to discuss the League of Nations in all its phases with us, but foresees endless trouble and controversy if immature conclusions are made public and the nations through their press become engaged in public argument in support of various methods. He has given us this clear warning, and it may easily embarrass our whole relations with him if we cannot meet his views.

LETTER, WISEMAN TO ARTHUR C. MURRAY, 30 AUGUST 1918

My dear Arthur,

It has occurred to me that you might be interested to have some description of the week I spent at Magnolia with the President and Col. House. The mail is just going, but I will do my best to give you some description—though I fear it will be disjointed.

I had arranged to spend a week with Col. House particularly because Gordon Auchincloss, his son-in-law, (whom you will remember is assistant counselor of the State Department) was taking his holiday there at the same time and we had planned some golf and tennis. The morning after I arrived, however, the President and his party reached Magnolia. They had come quite unexpectedly, having only decided upon the trip the day before.

I did my best to keep my name out of the papers and the reporters were very good about it and I think only one or two papers mentioned the fact that I was there.

This was sufficient, however, for the French Embassy to ring me up on the long distance telephone and ask if there had been any special significance in the conferences between the President, House and myself. I said they had been of the utmost importance since we had proved that the President could putt at least 50 yards on his iron shots if he would only follow through. In fact it was a most interesting time for me. The President, Mrs. Wilson and Admiral Grayson, his physician and Naval Aide-de-camp occupied a beautiful colonial house over-looking the sea and about a couple of hundred yards from Col. House's bungalow, where I was staying. A company of marines kept the public at a most respectful distance and a destroyer lying off the point guarded him from ambitious U-boat commanders. The President said he was delighted to find me there and insisted on my remaining with the party. Early in the morning about eight o'clock he would motor to one of the nearby golf courses and play a round before the course was crowded. He usually played with Grayson and Mrs. Wilson went nine holes with them.

On one occasion at Myopia the Club boor came up to him at the first tee, introduced himself, and offered to play a round with the President and show him the course. With the coldest look I have ever seen the President turned to him and said, "Thank you, I have a caddy." Out of ear-shot I asked him who his friend was, "Oh just a Boston ass" was the President's reply.

As a rule the President and Mrs. Wilson came to lunch at the House's bungalow and we all went over to dine with the President in the evening. In the afternoons they generally went for a motor drive through the really beautiful country along the North Shore. Of course I never discussed any of the questions of the moment unless the President raised the subject, but on one or two occasions the President himself suggested that after lunch he and I and Col. House should retire and talk business. In particular we discussed the League of Nations, the economic policy of the Allies, the President's Mexican policy and the possibilities of German peace efforts. I have, as you know, cabled Reading the substance of these conversations and I will try and elaborate on them in memoranda which, however, I am afraid will not be ready for this mail.

We talked a good deal of politics in England. The President knows England much better than I supposed. Apparently, when he was at Princeton, he used to spend his summer vacations bicycling or walking through England, particularly the Lake districts and at that time had quite a wide acquaintance among University men in England and Scotland. He thinks it was a mistake for us to have a Coalition Government on the ground that the mass of the people would suspect that the Government was controlled by the more reactionary elements and the representatives of capital and privilege. He is, I am afraid, a pretty extreme radical with that curious uninformed prejudice against the so-called governing class in England. I think he would prefer the Lloyd George of Limehouse rather than of the Guildhall. He does not seem to know much of the details of continental politics and I am much impressed with the way in which he relies upon House's advice in these matters.

He does not seem to have much sympathy for Italy and thinks she entered the war as a cold blooded business transaction. Nor has he very strong feelings about Alsace Lorraine, although he says that American opinion is very determined on this point; that they will pay their debt to

France by giving her back Alsace Lorraine. He has no sympathy whatever for Bulgaria or Turkey. He is convinced that there are genuine liberal elements in Austria and even in Germany who sincerely wish to follow democratic ideals, but admits that they are too small a minority to have any influence at present on the peoples, as a whole.

The German people, he believes, must be made to hate war, to realize that no military machine can dominate the world today. His personal hatred of the Kaiser, whom he has never seen, is almost amusing. The elected autocrat can see no good in the hereditary tyrant. Talking of the Crown Prince he said it made him furious to think the destinies of Germany might one day be in the hands of that young ass.

I was struck by his talking one day at some length on the question of Anti-British feeling in America. He ascribes it, of course, chiefly to the Irish. He does not believe in propaganda as a means of bringing the two countries closer together but thinks that the war will do much to help us understand each other better and that afterwards we shall gradually be drawn closer as we work together for the same ideals.

I find the President very interested in personalities. He was anxious to hear about our leading men, their characteristics and mode of life. He has interesting and novel ideas about the writing of history which is one of his favorite occupations. He misses, he says, the college life and the pleasant association with his fellow professors. . . . . .

NOTES OF AN INTERVIEW WITH THE PRESIDENT AT THE
WHITE HOUSE, WEDNESDAY, OCTOBER 16TH, 1918.
VERY SECRET

THE GERMAN NOTES:

The President had with him a few notes which he had made for me. He began at once to discuss the GERMAN NOTE. "They have said that they agree to my terms," he observed, "and if they were respectable people I should be obliged to meet them in a conference. Of course, we do not trust the present German Government; we can never trust them, and we do not want to discuss peace with them. But we must not appear to be slamming the door on peace.

"You must remember that there are many honest and sincere Americans who did not want us to go into this war—who think that it should end. And again there are many (particularly among the foreign born population, such as the Italians) who did not want their sons to be drafted. They are proud now at what their boys are doing, but they are not really deeply interested in the war.

"The spirit of the Bolsheviki is lurking everywhere, and there is no more fertile soil than war-weariness.

"There is grave unrest all over the world. There are symptoms of it in this country—symptoms that are apparent although not yet dangerous.

"We should consider too the condition of Germany. If we humiliate the German people and drive them too far, we shall destroy all form of government, and Bolshevism will take its place. We ought not to ground them to powder or there will be nothing to build up from.

"I am alarmed at the temper of some of our people now. They want us to devastate Germany in the same way that Germany has devastated other countries. I should be ashamed to call myself an American if our troops destroyed one single German town. I want us all on our side to end this war as finely as we began and show the world that we are the better fellow. The people you hear shouting that we must dictate terms in Berlin are not the real Americans. Theirs is not the voice of America. I think the Germans want peace—I think even the present German Government wants peace—and I even think it would be quite safe to meet them at a Conference table now; but I am not sure—at least I am not sure enough, and I will not take any chances with them. On the other hand, we must not fall into what may prove to be a German trap by allowing our answers to be used to stimulate their own war spirit and undermine ours.

"House and I have arrived at a formula which we think fairly sums up the positions:—'If the Germans are beaten, they will accept any terms; and if they are not beaten, we don't want them to accept any terms.' I think it should be possible to arrange an armistice which would safeguard us against any possible treachery. It would be best for our Naval and Military experts to recommend terms for an armistice. The heads of the governments will probably have to modify the terms because the soldiers and sailors will make them too severe. We must not make them impossible, or even humiliating."

AN INTERCEPTED MESSAGE:

The President showed me a copy of an intercepted wireless from SOLF to some German Commander in RUSSIA. The President was immensely interested in it. Every word, he said, breathed the old Prussian trickery and deceit. It was hard to see how we could ever trust such people.

THE AUSTRIAN NOTE:

I asked the President what he proposed to do about the Note from the Austrian Government. He replied that he would write an answer as soon as he had time—probably within the next two days. He would have to say that since his speech of January 8th outlining his fourteen points, two new facts had arisen which modified his declaration as regards AUSTRIA. These were the recognition of the CZECHO-SLOVAKS and the JUGO-SLAVS. He would support to the full their just claims. Otherwise he proposed to answer Austria in the same sense as he had answered Germany. I suggested that the Austrian Government might bring with them to the Peace Conference people who would claim to speak on behalf of the various nationalities of their Empire. The President replied very promptly—"We have already recognised Masaryk, Dmowski, and their groups, and we cannot listen to anybody else."

285

TURKEY:

The President said he had received a request from the TURKISH GOVERNMENT to use his good offices with the Allies to persuade them to discuss a separate peace. He should reply to the Turkish Government that he would communicate with the Allies: and to the Allies he should suggest, confidentially of course, that in his opinion it would be possible for them to make a satisfactory separate peace with Turkey; that such a move would materially hasten the German debacle; and that he would be glad if he could be of service in bringing about peace with Turkey.

THE FOURTEEN POINTS:

The President had with him a note of his fourteen points some of which he discussed briefly with me, as follows:—

(1). Treaties:

There should be no more secret treaties. International negotiations should be conducted publicly for the whole world to read so that everyone might know that the treaty did not threaten international peace.

(2). The Freedom of the Seas:

This was a question which would naturally interest GREAT BRITAIN more than any other country on account of the preponderance of her Navy and her position as a world-wide Empire. He admitted that the British Navy had in the past acted as a sort of naval police for the world—in fact for civilization. For his part he would be willing to leave this power to the discretion of the British people, who had never abused it, but he wondered whether the rest of the world would be willing to go on doing so indefinitely. Many nations, great and small, chafed under the feeling that their sea-borne trade and maritime development proceeded only with the permission under the shadow of the British Navy. He had always felt that the deepest-rooted cause of the present war was this feeling in Germany —an unjust fear and jealousy of the British Navy, but a feeling none the less real. I gathered that the President was searching for a remedy which he might suggest, but that he had found none; in his mind there is an idea that the great power of the British Navy might in some way be used in connection with the LEAGUE OF NATIONS and thereby cease to be a cause of jealousy and irritation.

It would be necessary, the President observed, soon after peace to have a Conference to revise international law, and particularly International Maritime Laws.

Since the beginning of the war he had recognised that the submarine introduced a new element in naval warfare which must modify existing international law. That was why, in his neutral days, he had not insisted more strongly on the strict observance of international law in his dealings with the British Government. The old American theory was that the highways of the sea should be free in war as in peace. It remained to be seen how far this must be modified.

The extent of territorial waters would also have to be enlarged owing to the greater range of modern guns, and the old-fashioned definition of "blockade" must be revised.

(3). Equal Trade Opportunities for All Nations Everywhere: and no economic boycott except as a penalty imposed by the LEAGUE OF NATIONS.

(5). German Colonies:

With regard to the German Colonies, the President observed that he had not much faith in government by international commissions. It was clear that the Colonies must not be given back to Germany; at least until we are satisfied that their form of government is very different from the present. For his part, he would be well content to see the German Colonies administered by Great Britain, whose Colonial government was in many respects a model for the world. He must warn the British, however, of the great jealousy of the other nations—including, he regretted to say, a large number of people in America. It would, he thought, create much bad feeling internationally if the German Colonies were handed over to us as a sovereign part of the British Empire. He wondered whether there was some way in which they could be administered in trust. "In Trust," I asked, "for whom?" "Well, for the League of Nations, for instance," he said.

(6). Russia:

I asked the President why he would not send any political Commissioner, or join in any political conferences with the Allies regarding action to be taken in Russia. "My policy regarding Russia," he said, "is very similar to my Mexican policy. I believe in letting them work out their own salvation, even though they wallow in anarchy for a while. I visualize it like this: A lot of impossible folk, fighting among themselves. You cannot do business with them, so you shut them all up in a room and lock the door and tell them that when they have settled matters among themselves you will unlock the door and do business." I suggested that in this case you would probably lock in a lot of Germans with them who would bolt the convention. He thought it was impossible to eradicate German influence from Russia. Hundreds and thousands of Germans had gone to live in Russia; had taken Russian names, and were apparently Russians. How could you get rid of the influence of these men? The Bolsheviki, he agreed, were impossible. He had watched with disgust their treatment of Lockhart, who had tried hard to help them.

The question of RUSSIA, he thought, should also be left to the Peace Conference. I protested that would be too late; that the stage was even now being set by the Germans, and we should find forces and conditions had been created in Russia which it would be difficult, if not impossible, to alter at a Peace Conference. The President said there was a great deal in that view, and the whole question was causing him great anxiety. I gathered the impression that it is not impossible that he will modify his policy regarding Russia.

(8). Alsace-Lorraine:

With regard to Alsace-Lorraine, he could not imagine why his pronouncement on this subject had been misunderstood. He meant, of course, that the Germans must give back Alsace-Lorraine—just that and nothing more or less.

(9), (10), & (11).

These questions will require most careful definition. He had, however, seen the maps and arguments prepared by his advisers, and thought it was quite possible to arrive at a fair and lasting settlement on the basis of self-determination.

(14).

A LEAGUE OF NATIONS should be the very centre of the Peace agreement. The pillars upon which the house will stand.

COLONEL HOUSE'S MISSION:

I showed the President Mr. BALFOUR'S cable expressing his gratification at the approaching visit of Col. House. "I was sure they would like me to send House," the President remarked. "He knows my mind entirely; but you must ask them to realise though how hard it is for me to spare him. On many problems he is the only person I can consult. I hope, the President added, that your Government will speak perfectly frankly to House. He will certainly be frank with them."

I suggested that it would be a good opportunity for Col. House to discuss peace terms generally with the Allies. The President rather demurred. He disliked the idea of settling peace terms without the enemy being present to state their case. It would give the impression of dividing the spoils amongst ourselves in advance. The same thing applied to the LEAGUE OF NATIONS—Germany ought to be present when the League of Nations is constituted. I asked if it would not be dangerous to go into conference with the enemy before we know each other's views, and whether there would be any objection to an informal exchange of views between, say, Colonel House and the British and French Governments. The President said, on the contrary, it would be of great advantage.

PEACE CONFERENCE:

Regarding the Peace Conference, he asked whether it would be possible to have the deliberations reported fully in the press from day to day. I said it seemed to me that would be quite impossible. "We should make it as public as possible then," he said. "For my part, I am deeply committed to the policy of open diplomacy."

WISEMAN,

THE ATTITUDE OF THE UNITED STATES AND OF
PRESIDENT WILSON TOWARDS THE PEACE CONFERENCE
[c. 20 OCTOBER 1918]

(1). THE PRESIDENT'S POSITION:

We are approaching the Peace Conference knowing very little of the American attitude towards the various problems which will be discussed.

There are two forces in the United States to be considered—public opinion and President Wilson. Sometimes they correspond, sometimes they differ. The President himself claims to be no more than the spokesman and interpreter of the American people. It is true that he responds very quickly to popular sentiment when it is expressed in an unmistakeable manner, but it frequently happens that opinions are fairly evenly divided and he must decide which is the true vox populi. Moreover, a man of Mr. Wilson's force in his unique position must inevitably influence public opinion, at any rate in his own country, to no small degree. There have been times, too, when the President has not hesitated to run counter to popular outcry. At the present moment his prestige in America is probably higher than it ever was. An unsuccessful war—a series of disasters to American forces on land and sea—would have put Roosevelt, Lodge, and his other political opponents and critics in a very strong position, but events as they have turned out have increased the President's personal authority.

It is well for us always to bear in mind that the President speaks for America and not the Republican leaders. Party politics are by no means shelved. If we should have any difference of opinion with the Administration, we might receive the enthusiastic support of powerful Republican interests, but we should, of course, find their very support our greatest handicap because the majority of Americans will always rally to the President in case of a dispute with a foreign country, and the ultra-British party have little political influence in America.

(2). THE AMERICAN VIEW OF THE WAR AND PEACE:

It is difficult to describe the point of view of the average American, untravelled and uninformed regarding foreign affairs. In a country of over a hundred million people, there must be many different points of view towards the war, but it is safe to generalise on certain broad lines. The American is undoubtedly an idealist. He was never afraid of Germany, or jealous of her. American troops go to Europe with a rather vague idea that they are going to democratize Europe, and put the Kaiser in particular, and all autocrats generally, out of business; an ingenuous notion that they want to make the rest of the world as democratic as they believe their own country to be.

Very few stop to follow this out to its conclusion, or translate their ideals into terms of frontiers and nationalities. They would be genuinely surprised and hurt if they were told that their ideas were quixotic or their motives guided by any kind of self-interest.

291

For all their idealism, the Americans are a people with shrewd common sense; and when the difficulties have become more apparent they will no doubt quite cheerfully accept a very much modified Utopia. In the meantime it is important that they should not come to believe that the British Empire is the chief obstacle to a world at peace.

They have been taught in their schools, and by recent German propaganda, to regard the British as a nation of Imperialists, who want to boss the whole world. It is safe to say that 90 per cent of the American people regard our treatment of Ireland with disapproval. The more friendly look upon it as a grave political blunder; the majority regard it as a blot on civilization.

Freer contact between the two peoples, owing to the war, has done much to offset this feeling. They are finding, to their genuine surprise, that we are not all like the traditional stage Englishman. A closer observation of the Irishman at home, and the Sein Fein dealings with the Germans in America, has done something to help them realise there may be two sides to the Irish question.

Against this we must put the growing consciousness that after the war there will be only two great powers left— Great Britain and the United States. Which is going to be the greater, politically and commercially? In that constantly recurring thought the explanation may be found of much of the friction that arises.

(3). THE PRESIDENT'S ATTITUDE:

All his life the President has been an uncompromising reformer. He did not hesitate to tear down old traditions and endanger the peaceful progress of Princeton University in his zeal for reform; and he will probably approach world-problems with very much the same spirit. He is by turns a great idealist and a shrewd politician; and he will not hesitate to attempt to put into practice his greatest ideals, though he will probably always under-estimate the difficulties and the opposition confronting him.

292

The President regards the war—or rather the peace which will follow it—as a great opportunity for re-modelling the whole structure of international affairs. He is not so much interested in the adjustment of this claim or that—the limitation of one power, and the strengthening of another—but his mind visualizes a new world in which there shall be no tyranny and no war. Mr. Wilson, however, is a student of history and a man of experience in public affairs, and he would be quite willing to admit that the outcome of this war will doubtless fall far short of his ideal. "Nevertheless," he would answer, "that is no reason why I should not try." The dangers of a too ambitious programme do not appeal to him.

It is important to understand something of the President's mind in order to follow his views on any particular problem which is likely to arise at the Peace Conference. It would be misleading, for instance, to take any one of the Fourteen Points of his speech of January 8th and separate it from the rest of the speech. Each of the fourteen propositions put forward simultaneously by the President is numbered to indicate that it constitutes a part of a complete and consistent whole.

In the President's mind, the whole future peace of the world is a single conception based on the LEAGUE OF NATIONS. If that fails—all else is useless. The formation of such a league is the only compensation to be looked for as an offset to the devastating effects of the war. All the other thirteen points are benefits which flow from the main idea. Should that fail to be put into operation, its proposed component parts become meaningless and disappear with it.

Of the President's fourteen conditions, Nos. 2, 3, & 5, are the only ones likely to bring him into conflict with the British point of view.

The 2nd. condition, referring to the Freedom of the Seas, would mean nothing without the League of Nations. If it meant anything it would be a declaration that the laws of war and of peace should be the same at sea, except as they may be varied by international action—the only expression of which we have at present is international law. Clearly, the clause can be taken only in connection with a League of Nations.

Now Article No. 3 deals with the subject of the removal of economic barriers and the instituting of equal trade conditions amongst such nations as shall consent to the making of peace and shall associate themselves together for its maintenance.

Article No. 4 in its turn calls for adequate guarantees to be given and taken for the reduction of armaments to the lowest possible point.

The rest of the conditions deal in broad outline with territorial adjustments; but Article 14, referring to the League of Nations, is the one which binds them all together, explains them, and in the President's view makes them possible. It provides for an association of nations which shall mutually guarantee the political and territorial integrity of the States of the Earth, both great and small. At once the other conditions become easier to understand, particularly the Freedom of the Seas and the removal of economic barriers; and, subject always to the plan of which they are part being put into actual operation, they become coherent and useful elements thereof. If there should be instituted a valid and operative League of Nations, freedom of the seas would appear to be a logical and proper corrollary. No war could under the postulated conditions come to exist except between the League as a whole and some non-assenting State, or some recalcitrant member. In that event—as indicated in condition No. 2—the seas would be closed by the power of the League to the vessels of the non-assenting State or recalcitrant member, and all trade with such nation by all other States would be prevented by the same power. This result would infallibly follow upon the creation of a League of Nations—for a League which did not concern itself with maritime matters would hardly be worth having; and the President does not consider prospective maritime laws under any other conditions.

(4). ATTITUDE TOWARDS THE GERMANS:

The American attitude towards Germany should be carefully considered, for it differs somewhat from the British point of view. The danger being that America inclines to thrust the whole responsibility for the war and the conduct of it upon the Kaiser and what is termed the Military Party. They are ready to believe that the rest of Germany has been an unwilling tool in the hands of their military masters. If Germany was to repudiate the Kaiser, and become a Republic, there would be an enormous reaction in America in her favour, and she might be received again very much like the Prodigal Son.

In any case it appears likely that the German delegates will come to the Peace Conference representing a beaten nation, and, in some respects at any rate, a different Government from that which began the war. They will be in a position not of expecting gains, but of hoping to save something from the wreck, and they will also be in a position to blame all the misdeeds of the war upon another government now out of power. In this way they may make a very insidious appeal to American sentiment.

The British Government, on the other hand, will have to demand a practical settlement of the problems, particularly such as Freedom of the Seas, and Colonial claims, which are essential and vital to the British Empire—while an idealistic America and a beaten Germany might be willing to try all sorts of extravagant experiments.

The one fundamental problem, however, which is the key-note to the whole American attitude, is the League of Nations. Here again American public opinion is probably more ready to experiment with the idea than the more cautious British. It is not improbable, however, that the President is considerably in advance of the general American public in his views on this subject. A new American national spirit has been created by this war, and America today is less international in sentiment than many European countries. It is possible that the people would be unwilling to pool any part of their national sovereignty even to a League of Nations devised by President Wilson.

It is easier to visualise difficulties than to suggest remedies. Our guiding spirit should be one of great patience. The American nation is making its first appearance as a great world-power. They have been flattered unduly by each of the Allies in turn, and will no doubt receive a subtle form of flattery from the enemy. We must remember that after peace is signed we shall by no means have finished with America. We shall not even have finished with President Wilson. During the difficult period of reconstruction, it will be necessary for the two nations to work together in harmony. There are some who think this is impossible, but such people do not know America. They do not realize that, in spite of jealousy and misunderstanding, the British and American peoples believe in the same things and follow the same ideals.

ANNOTATED BIBLIOGRAPHY

The following is an outline of the bibliography:

  I. Manuscript Collections
   A. In the United States
   B. In Great Britain

 II. Government and Documentary Publications
   A. American
   B. British

III. Contemporary Published Materials
   A. Newspapers
   B. Other

 IV. Published Diaries, Memoirs, and Letters
   A. American
   B. British
   C. Other

  V. Biographies
   A. American
   B. British

 VI. General Works

VII. Special Studies

NOTE ON SOURCES

The bulk of the raw material for this study came from unpublished sources. Reliance on these sources is necessary as well as desirable, because much of the data on the Anglo-American war partnership exists only in manuscript form. The British government has not published its diplomatic papers relating to the First World War. While the American government has printed most of its important "official" papers, it could not include in its publications "unofficial" materials such as the Wiseman Papers.

In the United States I have consulted all the government and private manuscripts that seemed relevant. In Great Britain I was initially restricted to the use of private papers. Then in 1967, following the decision of the British government to relax the "fifty-year rule" I was able in a short research trip to examine the Foreign Office records. The Lloyd George Papers became available after my work in England was done, but a search through them for specific Wiseman items was made for me.

I. MANUSCRIPT COLLECTION

A. IN THE UNITED STATES

Gordon Auchincloss Papers, Yale University Library
Some of the correspondence is of incidental importance, but the diary is very useful. The diary records Wiseman's visits to Washington, telephone calls between House or Wiseman and the State Department, and the difficulties Reading encountered in trying to see Wilson. Also in the diary are accounts of the 1917 and 1918 House trips to Europe.

Newton D. Baker Papers, Library of Congress
Contains a small but essential correspondence between Baker and Wilson regarding the amalgamation controversy and the Wiseman-House scheme to demote Pershing.

Tasker H. Bliss Papers, Library of Congress
Bliss's correspondence with Baker and General March is valuable concerning the Supreme War Council. Numerous Supreme War Council documents are in the collection.

Oscar T. Crosby Papers, Library of Congress
A small collection, but valuable for Crosby's account of the financial crisis of 1917 and for bits of information on his service with the Inter-Allied finance council.

Edith Benham Helm Papers, Library of Congress
The papers of one of Wilson's secretaries yielded one valuable item, a diary letter (May 2, 1919) saying that Wilson wished Wiseman to become ambassador. Important as testimony from outside the House entourage of Wilson's high regard for Wiseman.

Irving H. Hoover Papers, Library of Congress
The White House steward's papers include a log which recorded the visits of Wiseman and Reading (and presumably all others) to Wilson.

Edward M. House Papers, Yale University Library
This extremely important and large collection contains House's extensive correspondence, documents on a wide variety of subjects, and House's detailed diary. The latter is essential for tracing the actions of both House and Wiseman and reveals the closeness of their association. The correspondence with Wilson contains carbons of all of House's letters, including those which transmitted messages from the British. But the messages are not always identified, so that the student must consult the received letters in the Wilson Papers as well. Similarly, many enclosures in letters to House are now filed separately and are not always identifiable as to origin.

Robert Lansing Papers, Library of Congress
Lansing's correspondence is not very useful, but his desk diary records visits by Wiseman and Reading. His personal diaries and confidential memoranda are valuable and include, among other things, character sketches of Spring Rice, Northcliffe, and Reading.

Henry Cabot Lodge Papers, Massachusetts Historical Society
Useful for establishing the very close association of Spring Rice and Lodge and for confirming the well-known animosity between Lodge and Wilson.

William G. McAdoo Papers, Library of Congress
McAdoo's correspondence with Lansing, Wilson, and the

British indicates his uncompromising attitude toward the Allies in financial matters and his eagerness to direct foreign policy.

Vance McCormick Papers, Yale University Library
The correspondence deals largely with patronage matters. Nor are McCormick's privately printed diary and documents relating to blockade matters particularly useful. Many of the latter are in the House Papers also.

Walter Hines Page Papers, Harvard University Library
Of very slight use, except to confirm the unimportance of Page in Anglo-American relations, 1917-18. The most important of Page's letters are published.

John J. Pershing Papers, Library of Congress
Pershing's outline diary is useful for confirming that Wiseman interviewed him in May 1918. There is little of importance in the papers not published in his memoirs.

William Phillips Papers, Harvard University Library
Phillips' diary contains one capital entry regarding the relationship of Wiseman and Reading.

Frank L. Polk Papers, Yale University Library
A few useful letters from and to McAdoo and other Administration leaders. Polk's diary and confidential diary record numerous visits by Wiseman and occasionally divulge the subjects discussed.

State Department Records, National Archives
For the period under consideration, the General Records of the Department of State (Record Group 59) are available on microfilm. The easiest way to proceed is to consult the various pamphlets published by the National Archives to describe microcopies (e.g., the most important for this study: "Pamphlet Accompanying Microcopy No. 367, RECORDS OF THE DEPARTMENT OF STATE RELATING TO WORLD WAR I AND ITS TERMINATION, 1914-29). Microcopies 316, 367, 580, and 581 were useful. Generally, the important records have been published in *Foreign Re-*

lations, but there are exceptions, notably internal governmental memoranda.

Treasury Department Records, National Archives
The "Country Files" in the records of the Bureau of Accounts (Record Group 39) include the correspondence and interdepartmental memoranda regarding loans to Britain and the other Allies. Very important.

Woodrow Wilson Papers, Library of Congress
This vast collection includes important correspondence with Baker, Lansing, McAdoo, and House. The latter includes material transmitted from Wiseman. Essential for proving conclusively the Wiseman contact with the President.

Sir William Wiseman Papers, Yale University Library
The prime source for this book. These are the files kept by Wiseman in New York and include cables, letters, and memoranda to and from Wiseman and copies of many official cables between the Washington embassy and the Foreign Office. The files were culled by Wiseman and contain very little related to his intelligence work. They also contain almost nothing of a biographical or personal nature. A recent addition, known as the New Wiseman Papers and available on a restricted basis, consists largely of some business papers from the late 1940's and 1950's.

B. IN GREAT BRITAIN

L. S. Amery Diary, London
Vivid, daily impressions by a brilliant man in close touch with several British leaders, notably Milner. The diary (in the possession of Mr. Julian Amery) contains several references to Wiseman.

Arthur J. Balfour Papers, British Museum
This collection, excepting a few reserved items, became available in 1965 and covers the whole of Balfour's long political life. For 1917-18 it is very valuable for the correspondence with envoys and other government officials.

One bound volume contains Foreign Office communications with Wiseman and Reading, including a number of items not in the Wiseman Papers. Marginal notes by Balfour are enlightening and often entertaining.

Viscount Cecil of Chelwood (Lord Robert Cecil) Papers, British Museum
Particularly useful correspondence relating to the Russian intervention. Among other items are summarized abstracts of Wiseman's and Reading's dispatches concerning the American attitude toward intervention.

Austen Chamberlain Papers, University of Birmingham Library
Not very helpful, except for a few items regarding financial and economic matters. Chamberlain's private correspondence reveals considerable impatience with the American war effort and contempt for Wilson's independent diplomacy.

Elibank Papers, National Library of Scotland
Includes correspondence between Arthur Murray (later Viscount Elibank) and Wiseman. Nothing of any importance which is not also found in the Wiseman Papers at Yale.

Foreign Office Records, Public Record Office. Files FO 371 and FO 115, both huge, contain materials from and relating to the United States. In addition, file FO 800 contains the "private papers" of various officials. Of these the following were productive for this study:

Lord Balfour's Mission to United States, 1917
The records of Balfour's visit in April-May 1917. Valuable information concerning plans to recall Spring Rice and the hassle over sending Northcliffe to America. (I saw in the Foreign Office Library.)

Lord Robert Cecil's Private Papers, 1915-1917
The relevance of this small file is limited to the few items on British representation in the United States.

Sir Eric Drummond's Private Papers, 1916-1919
These are the records of Drummond's tenure as Balfour's private secretary. They include cables and notes from Wiseman, some not found elsewhere.

Private Secretary Archives 1917-1924, A. J. Balfour
Another of Drummond's files, containing several Wiseman items.

Lord Reading's Private Papers
The records of Reading as ambassador. Included are copies of cables to and from the Foreign Office, many of which are in the Wiseman Papers. There is also some correspondence with Wiseman, not found elsewhere, and several important exchanges with Lloyd George.

Sir C. A. Spring Rice's Private Papers, 1913-1918
Carbons of Spring Rice's reports to the Foreign Office and a few signed letters from Grey, Cecil, and Balfour. Of very little use for the period under study. (I saw in the Foreign Office Library.)

Lloyd George Papers, Beaverbrook Library, London
A search made for me of these papers produced only two or three items—e.g., handwritten notes from Reading to Lloyd George concerning Wiseman—not previously located in other collections.

Lord Lothian (Philip Kerr) Papers, Scottish Record Office
Consists largely of papers from a later period. Yielded one important document for this book.

Lord Milner Papers, New College (Oxford) Library
An important collection for foreign, military and colonial policies. Most of the material regarding Russia is of only indirect relevance to the present study. Milner's diary records a number of conversations with Wiseman.

Sir Horace Plunkett Papers, Plunkett Foundation, London
Of minimal use. Plunkett's diary records two meetings

with Wiseman. Plunkett had almost no influence in Anglo-American relations in 1917-18.

Sir William Wiseman's Private Papers, London.
A few letters and notes from famous people remain in the possession of Lady Wiseman.

II. GOVERNMENT AND DOCUMENTARY PUBLICATIONS

A. AMERICAN

Ray Stannard Baker and William F. Dodd, eds. *The Public Papers of Woodrow Wilson*, 6 vols., New York, 1925-27. The two volumes subtitled *War and Peace* contain Wilson's speeches of 1917-18.

Congressional Record, 1918, 65th Congress, 2nd Session.
Secretary Baker's testimony before the Senate Military Affairs Committee in January 1918, printed in Volume LVI, Part 2, pp. 1,411-96.

Department of the Army (Historical Division). *United States in the World War*, 17 vols., Washington, D.C., 1948. Consisting largely of documents, these volumes are essential to the study of American strategy and military cooperation with the Allies. Volumes Two and Three contain British as well as American documents relating to the Supreme War Council and the amalgamation controversy.

Department of State. *Papers Relating to the Foreign Relations of the United States, 1917*, Supplement 2, *The World War*, Washington, D.C., 1932.

————. *Papers Relating to the Foreign Relations of the United States, 1918*, Supplement 1, *The World War*, 2 vols., Washington, D.C., 1933.

————. *Papers Relating to the Foreign Relations of the United States, 1918, Russia*, 3 vols., Washington, D.C., 1931-32.

————. *The Lansing Papers, 1914-1920*, 2 vols., Washington, D.C., 1939-40. Combined these 8 volumes reproduce practically all the official diplomatic correspondence of importance, including the reports of House while he was representing Wilson in Europe. Indispensable.

James Brown Scott, ed. *Official Statements of War Aims and Peace Proposals, December 1916 to November 1918*, Washington, D.C., 1921. A convenient compilation from the pronouncements of all the major belligerents.

Senate. 74th Congress, 2nd Session, Special Committee on Investigation of the Munitions Industry, *Munitions Industry*, Report No. 944, 7 vols., Washington, D.C., 1936. Report of the Nye Committee, Volumes 5 and 6 contain subpoenaed correspondence between the British government and J. P. Morgan and Company regarding the "overdraft." This material is not available elsewhere.

Treasury Department. *Annual Report of the Secretary of the Treasury on the State of the Finances for the Fiscal Year Ended June 30, 1917*, Washington, D.C., 1918.

————. *Annual Report of the Secretary of the Treasury on the State of the Finances for the Fiscal Year Ended June 30, 1918*, Washington, D.C., 1919. These two volumes summarize, among other things, the Treasury's dealings with foreign governments. The 1918 volume goes through November 15, 1918.

B. BRITISH

Parliamentary Debates (5th Series), 1917-1918. Useful for discussions in June 1917 concerning Northcliffe's mission and for questions in April 1918 regarding the United States and the Paris Economic Conference.

"Recommendations of the Economic Conference of the Allies, held at Paris on June 14, 15, 16, and 17, 1916." *Command Paper 8271* (1916), in *British State Papers (Accounts and Papers)*, 1916, Vol. 34.

War Cabinet. *Report for the Year 1917.*

——. *Report for the Year 1918.* These are summary statements of War Cabinet acts. The 1917 volume includes an organizational chart of the government under the War Cabinet.

E. L. Woodward and Rohan Butler, eds. *Documents on British Foreign Policy, 1919-1939,* 32 vols., London, 1946-65. Official documents. Volume V of the First Series makes reference to Wiseman's activities in 1917-18, and prints two reports from Wiseman in July and August 1919 on the treaty fight in America.

III. CONTEMPORARY MATERIALS

A. NEWSPAPERS

Generally, the issues between the American and British governments were referred to, if at all, only vaguely by the press. The activities of Wiseman were almost totally unpublicized. His name appeared in the *New York Times* only twice and then with no indication of his real position. The newspapers that Wiseman watched carefully were: *Manchester Guardian, New York Herald, New York Times, New York Tribune,* and the London *Times.* The last-named was owned by Northcliffe and edited by Geoffrey Dawson whom Wiseman knew. Arthur Willert, Washington correspondent, and Wiseman occasionally gave Dawson leads for editorials to please the Americans. They also composed a laudatory article concerning Reading's work as ambassador. The New York *World* was edited by Wilson's friend, Frank Cobb whom Wiseman consulted in reporting American public opinion to London.

B. OTHER

"Across the Flood"—Addresses at the Dinner in Honor of the Earl of Reading at the Lotos Club New York, March 27th, 1918 (New York, 1918). Includes Lloyd George's

telegram to the American people and speeches by Reading, Charles E. Hughes, and George Harvey.

William G. McAdoo. "The Second Liberty Loan and the Causes of Our War with Germany" (n.p., n.d.). Speech to American Bankers Association, Atlantic City, N.J., Sept. 28, 1917. An indication that McAdoo placed American self-interest above an "idealistic . . . championship of universal democracy."

Lord Northcliffe. *Lord Northcliffe's War Book* (New York, 1917).

———. "What America is Fighting For," *Current Opinion*, LXIII, Oct. 1917, 234-37. Typical of the numerous inspirational pieces published by Northcliffe in the fall of 1917 in the United States.

Charles Hanson Towne, ed. *The Balfour Visit*, New York, 1917. Lists the personnel of the mission and prints Balfour's speeches.

IV. PUBLISHED DIARIES, MEMOIRS, AND LETTERS

Of the great number of these consulted, only those which yielded usable information are listed. Some half dozen of the following are essential.

A. AMERICAN

Ray Stannard Baker. *American Chronicle, The Autobiography of Ray Stannard Baker*, New York, 1945. Very readable. Includes description, based on diaries, of his contact on behalf of Wilson and House with British labor leaders.

———. *Woodrow Wilson, Life and Letters*, 8 vols., New York, 1927-39. Volumes 6, 7, and 8 are day-by-day accounts of the wartime presidency, with many valuable extracts from letters and other documents. Vital source.

George Creel. *Rebel at Large, Recollections of Fifty Crowded Years*, New York, 1947. Creel, who convinced

Wilson of the authenticity of the Sisson documents, was himself still convinced 30 years later.

E. David Cronon, ed., *The Cabinet Diaries of Josephus Daniels, 1913-1921*, Lincoln, Neb., 1963. Daniels was less important in war policy decisions than War Secretary Baker. The bulk of his diary entries are too trivial or terse to be useful, but a few regarding Wilson are revealing. Well edited.

David R. Francis. *Russia from the American Embassy, April 1916–November 1918*, New York, 1921. Interesting observations on the Russian situation by the ambassador who had little to do with the decision to intervene.

William S. Graves. *America's Siberian Adventure: 1918-1920*, New York, 1931. Difficulties of the commander of the American intervention force.

Joseph C. Grew [Walter Johnson, ed.]. *Turbulent Era: A Diplomatic Record of Forty Years, 1904-45*, 2 vols., Boston, 1952. Minimal relevance.

James G. Harbord. *The American Army in France, 1917-1919*, Boston, 1936. Informative account by Pershing's chief of staff and later commander of supply operations. Echoes Pershing's distrust of the British.

Mrs. J. Borden Harriman. *From Pinafores to Politics*, New York, 1923. A leading woman Democrat's gossip of Washington political-social life, with an interesting diary entry regarding Wiseman.

Burton J. Hendrick. *The Life and Letters of Walter H. Page*, 3 vols., Garden City, N.Y., 1922-25. Most useful for Page's descriptions of conditions in England and as indication of the dissimilarity of his and Wilson's views.

Herbert Hoover. *The Ordeal of Woodrow Wilson*, New York, 1958. Sketchy and unrevealing for the war months.

Edward N. Hurley. *The Bridge to France*, Philadelphia, 1927. Very useful. Reveals the British pressure on the

United States Shipping Board. Reproduces part of Reading's Lotos Club speech, which Hurley considered important.

Thomas W. Lamont. *Across World Frontiers*, New York, 1950. Reveals the unpublicized service of a Morgan partner to the Administration in its financial dealings with the Allies.

Anne W. Lane and Louise H. Wall, eds. *The Letters of Franklin K. Lane*, Boston, 1922. The Interior Secretary's letters reveal how rarely Wilson consulted the Cabinet before making decisions in matters of war and foreign policy.

Robert Lansing. *War Memoirs*, New York, 1935. Devoted primarily to the neutrality period. Lansing died before completing this work.

Henry Cabot Lodge. *The Senate and the League of Nations*, New York, 1925. Concerns neutrality and war policies also.

William G. McAdoo. *Crowded Years*, Boston, 1931. Long, discursive, self-praising, and not very useful.

Peyton C. March. *The Nation at War*, Garden City, N.Y., 1932. The army chief of staff's account of the building of the American Expeditionary Force. A few pages on the amalgamation controversy.

Elting E. Morison and Associates, eds. *The Letters of Theodore Roosevelt*, 8 vols., Cambridge, 1951-1954. Volume 8 contains letters opposing Wilson's policies and methods.

Charles Pergler. *America in the Struggle for Czechoslovak Independence*, Philadelphia, 1926. Useful on the tactics of Czech-Americans, but silent on Wiseman, whom Pergler undoubtedly knew.

John J. Pershing. *My Experiences in the World War*, 2 vols., New York, 1931. Unusually reliable and satisfying memoir. Includes numerous extracts from his diary and some of his most important correspondence with Secretary Baker.

William Phillips. *Ventures in Diplomacy*, North Beverly, Mass., 1952. Phillips, an assistant secretary of state, apparently had little contact with Wiseman. This book is most relevant to Phillips' career after the war.

Charles Seymour, ed. *The Intimate Papers of Colonel House*, 4 vols., New York, 1926-28. The connecting narrative by Seymour is almost as valuable as the many letters and diary entries. Wiseman and House collaborated with Seymour in the preparation of these volumes, and their correspondence shows that they were concerned not to offend anybody by the publication of sensitive material. As a result, much vital information in the House and Wiseman papers was omitted. There are also a few instances of significant alteration of the documents printed in order to render them inoffensive. These volumes cannot take the place of research in the original papers but are nonetheless the single most valuable source in print.

William S. Sims and Burton J. Hendrick. *The Victory at Sea*, Garden City, N. Y., 1920. Admiral Sims' account of anti-submarine warfare and naval cooperation with the British. Of minimal use in this study.

Edgar Sisson. *One Hundred Red Days*, New Haven, 1931. Sisson's account of his mission to Russia includes a description of Wiseman.

George S. Viereck. *Spreading Germs of Hate*, New York, 1930. German-American's description of German and British propaganda-secret service operations in America, including a few pages on Wiseman. Viereck and Wiseman became rather good friends after the war.

Emanuel Victor Voska and Will Irwin. *Spy and Counter-Spy*, London, 1941. A not very reliable account of Czech nationalist maneuvering in America and Europe. Describes Wiseman's Russian propaganda scheme (without attributing the scheme to Wiseman).

Edith Bolling Wilson. *My Memoir*, New York, 1939. The President's wife's book deals primarily with social and ceremonial matters. Only one reference to Wiseman.

Hugh R. Wilson. *Diplomat Between Wars*, New York, 1941. Wilson was chargé at the embassy in Switzerland. Of incidental use on the activities of Voska's Czechs.

B. BRITISH

Christopher Addison. *Four and a Half Years, A Personal Diary From June 1914 to January 1919*, 2 vols., London, 1934. Addison was minister of reconstruction in 1918. Second volume shows the relation of plans for domestic recovery to economic foreign policy. Also some information on Irish home rule.

L. S. Amery. *My Political Life*, 3 vols., London, 1953-55. Volume 2, covering the war years, is very enlightening on British strategy and imperial policy. Also valuable for the evolution of the Supreme War Council. Fascinating reading.

Arthur J. Balfour. *Retrospect: An Unfinished Autobiography*, 1848-86, Boston, 1930, ed. Mrs. Edgar Dugdale. Balfour died before bringing his account into 1917-18.

Lord Beaverbrook. *Men and Power, 1917-1918*, London, 1956. Rich account of British political struggles, based on Beaverbrook's memory as a participant and on his hoard of Beaverbrook, Lloyd George, and Bonar Law papers. Beaverbrook and Wiseman became close friends in their later years, and Beaverbrook acknowledges Wiseman's assistance in preparing this book. The book does not, however, cover the Wiseman-House-Balfour arrangement.

Robert Blake, ed. *The Private Papers of Douglas Haig, 1914-19*, London, 1952. Enlightening on controversies over strategy and Lloyd George's fight with Haig and Robertson.

Sir Tom Bridges. *Alarms & Excursions, Reminiscences of a Soldier*, London, 1938. Some account of the Balfour mission of 1917 and of Bridges' role in the amalgamation controversy. Usefulness impaired by such errors as a description of Wilson as a typical New Englander.

Sir C. E. Callwell. *Field-Marshal Sir Henry Wilson: His Life and Diaries*, 2 vols., London, 1927. Contains many important extracts from the diary of this political general.

Viscount Cecil (Lord Robert Cecil). *A Great Experiment*, New York, 1941. Almost totally concerned with the League of Nations after its founding, but includes Cecil's 1916 memorandum on peace-keeping.

Joseph Davies. *The Prime Minister's Secretariat 1916-1920*, Newport, Monmouthshire, 1951. Davies, an assistant to Lloyd George for shipping problems, describes the Balfour mission, Northcliffe's appointment to head the War Mission, and troop transportation. Appendix lists monthly shipping losses.

Admiral Sir Guy Gaunt. *The Yield of the Years*, London, 1940. Anecdotal account of his years at the Washington embassy before Wiseman usurped his place as liaison to House. Factually faulty. Denigrates importance of Wiseman.

Sir Auckland C. Geddes. *The Forging of a Family*, London, 1952. Useful information on the author, who was the manpower minister, and on Eric Geddes.

Lord Grey of Fallodon (Sir Edward Grey). *Twenty-Five Years, 1892-1916*, 2 vols., New York, 1925. Very useful background.

Stephen Gwynn, ed. *The Letters and Friendships of Sir Cecil Spring Rice*, 2 vols., Boston, 1929. The best of Spring Rice's often eloquent but minimally influential letters.

Lord Hankey (Sir Maurice Hankey). *The Supreme Command, 1914-1918*, 2 vols., London, 1961. Based on diaries. Useful, but Hankey, the War Cabinet Secretary, undoubtedly withholds much more than he tells.

Lord Hardinge of Penhurst. *Old Diplomacy*, London, 1947. By the permanent under-secretary of the Foreign Office, 1916-20. Praises Spring Rice, condemns Northcliffe, and fails to mention Wiseman. Indicates the professional's contempt for irregular diplomatic procedures.

Sir Samuel Hoare. *The Fourth Seal*, London, 1930. Reticent description of intelligence operations by a secret agent. Identifies, as do others, the chief of military and naval intelligence, but states that the Foreign Office intelligence chief (for whom Wiseman worked) can never be identified.

Major General Sir Alfred Knox. *With the Russian Army, 1914-1917*, 2 vols., New York, 1921. Stops short of the intervention. Lends support to Wiseman's and Wilson's belief that Knox, the most influential British military adviser on Russia, was a reactionary.

David Lloyd George. *War Memoirs*, 6 vols., London, 1933-36. A prime source, even though Lloyd George leaves much unsaid and occasionally distorts the facts. Includes many important documents.

R. H. Bruce Lockhart. *British Agent*, New York, 1933. The difficulties experienced by the envoy in Russia whose reports formed much of the information available to the British and American governments.

W. Somerset Maugham. *The Summing Up*, London, 1938. Maugham's memory of his espionage work, including his assignment under Wiseman (whom he does not identify).

Sir Frederick B. Maurice. *Lessons of Allied Co-operation: Naval, Military, and Air, 1914-1918*, New York, 1942. By Robertson's director of military operations who clashed with Lloyd George and Sir Henry Wilson over control of strategy.

Arthur C. Murray (Lord Elibank). *At Close Quarters, A Sidelight on Anglo-American Diplomatic Relations,* London, 1946. Short account of the Wiseman-Murray channel of communication. Prints several valuable letters.

―――――. *Master and Brother,* London, 1945. Largely concerned with Murray's brother, the Master of Elibank. Includes a few pages on Murray's service at the Washington embassy and his relations with Wiseman.

Sir Bernard Pares. *My Russian Memoirs,* London, 1931. By the student of Russia who spent several weeks there in 1917 and who furnished Wiseman information on the Russian situation. This memoir reveals nothing of his contact with Wiseman.

Lord Eustace Percy. *Some Memories,* London, 1958. Includes a brief account of his own experience in Anglo-American affairs and reference to the "semi-subterranean" activities of Wiseman.

Lord Riddell. *Lord Riddell's War Diary, 1914-1918,* London, 1933. Helpful extracts from the diary of the confidant of Lloyd George.

R. W. Seton-Watson. *Masaryk in England,* Cambridge, England, 1943. Sketchy reference to the connection of Emanuel Voska to Masaryk and English supporters of a Czech state.

Henry Wickham Steed. *Through Thirty Years, 1892-1922,* 2 vols., New York, 1924. Valuable background information from an influential editor. Brief coverage of Northcliffe's mission to America.

Sir Campbell Stuart. *Opportunity Knocks Once,* London, 1952. Vague recollections of a Northcliffe lieutenant and acquaintance of Wiseman. States that Lloyd George disliked Wiseman.

Norman Thwaites. *Velvet and Vinegar*, London, 1932. Flippant account of social exploits and undercover work by one of Wiseman's agents.

Sir Arthur Willert. *The Road to Safety; A Study in Anglo-American Relations*, London, 1952. The best of several memoir accounts of Wiseman (all listed here). Willert benefited from the use of Wiseman's papers and from Wiseman's own memories (which were not always accurate). Prints several Wiseman documents.

Sir Evelyn Wrench. *Struggle, 1914-1920*, London, 1935. Recollections and contemporary notes of the journalist who founded the English-Speaking Union. Useful on private efforts in Britain to strengthen Anglo-American ties.

C. OTHER

Thomas G. Masaryk. *The Making of a State; Memories and Observations, 1914-1918*, London, 1927. The first president of Czechoslovakia gives a brief account of his activities in Russia and Washington in 1917-18 and acknowledges help from Wiseman.

V. BIOGRAPHIES

A. AMERICAN

John Morton Blum. *Jos Tumulty and the Wilson Era*, Boston, 1951. Excellent on Democratic politics and Wilson's mode of governing.

————. *Woodrow Wilson and the Politics of Morality*, Boston, 1956. An important interpretation of Wilson's mind and purpose.

Lester V. Chandler. *Benjamin Strong, Central Banker*, Washington, 1958. Valuable account of the new Federal Reserve System's adjustment to the requirements of war. Nothing on Strong's role in mediating between McAdoo and the British.

Edward M. Coffman. *The Hilt of the Sword; The Career of Peyton C. March*, Madison, Wis. 1965. Scholarly biography. Of some use concerning relations between Pershing and the War Department.

C. H. Cramer. *Newton D. Baker: A Biography*, Cleveland, 1961. Better on Baker as mayor of Cleveland than on Baker as war secretary.

John A. Garraty. *Henry Cabot Lodge, A Biography*, New York, 1953. Brief on Lodge's attitude during belligerency. A more benevolent portrait of Lodge than that which an investigation of the Lodge Papers produces.

———. *Woodrow Wilson, A Great Life in Brief*, New York, 1956. Includes some psychological observations.

Arthur S. Link. *Wilson*, Vol. I, *The Road to the White House*; Vol. II, *The New Freedom*; Vol. III, *The Struggle for Neutrality, 1914-1915*; Vol. IV, *Confusions and Crises, 1915-1916*; Vol. V, *Campaigns for Progressivism and Peace, 1916-1917*. 5 vols. to date, Princeton, 1947-1965. This magnificent undertaking has so far progressed to the American entry in the war. Based on a staggering amount of research. Prerequisite to present book.

Elting E. Morison. *Admiral Sims and the Modern American Navy*, Boston, 1942. Useful on Anglo-American naval cooperation, which was much less problematical than military cooperation.

Frederick Palmer. *Newton D. Baker: America at War*, 2 vols., New York, 1931. Much detail but little analysis.

———. *Bliss, Peacemaker*, New York, 1934. Chiefly useful for its excerpts from Bliss's papers.

Rupert Norval Richardson. *Colonel Edward M. House, The Texas Years, 1858-1912*, Abilene, Tex., 1964. Disappointing, even for the years it covers. There is no adequate biography of House.

Arthur D. H. Smith. *Mr. House of Texas*, New York, 1940.

Mary Synon. *McAdoo*, Indianapolis, 1924. A campaign biography.

George S. Viereck. *The Strangest Friendship in History*, New York, 1932. Concerns House and Wilson. Based on what House chose to tell rather than on independent research.

Arthur Walworth. *Woodrow Wilson*, 2 vols., New York, 1958. The second volume is useful regarding Wilson's foreign policy but is marred by the lack of documentary citations.

B. BRITISH

Victor Bonham-Carter. *Soldier True; The Life and Times of Field-Marshal Sir William Robertson, 1860-1933*, London, 1963. Uses Robertson's letters to defend the general against Lloyd George.

Ian D. Colvin. *The Life of Lord Carson*, 3 vols., New York, 1932-37. The biography of the Ulster leader reveals the passion and complexity of the Irish problem.

Margaret Digby. *Horace Plunkett, An Anglo-American Irishman*, Oxford, 1949. Relates the arduous but largely ineffective efforts of Plunkett to aid Anglo-American relations and to solve the Irish problem.

Blanche E. C. Dugdale. *Arthur James Balfour, First Earl of Balfour*, 2 vols., London, 1936. By Balfour's niece. Still the best work on Balfour. Includes several useful documents.

A. M. Gollin. *Proconsul in Politics; A Study of Lord Milner in Opposition and in Power*, London, 1964. Useful on the great administrator but very general for the matters here studied.

J. L. Hammond. *C. P. Scott of the Manchester Guardian*, London, 1934. Includes two important contemporary accounts by Scott of conversations with Wiseman.

W. K. Hancock, *Smuts. The Sanguine Years, 1870-1919*, Cambridge, England, 1962. Very good discussion of the Imperial War Cabinet and of Smuts' influence in many areas of war policy.

H. Montgomery Hyde. *Lord Reading: The Life of Rufus Isaacs, First Marquess of Reading*, London, 1967. A popular biography, published after the present study was completed.

Admiral Sir William James. *The Code Breakers of Room 40: The Story of Admiral Sir William Hall, Genius of British Counter-Intelligence*, New York, 1956. The fullest treatment of British counterintelligence, based on Hall's private papers.

Donald McCormick. *The Mask of Merlin, A Critical Biography of David Lloyd George*, New York, 1964. Skillful dissection of the man's personality but not of his policies.

Frank Owen. *Tempestuous Journey: Lloyd George, His Life and Times*, New York, 1955. The best of several biographies, none of which is wholly satisfying.

Reginald Pound and Geoffrey Harmsworth. *Northcliffe*, New York, 1960. Long and detailed. Based on several manuscript collections, including the Lloyd George Papers. The chapters on Northcliffe's mission to America and his relations with Lloyd George are very helpful.

Marquess of Reading. *Rufus Isaacs, First Marquess of Reading*, 2 vols., New York, 1940-45. By the ambassador's son. Volume 2, containing numerous extracts from Reading's papers, is very helpful. Wiseman assisted in the preparation of the book but is rarely mentioned in it. Must be used with caution.

John Terraine. *Douglas Haig, The Educated Soldier*, London, 1963. Defense of Haig. Useful discussion of the difficulties in achieving unified Allied command.

Sir John Evelyn Wrench. *Alfred Lord Milner, The Man of No Illusions, 1854-1925*, London, 1958. Notes the attention Milner paid in 1918 to Wiseman's reports.

————. *Geoffrey Dawson and Our Times*, London, 1955. Incidentally useful regarding the press and politics.

Kenneth Young. *Arthur James Balfour*, London, 1963. Indebted to Dugdale. Some interesting observations on Balfour's personality and philosophical studies, but virtually useless on Balfour's foreign policy. The greatness of Balfour has yet to be captured in print.

VI. General Works

H. C. Allen. *Great Britain and the United States*, New York, 1955. Competent survey.

Howard F. Cline. *The United States and Mexico*, rev. ed., New York, 1963. Concentrates on the twentieth century. Useful chapters on the war years include information on British involvement in Mexico.

C.R.M.F. Cruttwell. *A History of the Great War, 1914-18*, Oxford, 1934. A general military history, of outstanding quality.

John Dos Passos. *Mr. Wilson's War*, Garden City, N.Y., 1962. Inappropriately titled history for the general reader. Well written, episodic treatment of all aspects of American participation in the war.

Sir James E. Edmonds. [*History of the Great War Based on Official Documents*]. *Military Operations, France and Belgium, 1918*, 5 vols. and a volume of appendices, London, 1935-47. Detailed coverage of the war during the period of American participation. Appendices contain useful documents.

Sir James E. Edmonds, comp. *A Short History of World War I*, London, 1951.

Thomas G. Frothingham. *The Naval History of the World War*, 3 vols., Cambridge, Mass., 1924-26. Volume three covers American participation.

A. Whitney Griswold. *The Far Eastern Policy of the United States*, New York, 1938. Useful for relating the Russian intervention to traditional American policy.

Edgar Holt. *Protest in Arms: The Irish Troubles, 1916-1923*, New York, 1961. General narrative of the struggle between Dublin and London. Least emotional account available.

Richard W. Leopold. *The Growth of American Foreign Policy: A History*, New York, 1962. The best general diplomatic history of the United States in the twentieth century.

Arthur S. Link. *Woodrow Wilson and the Progressive Era, 1910-1917*, New York, 1954. Essential background. Superb chapter on American-Mexican relations.

R. B. Mowat. *A History of European Diplomacy, 1914-1925*, London, 1927.

Robert E. Osgood. *Ideals and Self-Interest in America's Foreign Relations: The Great Transformation of the Twentieth Century*, Chicago, 1953. Provocative analysis of foreign policy from the time of the first through the time of the second Roosevelt. Trenchant criticism of Wilson's idealism.

Frederic L. Paxson. *America at War, 1917-1918*, Boston, 1939. Competent summarization of activities on the home and battle fronts.

Sidney Ratner. *American Taxation, its History as a Social Force in Democracy*, New York, 1942. Adequate treatment of McAdoo's tax and financial policies.

R. W. Seton-Watson. *A History of the Czechs and Slovaks*, London, 1943. Standard synthesis.

Charles Seymour. *American Diplomacy During the World War*, Baltimore, 1934. Lectures surveying the neutrality and belligerency periods.

Daniel M. Smith. *The Great Departure; The United States and World War I, 1914-1920*, New York, 1965. Short survey with very little attention to the belligerency period. Up-to-date bibliography of secondary materials.

A.J.P. Taylor. *English History, 1914-1945*, New York, 1965. Brilliant, opinionated, first-rate reading. Taylor's knowledge of British politics during the First World War is probably unexcelled.

VII. Special Studies

Thomas A. Bailey. *The Policy of the United States Towards the Neutrals, 1917-1918*, Baltimore, 1942. Concludes that the United States as a belligerent was as respectful of the rights of neutrals as possible. Helpful regarding the coordination of American and British policies.

Ruhl J. Bartlett. *The League to Enforce Peace*, Chapel Hill, N.C., 1944. The story of the private planners whose zeal vexed Wilson in 1918.

Daniel R. Beaver. "Newton D. Baker and the Genesis of the War Industries Board, 1917-1918," *The Journal of American History*, LII (1965), 43-58. Struggle within the government for control over war production and allocation. Reveals, among other things, McAdoo's extreme sensitivity regarding the appointment of anyone involved with J. P. Morgan and Company.

———. *Newton D. Baker and the American War Effort, 1917-1919*, Lincoln, Nebraska, 1966. Very helpful on the difficulties of establishing and supplying the A.E.F. in Europe, of command arrangements, and of planning for 1919. Generous excerpts from documents and correspondence.

Giles T. Brown. "The Hindu Conspiracy, 1914-1917." *The Pacific Historical Review*, XVII (1948), 299-310. A description of some incidents of the Indian independence movement and how American police and courts treated the "conspirators."

Edward H. Buehrig. *Woodrow Wilson and the Balance of Power*, Bloomington, Indiana, 1955. Study by a political scientist indicating that there was "realism" as well as "idealism" in Wilson's foreign policy.

Roy W. Curry. *Woodrow Wilson and Far Eastern Policy, 1913-1921*, New York, 1957. Includes a section on Russian intervention.

C. Ernest Fayle. *The War and the Shipping Industry*, London, 1927. Recounts the losses in the British merchant marine. Statistics.

Claude E. Fike. "The Influence of the Creel Committee and the American Red Cross on Russian-American Relations, 1917-1920," *The Journal of Modern History*, XXXI (1959), 93-109. Useful description of the muddle caused in Russia and Washington by amateur diplomats.

Peter G. Filene. *Americans and the Soviet Experiment, 1917-1933*, Cambridge, Mass., 1967. A study of popular attitudes, including a chapter on the intervention of Siberia and North Russia.

Lawrence E. Gelfand. *The Inquiry: American Preparations for Peace, 1917-1919*, New Haven, 1963. Thorough and useful account of the composition and function of House's peace planners.

Alexander L. George and Juliette L. George. *Woodrow Wilson and Colonel House: A Personality Study*, New York, 1956. An attempt through the use of psychological tools to determine why and how Wilson made the decisions he did. The authors remark that flattery was used by House and Wiseman upon Wilson.

Louis L. Gerson. *Woodrow Wilson and the Rebirth of Poland, 1914-1920: A Study in the Influence on American Policy of Minority Groups of Foreign Origin*, New Haven, 1953.

Henry F. Grady. *British War Finance, 1914-1919*, New York, 1927. Chiefly concerned with organization and operation, but not policy. Useful.

Paul Guinn. *British Strategy and Politics, 1914 to 1918*, Oxford, 1965. Primarily an investigation of the interaction of domestic politics and military considerations. Indirectly helpful.

George F. Kennan. *Soviet-American Relations, 1917-1920*, Vol. I, *Russia Leaves the War*; Vol. II, *The Decision to Intervene*. 2 vols. to date, Princeton, 1956-58. Immensely helpful. Extensively researched, well written, and full of insights.

————. "Soviet Historiography and America's Role in the Intervention," *The American Historical Review*, LXV (January 1960), 302-22. Demonstrates how well, though mistakenly, Wilson's intervention fits into doctrinaire Soviet interpretations of history.

Mary Klachko. "Anglo-American Naval Competition, 1918-1922," dissertation, Columbia University, 1962, Ann Arbor, Mich., University Microfilms, 1963. An investigation of the race that began in the closing phase of the war. The author interviewed Wiseman in 1956.

Christopher Lasch. *The American Liberals and the Russian Revolution*, New York, 1962. An outstanding study, explaining, among other things, the rationale of liberals supporting intervention.

————. "American Intervention in Siberia: A Reinterpretation," *Political Science Quarterly*, LXXVII (1962), 205-23. Recognizes the rescue of the Czechs as the immediate cause of the decision to intervene. Stimulating observations.

N. Gordon Levin, Jr. *Woodrow Wilson and World Politics: America's Response to War and Revolution*, New York, 1968. A stimulating analysis of Wilson's goals in the context of "traditional imperialism and revolutionary socialism." Published after the present study was completed.

Arthur S. Link. *Wilson the Diplomatist: A Look at His Major Foreign Policies*, Baltimore, 1957. A set of lectures analyzing Wilson's assumptions and techniques. Almost nothing specifically on the period of belligerency.

Seward W. Livermore. *Politics is Adjourned: Woodrow Wilson and the War Congress, 1916-1918*, Middletown, Conn., 1966. Demonstrates that partisan politics was not adjourned. Here one can trace Congressional criticism of the Treasury's spending and the War Department's inefficiency as well as Republican attacks on Wilson's peace program.

Thomas C. Lonergan. *It Might Have Been Lost*, New York, 1929. An early study of the amalgamation controversy, containing excerpts from official British documents.

Francis Bullitt Lowry. "The Generals, the Armistice and the Treaty of Versailles, 1919," dissertation, Duke University, 1963, Ann Arbor, Mich., University Microfilms, 1964. Primarily a study of the armistice's military terms, their implementation, and their relation to the peace treaty. Minimal help.

Sir Bernard Mallet and C. Oswald George. *British Budgets (Second Series), 1913-14 to 1920-21*, London, 1929. Includes a capsule treatment of how Britain financed the war.

Victor S. Mamatey. *The United States and East Central Europe, 1914-1918: A Study in Wilsonian Diplomacy and Propaganda*, Princeton, 1957. A model study of international history. Omits any reference to the Voska-Wiseman collaboration.

Laurence W. Martin. *Peace Without Victory: Woodrow Wilson and the British Liberals*, New Haven, 1958. Useful and succinct study of the influence of the one upon the other regarding war aims.

Arno J. Mayer. *Political Origins of the New Diplomacy, 1917-1918*, New Haven, 1959. A brilliant study of the impact of the war on liberal thought and the latter on international relations. Lord Robert Cecil's contribution to the January 1918 British statement of war aims is not mentioned and would not fit the author's attribution of liberal war aims to parties of the left.

Stanley Morison. "Personality and Diplomacy in Anglo-American Relations, 1917," in Richard Pares and A.J.P. Taylor, eds., *Essays Presented to Sir Lewis Namier*, London, 1956, 431-74. A favorable assessment of Northcliffe, resulting from a selective use of the House and Wiseman Papers. Morison was once a Northcliffe employee.

James William Morley. *The Japanese Thrust into Siberia, 1918*, New York, 1957. Impressive study, based on Japanese, Chinese, Russian, and American sources. Very useful.

Harley Notter. *The Origins of the Foreign Policy of Woodrow Wilson*, Baltimore, 1937. The standard account of Wilson's early thought on foreign policy.

Alexander D. Noyes. *The War Period of American Finance, 1908-1925*, New York, 1926. Survey of private and public financial developments. Not altogether satisfactory, but the best work available.

Julius W. Pratt. "Robert Lansing," in Samuel Flagg Bemis and Robert H. Ferrell, eds., *The American Secretaries of State and Their Diplomacy*, New York, 1927—X, 47-175.

Harry R. Rudin. *Armistice 1918*, New Haven, 1944. Exhaustive account of the negotiations, with many useful excerpts from relevant documents.

Sir James Arthur Salter. *Allied Shipping Control; An Exper-iment in International Administration,* London, 1921. De-scription, documents, statistics.

Marion C. Siney. "British Official Histories of the Blockade of the Central Powers during the First World War," *American Historical Review,* LXVIII (January 1963), 392-401. Review article with helpful comments on Amer-ican policy.

Gaddis Smith. "Canada and the Siberian Intervention, 1918-1919," *American Historical Review,* LXIV (July 1959), 866-77. In explaining how Canadian policy differed from American and British, the author also indicates contra-dictions between the latter two.

John L. Snell. "Wilson on Germany and the Fourteen Points," *Journal of Modern History,* XXVI (1954), 364-69. Prints the Wiseman-Wilson interview of October 16, 1917, with a commentary.

――――. "Wilsonian Rhetoric Goes to War," *The Historian,* XIV (1952), 191-208. Describes how Wilson "innovated and organized the first top-level ideological campaign of the twentieth century." Useful.

――――. "Wilson's Peace Program and German Socialism, January-March, 1918," *Mississippi Valley Historical Re-view,* XXXVIII (September 1951), 187-214. Concludes that Wilson's words hastened victory over Germany.

Leonard Stein. *The Balfour Declaration,* New York, 1961. Thorough and well-documented study of the origins and immediate responses to the famous declaration.

Leonid I. Strakhovsky. *American Opinion About Russia, 1917-1920,* Toronto, 1961. Lecture series which draws on recent scholarship and contemporary periodicals to dem-onstrate the official and popular misconceptions about Russia. Peripherally helpful.

――――. *The Origins of American Intervention in North Russia (1918),* Princeton, 1937. Superseded by Kennan.

Charles C. Tansill. *America and the Fight for Irish Freedom, 1866-1922*, New York, 1957. Polemical, but useful for its documentation.

A.J.P. Taylor. *Politics in Wartime, and Other Essays*, London, 1964. Essays on British politics. Stresses the power of the press, especially Northcliffe's, over Lloyd George.

——. *The Trouble Makers: Dissent Over Foreign Policy, 1792-1939*, London, 1957. Lectures on liberal dissent, including one on the Union of Democratic Control's influence on Lloyd George's war aims.

Seth P. Tillman. *Anglo-American Relations at the Paris Peace Conference of 1919*, Princeton, 1961. Excellent. Although primarily devoted to the peace conference, the book reaches back into the period of belligerency as well.

David F. Trask. *The United States in the Supreme War Council; American War Aims and Inter-Allied Strategy, 1917-1918*, Middletown, Conn., 1961. Sharply focused and very useful.

Richard H. Ullman, *Anglo-Soviet Relations, 1917-1921*, 2 vols. to date, Princeton, 1961-68. The first volume, *Intervention and the War*, in this projected series concludes in late 1918, and emphasizes the dominance of the War Office over the Foreign Office in Russian policy. Patterned after Kennan's Soviet-American study and based to a considerable extent on the Wiseman and Milner Papers. Very useful.

Betty Miller Unterberger. *America's Siberian Expedition, 1918-1920: A Study of National Policy*, Durham, N.C., 1956. Thorough and very useful examination of State Department records, private papers, and the press. Her conclusion that Wilson's "basic" reason for intervention was to restrain Japan and "preserve the open door in Siberia and North Manchuria" is unconvincing.

Robert D. Warth. *The Allies and the Russian Revolution, From the Fall of the Monarchy to the Peace of Brest-*

Litovsk, Durham, N.C., 1954. Useful for the period it covers.

D. C. Watt. *Personalities and Policies; Studies in the Formulation of British Foreign Policy in the Twentieth Century*, London, 1965. A collection of important essays attempting to isolate the persons who influenced and determined British foreign policy. The second essay, "America and the British Foreign-Policy-Making Elite, from Joseph Chamberlain to Anthony Eden, 1898-1956." includes brief mention of the Wiseman-House arrangement. Extremely valuable bibliography.

John A. White. *The Siberian Intervention*, Princeton, 1950. Covers both Allied and American aspects.

William A. Williams. "American Intervention in Russia, 1917-1920," *Studies on the Left*, III (1963), No. 4, 24-40; IV (1964), No. 1, 39-56. Concludes that American intervention was "anti-Bolshevik in origin and intent. . . ."

Trevor Wilson. *The Downfall of the Liberal Party 1914-1935*, London, 1966. Includes an excellent analysis of Lloyd George and the "coupon election" campaign of November-December 1918.

Henry R. Winkler. *The League of Nations Movement in Great Britain, 1914-1919*, New Brunswick, N.J., 1952. Examination of the sources of support in Britain for the League. Useful on Cecil's advocacy of the league.

David Wise and Thomas B. Rose. *The Espionage Establishment*, New York, 1967. Without revealing their sources, the authors give a brief history of the British Secret Service and identify "C." Not a scholarly book.

Sir Llewellyn Woodward. *Great Britain and the War of 1914-1918*, London, 1967. A wise and comprehensive military history which includes British domestic developments and diplomacy. Not concerned directly and in detail with the topic of the present study. Published after the present study was completed.

INDEX

329